LINGUISTIC CONVERGENCE

AN ETHNOGRAPHY OF SPEAKING
AT FORT CHIPEWYAN, ALBERTA

This is a volume in

LANGUAGE, THOUGHT, AND CULTURE
ADVANCES IN THE STUDY OF COGNITION

Under the Editorship of

E. A. HAMMEL

Department of Anthropology
University of California, Berkeley

A complete list of titles in this series is available from the publisher.

LINGUISTIC CONVERGENCE

AN ETHNOGRAPHY OF SPEAKING AT FORT CHIPEWYAN, ALBERTA

Ronald Scollon
Suzanne B. K. Scollon

Alaska Native Language Center
University of Alaska
Fairbanks, Alaska

ACADEMIC PRESS
New York   San Francisco   London
A Subsidiary of Harcourt Brace Jovanovich, Publishers

ACADEMIC PRESS, INC.
111 Fifth Avenue, New York, New York 10003

United Kingdom Edition published by
ACADEMIC PRESS, INC. (LONDON) LTD.
24/28 Oval Road, London NW1 7DX

Library of Congress Cataloging in Publication Data

Scollon, Ronald, Date
    Linguistic convergence.
    (Language, thought, and culture series)
    Bibliography: p.
    1. Fort Chipewyan, Alta.--Languages. 2. Alberta--
Languages. 3. Sapir--Whorf hypothesis. 4. Languages in
contact. I. Scollon, Suzanne B. K., joint author.
II. Title.
P379.S3   301.2'1   78--67886
ISBN 0--12--633380--7

PRINTED IN THE UNITED STATES OF AMERICA

79 80 81 82   9 8 7 6 5 4 3 2 1

CONTENTS

4
BUSH CONSCIOUSNESS AND MODERNIZATION   177

5
SOCIAL ATOMISM AND SPEECH COMMUNITY   211

6
SOME NEW PROBLEMS   247

PREFACE

This book is a discussion of one case in which there is a significant relationship between the structure of language in a speech community and the world view or, to use a term which we introduce, "reality set" of the people who are members of that community. As such, it is an investigation of the issue of linguistic relativity through ethnographic techniques of description and analysis.

The setting for this study is the northern Canadian community of Fort Chipewyan, Alberta. In this town of about 1500 people, four languages—Chipewyan, Cree, French, and English—have coexisted for over a century. The structural result of this coexistence is a considerable amount of convergence among these languages. This book provides a description of the linguistic history of this community; a description of the current structure of two of these languages, Chipewyan and English, as represented in the narrative performance of one narrator; and an analysis of the reality set which we are calling the "bush consciousness." This reality set is the milieu in which linguistic convergence has been fostered at Fort Chipewyan. As a specific case it is planned to be the foundation for a set of studies of the social and cognitive bases of multilingualism and linguistic change.

Among the most persistent problems of methodology in studies of the

Canadian subarctic is that of finding reliable sources of material. Many researchers have found it nearly impossible to work in this area and where they have succeeded it has been only with difficulty. We argue that the conflict between the bush consciousness and the modern consciousness of the researcher lies at the heart of these methodological problems. Thus this book develops a historical and methodological context for the understanding of linguistic and ethnographic research in the Canadian subarctic.

It is a measure of the difficulty of the problem of linguistic relativity that in some ways this book appears to be about several things at once. Ethnographers of speaking will find it of interest because of the holistic view of the language of a speech community that it adopts. This we take as our organizing perspective. Folklorists may be interested in the detailed discussion of the framing of narrative as performance. Sociolinguists will find the discussion of phonological variation parallel to other discussions in the literature, with two differences. In most cases, phonological variation has been studied in urban communities of reasonably technologically developed societies. In these cases, variation is normally tied to such factors as group membership or variation in the mode of interactions in the social setting. In the present case, the phonological variation we discuss is reflective of reality set and so integrates interests of both sociolinguists and ethnolinguists. Our treatment of the linguistic history of Fort Chipewyan will be of interest to ethnohistorians as well as to anthropologists interested in problems of change and acculturation. The history of education first in French and then in English at Fort Chipewyan should interest educators concerned with bilingual education. A further problem of interest to educators is the conflict between reality sets and the effects this has on communication between people at Fort Chipewyan and outsiders. The structural details, which are given for Chipewyan and English and extend into an analysis of clause structure, present valuable material to Athabaskan linguists. We can hope that Algonquianists will find these matters of enough interest to undertake parallel studies of Cree in the same area. Finally, our treatment of the history of linguistic and ethnographic work in the Fort Chipewyan area is a contribution to the history of attitudes and presuppositions held among researchers throughout the past five decades. In this treatment we see that the history of language at Fort Chipewyan becomes the history of ourselves.

The book is organized around a single short narrative, told first in Chipewyan and then in English. Special attention is paid to the embedding of this narrative as a performance in the social context since it forms the basis for all of our discussions of linguistic structure and convergence which follow. After an understanding of the performance and the linguistic structure has been reached, we develop an analysis of the two reality sets, the bush consciousness and the modern consciousness, especially as these relate to language. This discussion of reality set is followed by a discussion of the social and linguistic world in which the bush consciousness exists. These then form the descriptive and analytical core of the book.

As a means of introducing the descriptive core, and of setting the problem, we give the history of both our work at Fort Chipewyan and, preceding that, the work of Fang-Kuei Li. Following the core description, we return to this historical theme and look at the work of other linguists and ethnographers in the area. The problem we face begins with the assumption that the changes we observed were changes that had taken place since Li's work in 1928. As it becomes clear that these supposed changes go back at least to 1876, we are forced to view Li's work as exceptional. The book closes with a discussion of the perspective within which we set Li's and, hence, our own work. We see the problem of linguistic change as being not only a question of change in the phenomenon under study, but also a matter of change in the descriptive and analytical cannons of linguists and ethnographers.

ACKNOWLEDGMENTS

The research contract that allowed us to do this work at Fort Chipewyan was given by the Urgent Ethnology Programme of the Canadian Ethnology Service, National Museum of Man, Canada from September 1976 to August 1977. Our work in the preceding summer of 1976 was supported by the National Endowment for the Humanities Summer Stipend Program. We wish to express our gratitude to these two institutions for their support.

At Fort Chipewyan, we are indebted to several hundred individuals for their help and interest in our work even where our intentions and goals must have remained highly unintelligible. The Athabasca Cree-Chip Band, through its manager Lawrence Courtoreille, gave us encouragement and support. Fred Marcel, the Chipewyan chief, was especially helpful in the early stages of getting to know people. We wish to thank the Advisory Council through Maureen Clarke for its assistance in arranging a place to stay, as well as in providing invaluable knowledge about the settlement and its relation to the larger provincial structure. The generous help of Dickie Mah and his family extended far beyond a very enjoyable Chinese New Year. We hope they will continue to prosper.

In the pages to follow, our indebtedness to Ben Marcel will become clear. We wish to thank him here for many enjoyable encounters and for his goodwill in helping us understand Chipewyan stories. We also wish to thank Philip Mandeville for his generous help in understanding his own and his father's life and work.

Intellectual debts are largely acknowledged in the references cited throughout the text. In several cases, however, there are debts far greater than a simple reference can convey. We owe a great deal to discussions with George Grace. His concern with questioning our traditional assumptions about the nature of language and of linguistic description is foundational to our work. The close correspondence between our work and that of John Gumperz in Kupwar Village reflects the importance of his original insights in our thinking. Discussions with him of this work based on his reading of an earlier version have been of invaluable importance. This research has been founded on the work of Dell Hymes. This debt is so central that we have chosen to cite only a few key references; a more accurate accounting would have considerably extended the references. For those of us who have not known him personally, his work is nevertheless a source of challenge and excitement. Michael Forman's commitment to excellence in teaching at the personal level leaves him little time for publication. As a result, we find it difficult to indicate the extent of our indebtedness to him with any scholarly accuracy. We have relied heavily on his critical judgment in first formulating this research, in doing the fieldwork itself, and finally in working through several drafts of this book.

Finally, Fang-Kuei Li has never failed to give generously of his time, his original field materials, and his counsel. As our teacher he continues to set for us a standard of insight, scholarship, and careful statement that guides us in our work.

1

FROM SOCIOLINGUISTICS
TO ETHNOLINGUISTICS

THE CHIPEWYAN WORK OF FANG-KUEI LI

In late June of 1928, Fang-Kuei Li arrived at Fort Chipewyan, Alberta. Some 6 weeks later, in early August, he left to go downriver to Fort Smith for a brief visit before the short northern summer ended. In the little more than 6 weeks that he had stayed at Fort Chipewyan, Fang-Kuei Li had written down 10 books of Chipewyan stories in phonetic notation and some 2800 file slips of verb paradigms, also in phonetic notation. For nearly 50 years this work has stood as the foundation of our academic knowledge of the Chipewyan language, and for many researchers Fang-Kuei Li's publications on Chipewyan have been their introduction to the entire Athabaskan family of languages. As students of Li's we often wondered how he could accomplish work of this importance in such a short field period. The research we are reporting here has grown out of this wondering.

When Li arrived at Fort Chipewyan in 1928 he had just completed his Ph.D. under Edward Sapir at the University of Chicago. It was his third degree in as many years. He was 26 years old. Sapir described his student in a letter to Ruth Benedict as "a very able Chinaman [Benedict 1959]." From Li's performance at Chicago it is clear that he was indeed "very able."

Because it was brief, it is possible to give a capsule description of Fang-Kuei Li's American education. He arrived from China in 1924 and began his studies in linguistics at the University of Michigan. Just a little over a year later in 1926 he received his B.A. The emphasis of his training at Michigan was on phonetics.

He then went to Chicago where he took classes with Edward Sapir as well as Leonard Bloomfield. Sapir asked Li if he had an interest in Athabaskan and in learning field methods. Li had come to America to learn American field methods for recording unwritten languages. He intended to work on the unrecorded languages of China and so he was very pleased to have the opportunity to work directly with Sapir.

Sapir took him to his home where he had invited a Navaho man to come. Li's training consisted of being instructed to write down everything the informant said but without the benefit of seeing Sapir's notes. Because of the speed and insightfulness of Sapir's questioning, Li found he was unable to do more than make his own record. He did not himself ask questions.

Apparently Sapir was satisfied with Li's abilities because he soon gave Li his Sarcee field notes with the instruction to see what he could do with them. Within 3 months Li had written "A Study of Sarcee Verb-Stems" (Li 1931) which was accepted in 1927 as his master's thesis.

That summer Sapir took Li with him to California so he could learn in the field. Again, Li's training was simple in conception though in fact a trial by fire. He again duplicated Sapir's notes as Sapir elicited material from his Hupa informant. This time, though, he was able to ask a few questions.

After only a week or so with Sapir, Li then struck off on his own to record Mattole and Wailaki. Upon returning to Chicago, Li wrote up his Mattole material and this was accepted as his doctoral dissertation (Li 1930). His official graduation was delayed somewhat because he had neglected to take his German and French reading examinations. By 1928, however, Li had substantially completed his American education with a Ph.D. degree. During the preceding 3 years he had studied among the usual linguistic topics at least 18 languages, 5 of them in the Athabaskan family. These were Navaho, Sarcee, Hupa, Wailaki, and Mattole. He had also acquired some familiarity with Chasta Costa and Kutchin. Of these 7 he had actually done fieldwork taking phonetic dictation in Navajo, Hupa, Wailaki, and Mattole. It might be added parenthetically that much of this study had been done through the medium of a language, English, which Li had known only to write, not to speak, before arriving in America in 1924.

Before Li returned to China, Sapir arranged for a small amount of money to support a field study of Northern Athabaskan. Goddard had published some material on Chipewyan (Goddard 1912), as had Petitot (1876, 1888) and Legoff (1916). As valuable as this material was, none of it had indicated tone. Since working on Sarcee and Kutchin, Sapir had become interested in Athabaskan tone. Sapir is also known to have had a basic mistrust of Goddard's linguistic abilities. Li, as a native speaker of several Chinese languages, was a natural choice to extend Sapir's reach into Northern Athabaskan where he could continue toying with his idea of an Athabaskan–Sino-Tibetan connection. Sapir was by then convinced of Li's remarkable abilities and especially convinced of Li's ability to take quick, accurate phonetic dictation which would include the marking of tone.

When Li arrived at Fort Chipewyan in June of 1928, then, he was well prepared to record Chipewyan texts quickly and accurately. Fortunately he met his match at Fort Chipewyan in the person of François Mandeville. This equally remarkable man worked with Li for 8 hours a day for 6 weeks, dictating texts, explaining forms, translating, and giving verb paradigms.

Their method of working was for Mandeville to dictate a text carefully, but as quickly as Li could write it. From the handwriting in Li's originals it is obvious that this was rather rapid. When they came to the end of the text, they would then go back to the beginning and make a word-by-word translation. Mandeville gave this translation in English and sometimes in French, and Li recorded it in English. That is, in some cases he translated French into English in his notes.

While they made this translation, Li would stop at each stem and ask Mandeville for a full paradigm where it existed. These notes were recorded on separate file slips. At the end of the already long day of dictation, Li would spend the bright summer night going over the notes, cross-referencing and trying to learn as much as possible to prepare for the next day's work.

In a little more than 6 weeks Li and Mandeville had recorded 19 stories in Chipewyan. These were personal narratives of events in Mandeville's life, traditional myths, legends, and several accounts of the old way of life. There were also two shorter stories which Mandeville told in Dogrib. Li also recorded a short story which was told by another narrator, Baptiste Forcier. When Li left Fort Chipewyan, he went on with François Mandeville to Fort Smith, where for a short period of time he recorded some texts in Hare.

Li's publications on Chipewyan began to appear after he returned to China. In 1933 he published his "Chipewyan Consonants" (Li 1933a) in

China and his "A List of Chipewyan Stems" (Li 1933b) in America. These two articles were the long-awaited reports on Chipewyan. The first reasserted Sapir's reconstruction of Proto-Athabaskan, and the second gave the stems which were necessary to proceed with further comparative work.

In 1946 he finally published his "Chipewyan" (Li 1946). This grammatical sketch was published as part of a volume planned by Sapir to honor Franz Boas, who had been the guiding force behind American linguistics. Li's sketch remains to this day a monument in the history of Athabaskan linguistics as well as a very practical working guide to the Chipewyan language.

In 1964, 18 years later, Li published one of the shortest of the 19 texts with a translation and grammatical notes (Li 1964). But until 1976 the remainder of the texts were still unavailable. These have finally appeared in an edition which R. Scollon prepared in collaboration with Fang-Kuei Li (Li and Scollon 1976). Thus 48 years elapsed between the original recording of these texts and their publication. The field notes which will be the basis for a lexicon of the language remain in manuscript form and it will be some years before they will also be available.

THE BOASIAN TRADITION IN
LINGUISTIC ELICITATION

From Fang-Kuei Li's publications on Chipewyan it can be seen that he was working within the general plan of research first organized by Franz Boas and then carried on by Boas's students such as Sapir. The original Boasian goal so far as American languages were concerned was to record as many of them as possible before contact with the advancing American frontier made this recording impossible.

Sapir's linguistic goals were somewhat more specific. He was working at the reconstruction of Proto-Athabaskan as a means of testing and demonstrating the method of comparative reconstruction for unwritten languages. This method had been amply tested in the Indo-European family, and Sapir was pursuing the method with Athabaskan while Bloomfield was doing the same with Algonkian. Sapir, of course, had much broader interests as well, as his writings on culture and personality show (Sapir 1949). It is clear, though, that Li did not share Sapir's wider interests, but rather was concentrating his efforts on linguistic reconstruction.

In making linguistic reconstructions, one of the most crucial considerations is the validity of the cognate sets. The words to be compared must be known to be truly comparable; that is, they must be the descendants of the same word in the original language or the set is invalidated. When eliciting words in a language not one's own, it is often difficult to know that a word is being accurately translated. The recording of texts was established as a useful means of obtaining coherent prose of a sufficiently high interest and value to the narrator that the task of dictation could be sustained for a long enough period of time to collect large amounts of fairly natural material for analysis. The coherence of the text guaranteed that the linguist and his informant really knew what a word meant because it was found in a larger context.

In its earliest form this kind of text recording served multiple purposes. It was used for linguistic analysis as well as for the ethnographic detail it embodied. With the specialization that began to develop in the 1920s, the Boasian tradition began to fragment. Certain researchers began to collect texts which were recorded only in English. In some cases these English texts were further polished by the ethnographer or folklorist so that all linguistic resemblance to the original was lost. Only the plot and basic themes of the original remained in these translated and paraphrased texts.

At the other extreme, linguists began collecting texts solely for the purpose of linguistic analysis. The content of the texts was taken to be only of marginal interest. Fang-Kuei Li's Chipewyan work falls into this latter group. His first publications covered consonants and stems (5 years after the original work). Then he wrote on phonology and morphology 18 years after the original work. Finally, 36 years after the original fieldwork, the first text appeared. This was followed in another 12 years by the full set of texts.

This narrowing of interests allowed researchers to be trained much more highly in their specialties. At the same time it is possible that this specialization removed an important control over the work of linguists and ethnographers. Although the linguistic work that Li did on Chipewyan is of very high quality, there remains a rather important question of the place of his sample in the larger speech community. His work does not tell us how other speakers speak, nor does it even tell us how François Mandeville spoke in any other situation. There is nothing in Li's reports of his work to tell us whether Chipewyan was a moribund language with this one speaker remaining or if it was vigorous. We do not know except by inference whether other languages were spoken in the same community and, if so, what place among them Chipewyan would have.

The splitting of the Boasian framework into separate specializations also implied that a position had been taken on the question of the relation between language and culture. It was implicit in linguists' work that it was not necessary to know a great deal about the culture to record the language accurately; at the same time, ethnographers and folklorists at least implicitly gave up any chance to discover a connection between language and culture by entrusting the study of language to linguists.

It is only fair to remember that for the purpose of historical reconstruction very useful work has been done without knowing anything more about a speech community than that one's informant is the most conservative speaker available. We can have the confidence that Li would have established and, in fact, did establish that much. But as the field of linguistics has evolved in the past 50 years, first drifting away from its concern with language in its social context and later drifting back, we now wish to have answers to questions about the speech community in which Fang-Kuei Li's work took place. These are among the questions that have led to the research reported here.

A SOCIOLINGUISTIC STUDY OF A CHIPEWYAN SPEECH COMMUNITY

In this research we were originally pursuing two related goals. The first was to do an ethnographic study of speaking in the community of Fort Chipewyan, Alberta, with a focus on the uses of Chipewyan narratives. We were particularly interested in the attitudes of speakers toward the use of Chipewyan by children. We were further interested in investigating the extent to which the forms of speech are related to the situation in which narratives are used. In spite of Li's important collection of narratives we knew very little about the place of such narratives within the speech community.

Toelken (1969) had shown remarkable differences in the same stories between the texts Sapir recorded as elicited texts in the Boasian tradition and the texts he himself was able to record in a natural setting of storytelling to children. Tedlock (1972a, b) further showed the importance for translation of such features as intonation, voice quality, and pauses which indicate features of the performance. Unfortunately, these features are not indicated in Li's Chipewyan texts. Moreover, Li did not investigate nonnarrative speech in use.

During the year preceding our field study, R. Scollon had worked with Fang-Kuei Li on translating and editing his texts for publication. In doing that work he had noted that there was internal evidence within the body of texts that the interaction between the linguist and the informant had changed over the period of the dictations. The later texts were much more smoothly dictated and were more stylistically consistent than the earlier texts. Frequent use of the marker *sni* ('they say' or 'it is said') in the early texts and much less use of this marker in the later texts also indicated a change in the situation (Toelken 1969). In addition, second-person references to the linguist were present in the early texts but absent in the later ones.

The question that arose was: In addition to the expected increased familiarity of the linguist with the language, to what extent do these changes also represent the linguist's increased sensitivity to the constraints of the form of the texts and to what extent do they also represent the informant's sensitivity to the linguist's interests? Richardson (1968) reported that the form of sentences may depend on the overall context of the discourse. Word order in narratives is quite different from word order in conversation, especially in the placement of adverbials. Lacking a fuller study of the use of narratives, or of speech to outsiders, any grammatical work done on Li's texts must be regarded as representing the speech of a single speaker who was speaking under the unusual conditions of dictation. The first goal of the research that we proposed, then, was to try to establish the place of Li's texts by comparing them with texts recorded in settings of naturally occurring narratives.

The second goal of this research was to study with native speakers, including children, a number of grammatical problems raised in R. Scollon's preliminary analysis of Li's texts. These problems centered on the difficulty in maintaining a clear distinction between lexical structure and syntactic structure on the one hand, and the use of several types of topicalization on the other. Both of these studies required the judgments of native speakers, and the study of topicalization further required the examination of actual performances where the information structure at the time of the utterance could be analyzed.

Our reasons for wanting to do this study began to develop in two separate areas, in doing research in child language (R. Scollon 1974, 1976a) and in doing field work on the Kutchin language in the summer of 1972 in Arctic Village, Alaska (R. Scollon 1975). In working with children it became increasingly clear to us that even as comparatively simple a linguistic system as that of a young child could not be regarded in isolation from the context of the use of that system. We found that the speech of the child could only be understood as situated speech and, further, that by taking this perspective, one could show a relationship between syntactic developments and the discourse structure of earlier interactive speech between the child and other speakers.

During the time we were doing research in children's language we took a 2-month field trip to Arctic Village. This was our first field experience with an Athabaskan language. We had understood from the literature

(Sapir 1921) that Athabaskans were extremely conservative and that borrowing in Athabaskan languages was rare, even in cases of frequent or prolonged contact with other groups. In Arctic Village, however, we found that the two historically separable languages, Kutchin and English, were virtually inseparable in actual use. Complex situations had been reported frequently for other languages and in highly urbanized communities, but with a few exceptions, such as Darnell's (1971) work in the Cree community of Calling Lake, Alberta, remote northern communities had been regarded as rather less complex.

In working over our field notes, and especially our tapes, it became increasingly clear that any linguistic study, however narrowly focused, must take into account patterns of use in the speech community of the study. Both in our child-language research and our Athabaskan work we also felt a need to develop methods of recording and analysis which would be more sensitive to speech as it occurred naturally, in contrast to speech elicited according to the linguist's preconceptions.

Over the preceding 2 years we had felt that these two lines of our work were converging on what Hymes (1972, 1974) has called the ethnography of speaking. Work currently being reported within this framework (for example, Bauman and Sherzer 1974) was dealing with just the kinds of questions that we had been raising in our own work (R. Scollon 1976a, b, c, 1977). In this research, then, we were proposing to unite our Athabaskan work with our work in child language, especially those aspects dealing with the relationships between discourse structure and syntactic structure within texts and the relationships between texts and the situations in which they occur.

These were our original purposes in this research, but as we worked in the field it became increasingly clear that of the two goals, the first goal, of studying the place of Li's texts in the modern context, was more important than the second goal of pursuing grammatical questions, and that in place of the second, a third focus had emerged. It was immediately obvious on arriving in Fort Chipewyan that linguistically it was a rather complex community and that before much else could be done a rather penetrating study of the speech community would have to be done. As we began to understand the role of Chipewyan we began to realize that there never would be a "good informant" to work with and that the questions of grammaticality would have to be studied obliquely if at all.

In Fort Chipewyan there is a long history of four languages in contact: English, French, Chipewyan, and Cree. These four have influenced each other to such an extent that considerable convergence has occurred. In light of Sapir's long-standing assertion that Athabaskan languages are very conservative (Sapir 1921) and our own research in Arctic Village (R.

Scollon 1975), it seemed that a more important immediate goal of this research should be to determine the extent to which Chipewyan has been influenced by other languages in this community.

THE PROBLEM OF THE MULTILINGUAL SPEECH COMMUNITY

The literature of sociolinguistics had dealt with multilingual speech communities as one of its central concerns. The question raised by Fishman (1972) of "Who Speaks What Language to Whom and When" has set the problem for many researchers. In looking more carefully at the phrasing of this question, however, it is clear that our interests are basically quite different from those of sociolinguists. This is partly a result of the nature of the speech community at Fort Chipewyan.

As Fishman has phrased the central sociolinguistic question both a certain kind of explanation and a certain set of basic assumptions are implied. The answer to the implicit "why" in Fishman's question is assumed to lie in various social factors such as socioeconomic grouping (Labov 1970, 1972a), the marking of ethnic identity (Barth 1969, 1972), or in special uses of languages such as to mark literary styles in contrast to colloquial styles (Ferguson 1959). As Gumperz and Hernandez (1972) have put it, in these studies of the emblematic uses of language, "The assumption is that the presence or absence of particular linguistic alternates directly reflects significant information about such matters as group membership, values, relative prestige, power relationships, etc. [p. 87]." In their own work Gumperz and Hernandez go on to point out that it is not the language itself that is necessarily indicating this social information, but rather it is the choice of one variety over another which conveys information in situations which have come to be known as code switching. "What the linguist sees merely as alternation between two systems serves definite and clearly understandable communicative ends. The speakers do not merely switch from one variety to another, they build on the coexistence of alternate forms to convey information [p. 98]."

The problem that sociolinguists have set for themselves is that of accounting for multiplicity of linguistic codes, and the explanations that are given relate to the communication of social information. This problem and this information have assumed, to begin with, that the definition of the speech community is unproblematical. That is, Fishman has not asked his first question: What is the domain within which we might reasonably ask "Who Speaks What Language to Whom and When?" Hymes (1974) and Gumperz (1968) have both emphasized the importance of the concept of the speech community as the foundation for further sociolinguistic work.

At the same time they and others have raised questions about the terms of Fishman's question: "who," "language," "speak," and "when." The literature of the ethnography of speaking (Bauman and Sherzer 1974, Gumperz and Hymes 1972, Hymes 1974) has quite fully discussed the problems involved with such matters as the isolation of linguistic varieties, participant status, and the structure and functioning of speech events and situations. More recently the focus of sociolinguistic work has become the face-to-face interaction where the interest is in the ongoing negotiation of such things as ethnic identity and other forms of group membership (Gumperz n.d., Goffman 1976).

Two assumptions underlie much research in sociolinguistics. The first of these is the assumption of the importance of social groups and the necessity of communicating information about these groups linguistically. We do not intend to suggest that social information has not been significant in the studies reported in the literature. We do want to suggest, however, that the importance of social groups is itself variable across cultural groups and so may therefore figure in much less significant ways in some speech communities than in others. We feel that the community at Fort Chipewyan is an example in which social grouping is of rather lesser importance than in any community we have encountered in the sociolinguistic literature and so social factors may be considerably less significant in linguistic functioning.

The second assumption that has run through the sociolinguistic literature despite the appearance of the contrary is that the normal state of affairs is that each speech conmunity should speak only one language. We are aware, of course, that this is the basic assumption by which linguists have traditionally related language and society. We are also aware that much of sociolinguistic research is seen as arguing against this assumption. We would argue, however, that the concern of sociolinguistics with multilingual communities reflects in part the assumption that multilingual communities are what need to be explained (Sankoff 1972).

To set this assumption in relief we only need to assume the opposite: that multilingual communities are the normal state of affairs. If we really assumed this at some pretheoretical level, we would no doubt find multilingual communities uninteresting and would instead find sociolinguistics both centrally preoccupied with speech communities in which a single language is used and also seeking explanations of this fact among various social factors.

This assumption is not as hypothetical as we have expressed it here. It is, in fact, the assumption made by many people at Fort Chipewyan. We found after some time that part of the difficulty we experienced in investigating the linguistic situation at Fort Chipewyan could be attributed to our approaching the community with assumptions about the nature of language that were quite different from the ones held there. Where we sought an explanation for the continued presence of Chipewyan, Cree, English, and French, people in the community were seeking an explanation for the insistence on the use of a single language by such outside institutions as the school and the church.

This difference in central assumptions may in the end be of little importance to this research since we ultimately intend to seek an explanation for one case in which a discrete language was recorded at Fort Chipewyan, the Chipewyan of François Mandeville. We have raised the question here as a means of narrating how the present position of this work was developed. By taking the speech community's point of view we are faced with an apparent contradiction. Although multiplicity of languages is taken as the normal state of affairs, there has been, in fact, a considerable amount of convergence among the languages used at Fort Chipewyan. If we take the traditional linguistic position that for each community there should be one language, we will seek no further explanation. Four languages are converging on one because that is the nature of language. Of course, the traditional linguist looks with horror upon conditions that suggest convergence of languages, so we might better characterize that position as saying that all but one language should die out leaving only lexical remnants borrowed into the remaining language. The point here, however, is that if we assume that there should be only one language at Fort Chipewyan, the convergence of languages there does not need to be explained. On the other hand, if we assume that multiple languages are normal, then we must seek out the explanation for the convergence that has taken place.

We may anticipate our later discussion by saying now that we feel the explanation for linguistic convergence at Fort Chipewyan lies in the characteristic way in which things are known by people in that community. That is, our explanation of linguistic convergence now looks to the worldview of the speakers. Thus our work which began in a sociolinguistic framework has become decidedly more ethnolinguistic than sociolinguistic. We are of course engaged in what Fillmore (1977) might call "exchanging mysteries." That is, we have decided to treat linguistic convergence as problematical and are seeking to explain that by reference to worldview. At the same time we are treating more central sociolinguistic issues, such as the role of communications about social groups, as either not relevant or uninteresting. Ultimately we will develop more fully our reasons for making this exchange of mysteries, but for now we will say only that we feel that this point of view more closely approximates what would be taken as a problem of significant interest in the speech community at Fort Chipewyan.

In the chapter to follow we will begin our discussion with the context of the informant narrative performance. Our purpose in this discussion is twofold. We are first of all concerned with the historical problem of relating the Chipewyan material elicited by Fang-Kuei Li to the context in which it was elicited. For this we need a fuller understanding of the relationship between the linguist and the informant in the situation of elicitation. At the same time, we feel that a rather full discussion of the performance context of oral narratives is necessary as background for our later discussion of linguistic convergence. In the literature on linguistic convergence and multilingual speech communities (e.g., Gumperz and Wilson 1971; Jackson 1974) there is very little discussion of the context in which samples have been recorded. To provide an example of linguistic convergence in which the context is rather fully described we are limiting most of our discussion to the study of a single narrative which was told first in Chipewyan and then in English within the same setting. Although this limits in various ways the generality of our statements about the community, it allows us to keep our discussion well grounded in the context of language use. Chapter 2, then, describes in some detail how our sample text is integrated into the situational context.

In the third chapter we will then look more closely at the linguistic convergence itself. Although the convergence we have observed has affected all of the languages at Fort Chipewyan, our example, by being in Chipewyan and English, necessarily limits the present discussion to primarily these two languages. The third chapter, then, presents in a basically descriptive format the phenomenon we are seeking to explain.

We have said that we feel the explanation for linguistic convergence at Fort Chipewyan lies in the worldview of the speakers. Because of a number of difficulties with the term ''worldview,'' we have felt it useful to develop a new term, ''reality set,'' which can be more directly related to the current literature in the social construction of reality (Berger, Berger, and Kellner 1973; Berger and Luckmann 1966). The fourth chapter is a discussion of the reality set we have called the ''bush consciousness'' and the relationships between this reality set and linguistic structure and use.

Our primary descriptive fact is the convergence of four languages at Fort Chipewyan. Our explanation is in the relationship of language to the bush consciousness. In the fifth chapter we then back up one more step to place the bush consciousness in context. That chapter discusses the history and social structure of the speech community as an explanation of how the bush consciousness is grounded in the social and cultural context. In a sense this is our explanation for our explanation.

The final chapter then seeks to frame our whole discussion within the history of Chipewyan studies and the development of theoretical frameworks in linguistics and ethnography. This chapter closes out the study by finally relating the Chipewyan work of Fang-Kuei Li to our own fieldwork.

2

THE CONTEXT OF THE INFORMANT NARRATIVE PERFORMANCE

FRAME

We begin on the narrative ground of this research. To do this we will first give a short narrative. This story which was untitled in the original took about 5 minutes to tell and so is not too long for us to look at in some detail.

1. *Once I hunted beaver. Being by myself I quickly traveled far across the Saskatchewan line where I thought there were many beaver.*

2. *There were not many beaver at that time. I left from Jackfish then.*

3. *Well, after traveling three days from there I still hadn't found any beaver. Then, on the third night I found some beaver and killed three of them.*

4. *Going on from there, there were many lakes and creeks all over. I came to a big river, Wolf River, which was not far and there I got two more beavers.*

5. *From there I crossed a big river and, passing a big hill, I came to Bear Trap Lake. That's what it is called. There are always beaver there. Then I got two more. (A little further) on the way was*

another lake where I got another two. Then coming back that same day I got still two more. So by evening I had killed six beavers.

6. *I decided to come back again from there the next day since I couldn't do anything there. There were no beaver, so I camped there.*

7. *Then as I was coming back, because I couldn't find any beaver, I came to Archer Lake, a big fishing lake where I have my trap line now. While I camped there it snowed a lot at night. The next morning you could only go straight ahead.*

8. *Well, there's a long, narrow lake where in the spring you can always see a lot of bears. There is a rapids and the fish are killed there. That's what the bears live on. In the spring there are always many of them there.*

9. *I had just about made it to the end of that lake when all of a sudden I saw a bear there not far from where I had to go. He was passing on the bear-crossing ahead.*

10. *Well, I only had a twenty-two with me. It was a nice, long single shot twenty-two. I didn't want to kill the bear but just to scare him away. I wanted to scare him by shooting a little away from him.*

11. *Well, it was quite close. I could tell by where the shells hit the ground. He just jumped back and came forward again. So I shot again.*

12. *The bear was coming up close and then going back into the bush again. He kept doing that.*

13. *Then finally, he went into the bush and didn't come out again. Then I thought I heard him roar in the bush. I thought maybe I had hit him. A bear will roar like that when he's going to die. So I thought I had hit him.*

14. *Well, I just went on. There's a trail by the lake going over the hill and as I came over the hill the bear charged me.*

15. *He came up about ten feet away and then stopped. Then he turned back. He went back into the bush but then charged out again. I still didn't shoot him. He came right up to where he had turned back before and then went back into the bush and came out again.*

16. *Now he was not far away. He was about eight feet and he kept coming back. My dog just went behind me and watched from there.*

17. *So then I shot him in the head. I couldn't miss because he wasn't far away. Then he collapsed. I shot him twice again. He was dead.*

18. *Then three bear cubs came from behind him.*

19. *I told them, "I'm very sorry. If I had known you were there I wouldn't have shot her. But I didn't know."*

20. *Well, I couldn't do anything for them. They would have died that way, anyway. So I took my butcher knife out of my back sack and after running them all together, I killed and butchered them.*

21. *There was a lot of good meat anyway. They were young and fat and in good shape. So I got all the meat together and the fat and packed it. My dog's pack wasn't heavy anyway. I got everything from those bears and then I camped there at that big lake.*

22. *So after camping there one night, I returned home.*

This narrative as it appears here is much like other Athabaskan narratives which have appeared in ethnographic accounts (Goddard 1912; Li and Scollon 1976; Lowie 1912; Mason 1946; Petitot 1888). It is presented in a reasonably idiomatic English which does not, however, disguise the basically Athabaskan character of the narrative. Ethnographers and folklorists have accomplished a great deal with narratives in this format. For our own sake here it might be useful to begin by seeing what can be said about the cognitive world of the narrator on the basis of this one narrative in this format.

At the first level of understanding, we can see several fairly transparent things about the narrator. He is a trapper, or at least he was at the time of the story. The time of the story is not well established except as being in the past, but the statement that there were not many beaver at that time indicates that it probably occurred during the 1920s or 1930s when the country around Fort Chipewyan was said to have been cleaned out of beavers (Fumoleau 1975).

The mention of his staying at Jackfish shows the narrator to be a Chipewyan because Jackfish is a Chipewyan reserve. This is, perhaps, the only overt indication of Athabaskan identity. As we shall see there are various other indications as well.

There may be several ways of interpreting the narrator's hesitation in shooting the bear at the climactic point of the story. His rifle was only a .22 and shooting at less than a certain distance would, perhaps, be more dangerous than not shooting at all. We feel, though, that we should believe the narrator when he says that he does not want to shoot the bear. He was in no immediate need of meat, having killed 11 beavers in the preceding 4 days and being on his way home. We feel, instead, that his hesitation in shooting is due to a deep respect for living things. It is with genuine regret that he tells the cubs that he is sorry for shooting their mother.

Here it is important to think about the narrator speaking to the cubs. There is no indication that this is anything but simple, direct speech to the animals intended to be understood by them. He does not say that he thought about saying this or that he felt sorry for them. He speaks to them directly. This is in partial sympathy with a view expressed by another person at Fort Chipewyan that there had been three creations. In the first creation everything could talk, the trees, animals, meat, or any other thing in the creation. This was the first and natural state of the world.

In the second creation the angels and the devil fought with each other and as a result many of the spiritual powers had been lost. The ability to speak had been restricted to only certain parts of the creation.

Finally in the third creation came Jesus, the whitemen, and the loss of speech to all but men. There were nevertheless some rare people who retained the ability to speak to and to understand animals. Some of these had lived for part of the time as animals and for part of the time as humans. The narrator in this case simply assumed this background and tells us that he spoke to the bear cubs. We are meant to understand this as a normal speech event.

We can also see that the narrator is careful to observe the prescribed ways of treating a bear which has been killed. He tells us that he "got everything" from the bears. This reminds us of the story told by François Mandeville of the man who hibernated with a bear (Li and Scollon 1976). The bear instructed him in the appropriate ways of treating bears with the injunction that he teach the people. The bear says,

> *Now when I am killed, eat me all up. And all of the people who are camped together must eat my flesh* [*p. 264*]

A little later when the people arrive we are told,

> *Then they killed the bear. They cut the bear up. Then they packed off all the bear meat* [*p. 264*].

The teachings of the bear as narrated by François Mandeville have been incorporated into the narrative we are now considering as the usual way of acting.

If we look at the less overt level of the structure of the narrative, the similarities with Mandeville's narratives indicate that this narrator is working within the same tradition. The story is untitled as we have mentioned above. In the collection of 19 stories told by Mandeville, none were originally titled. The titles that were recorded had been requested by Li (R. Scollon 1976b) and given only after the story had been told.

The structural organization of this story may be outlined as follows:

  a. Initial (1)
  b. Beaver hunt (1–7)
  c. Bear encounter (8–21)
  d. Final (22)

Within each of the two major sections there are further structural divisions.

  b. Beaver hunt
      1. Orientation (1–3)
      2. Kills three (3)
      3. Kills two (4)
      4. Kills six (5)
      5. Returns (6)
  c. Bear encounter
      1. Orientation (7–8)
      2. Big bear
          i. Sights (9)
          ii. Shoots (10–13)
          iii. Sights again (14–16)
          iv. Kills (17)
      3. Bear cubs
          i. Sights (18)
          ii. Regrets (19)
          iii. Kills (20)
          iv. Takes everything (21)

We can first focus on the initial and final. In Li's collection (Li and Scollon 1976) there are three stories which are Mandeville's own experience. They begin as follows:

> *Once in the winter we hunted beavers (1976:386).*
>
> *Once I shot a moose (1976:368).*
>
> *Once I made a canoe (Li 1964:132).*

From these we can extract the structural form for initials as, *Once* + (time) + verb. The initial in this story, of course, fits nicely into this pattern.

Generally, finals are less regular in the Mandeville texts (R. Scollon 1976b), but in this case the similarity between Mandeville and this narrator is striking. Mandeville (1976) ends his beaver hunt narrative with

In that way I returned home [p. 416].

This narrative ends

So after camping there overnight, I returned home.

This return to home reflects the generally cyclical structuring of Chipewyan narratives. Central characters start out in camp with the people, go out for the principal action of the narrative, and then return home again at the end. In this case the narrator places himself in this camp at Jackfish by implication in the second paragraph.

Toelken (1969) has suggested that a four-part structuring is characteristic of Navaho and perhaps Athabaskan narratives. At the most general level, this story has a four-part structure which is in turn divided into five parts (b, 1–5) and three parts (c, 1–3). Within the three-part section, however, there are two sections subdivided by four. These are (2, i–iv) and 3, i–iv). There seems to be here a more complex structural pattern, with Athabaskan patterning for the whole piece and for the lowest level of narrative action. The question we would want to ask is: To what extent do the five-part and three-part sections of the structure represent departures from an Athabaskan structure? The answer to this question would require looking into other narratives and may be deferred for the moment. Preston (1975), however, tells us that Eastern Cree narratives are organized around a three-part structure. We are also, of course, aware of the prevailing three-part structuring of European folklore (Jacobs 1959). We can suggest here that where this narrator departs from a four-part structuring of his story, this may represent the influence of either a Cree or a European tradition.

Finally, we can look at the two sections (c, 2) and (c, 3). In Mandeville's stories R. Scollon found that when Mandeville narrated hunting, certain actions were always treated as separate structural units (Scollon 1977). These were the sighting of game, attacking and killing, the assessment of the kill, and the review of further prospects. The encounter with the bears was not a hunt, and yet this narrator separates sighting, killing, and his assessment (that is, his regret over having killed the mother bear). This indicates a sense for the structuring of narrative action which is much like Mandeville's.

We have seen, then, that the narrator of this story is a Chipewyan trapper who was probably living and trapping during the 1920s or 1930s. His narrative performance appears to fall within the same narrative tradition that François Mandeville worked within. Presumably a larger collection of stories by the same person would take us a long way toward understanding both this narrative tradition and the cognitive world of the narrator.

This is the direction in which many ethnographic and folkloristic studies have gone in the past. Recently, however, in American folklore more attention is being given to the context of the performance of narratives (Darnell 1974; Hymes 1975; Tedlock 1972a,b). In this case we become interested in knowing more about the narrator. We want to know, for example, something about his performance history. Is this story an immature performance of someone else's narrative or the well-rehearsed performance of a mature narrator? Where does this narrative fit into his repertoire?

At the same time we also wonder why this story was told. Was it for entertainment, instruction, display of qualities of bravery, display of linguistic or narrative expertise? Any of these purposes are likely to affect the story as it is told, and that, in turn, would affect what could be inferred from a reading of the story.

The story as presented thus far tells us nothing about how the story was told. We would like to know first of all in what language it was told. Are we reading a translation, a paraphrase, or a direct transcription of the narrator's own words? We would also like to know what gestures were used or if they were used. And we would like to know about how loud and how fast and how fluently it was told.

Our approach now will be to look at some of these questions in detail. Rather than comparing many texts at the same level of analysis, we will look at this one text in many of its levels of performance and analysis. In doing so we have relied heavily on the work of Goffman (1974) for our conceptual framework. We can begin with the concept of frame.

The person who told this story was Benjamin Marcel (b. 1901). Marcel is registered in the Athabasca Chipewyan Band and his younger brother is Fred Marcel, the present Chipewyan chief. Marcel (Benjamin, unless otherwise clarified) is said to be a good storyteller by people in three generations, but it is also said he only does this storytelling "sometimes."

In the 1920s or 1930s Marcel went out from his camp at Jackfish for beaver. The level of primary activity which the story tells about was this trip. For our purposes it is probably best to follow Goffman (1974) and think of this as a strip of activity or string of events without further questioning the reality status of those events. We can think of this first level as simply the events of Marcel's life.

We can presume that Marcel had organized these events into larger pieces at some time before telling us this story. Our reason for thinking so is that we can point to a high degree of similarity in various different accounts of these events. It is in fact quite likely that he had told this story many times in the 50 or so preceding years. We also have Fred Marcel's comment that we cannot remember everything but only select interesting and important things and those we remember without changing.

This organizing of a string of events into larger pieces we can think of as framing those events. Where they become a part of a narrative, we can think of this as narrative framing. We see, of course, that not everything that happened between leaving Jackfish and returning is included in the narrative frame. We have no details of how Marcel made camp, slept, ate, located himself, traveled, or clothed himself. In the act of creating the narrative frame, the narrator selects certain events as significant and others as unimportant, and thus the events come to be thought of as a beaver hunt rather than as a long walk into Saskatchewan, or as four nights in a life, or as any other of the many possible characterizations of those same events.

The third level was framed when Marcel told R. Scollon this story in English at his own house one evening while we were visiting him. On that occasion R. Scollon asked him if he would be willing to tell the same story again some time so that it could be tape-recorded. Marcel agreed and some 2 weeks later came to our house. He first told the story in Chipewyan and then told it in English. This English version was also recorded. We will leave open for now the question of whether the second version in English was a translation of the Chipewyan version or a paraphrase of the first English version.

We can think of this story, then, in a set of successive frames. We begin with the string of events and end with the English version of the story told to us on tape. Each of these frames has transformed the preceding frame in some way. This framing may be sketched as shown in Figure 2.1.

There are several things to think about here. At each level of framing the preceding level is part of the known world or the context of the narrative. When Marcel performed the narrative at (e) in English, he knew we all knew he had just told the story in Chipewyan (d). Again, when he was telling us the story in Chipewyan (d), he knew that he had told R. Scollon this same story before in English (c). Before we can look for meaning in the narrative or in the language used in performing the

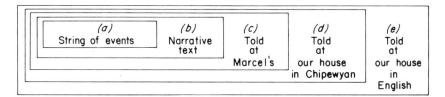

FIGURE 2.1. The story as a set of successive frames.

narrative it may be rather important to look into the effects of these earlier frames on the narrative.

There is another kind of framing, however, that must be considered before we can make much sense of the comparison of the performance frames. We are not really comparing Marcel's story at his house to the same story told at our house. We are comparing our notes taken after that first visit with our tapes and transcriptions of the second set of performances. We need to consider, then, what sort of framing or transformations of the original text takes place in going from the spoken word to typed English versions. These can be charted and then that chart can be superimposed on Figure 2.1 as shown in Figure 2.2.

Successive frames or transformations of the original experience by Marcel have been shown from left to right and have been given the letter labels (a), (b), (c), (d), and (e). Successive transformations of those frames in which R. Scollon was the author of the change have been listed vertically and have been given number labels; thus we have (c.1), (d.1) and (d.2), (e.1) and (e.2) and (de.1), (de.2), (de.3), and (de.4). At each of these framings a text was produced that was different in some important ways from the texts which had preceded it, and we would now like to look in some detail at what these differences were.

The first story that R. Scollon heard was told at Marcel's house during a visit and was not tape-recorded. After leaving the house he wrote out a note of some eight pages commenting on the whole visit. The section dealing specifically with this narrative is about one paragraph long. This paragraph is the text which is labeled (c.1). It may be quoted in full here.

> *BM told me about one time a bear kept coming up to him and finally it came up so close he had to kill it. Then just after that three cubs came up. When he saw the cubs he said he told that bear he was sorry he had killed her because he didn't know she had cubs. Earlier he had said that at Jackfish he had no one to talk to, no dogs even. So I gather that he feels talking to animals was ordinary. When I said maybe he would talk to himself he said no, he didn't* [Obs. VII: 29, 30].

FIGURE 2.2,

It is worth noticing now that in writing the note R. Scollon made no comment on the first section of the narrative, the beaver hunt. We cannot be sure now if he was told that part the first time. In this and other details we can see that the text of (c.1) represents a considerable transformation of the original, with everything but a few details of the second section having been lost. The original focus in writing the note was on Marcel's speaking to the bear(s). At that time our interest was in establishing who could be counted as a participant in a normal speech event, and that was what R. Scollon had been searching for in suggesting Marcel might talk to himself when he lived alone at Jackfish. Thus for us in the first occasion this was a narrative about language and participant status.

The second telling of the story (d) was tape-recorded and is about 4 minutes long. Marcel was acutely aware of this framing and in fact covered the microphone with his hand before beginning and then requested that the tape be turned off at the end. This text begins in English as follows:

> *Wait*
>
> *I tell you one time*
> *I going to hunt the beaver.*
> *So that's what I tell you first.*
> *Well ʔįɫá tsákayaú si θani.*

The first *wait* was said when R. Scollon turned on the tape recorder. The next paragraph was said with Marcel's hand over the microphone. Then after saying what the story would be about, Marcel begins with the formal initial of the story. From this we can see that Marcel felt it was important to frame the recorded narrative with an unrecorded introduction. He was apparently quite uncomfortable with the abrupt beginning of the narrative that had been threatened.

It can be seen that Marcel intended to record just the formally structured narrative from both this beginning frame and the ending frame. The story ends like this:

> *sɛkúɛ nɛsdja.*
> *now tθ'i ʔɛyɛr ots'én ʔúɫį that's all I know*
> *Stop it.*

The final of the narrative frame concludes with *nɛsdja* 'I returned'. Then Marcel switches to a mixed English–Chipewyan formula to close not the narrative but the performance. This formula is used very frequently now in narratives that occur more or less naturally. Another narrator used this in all her stories, both in stories told to us and in stories told to schoolchildren.

Following the performance close there is a pause, and then, because R. Scollon did nothing toward stopping the tape recording, Marcel said, *Stop it*, and waited until the tape recorder was turned off before resuming speaking. This *stop it* nicely parallels the *wait* with which he began the performance. It is clear that Marcel wished to be in control of the recording of his speech.

After R. Scollon had turned off the tape recorder, Marcel began to tell us what he had said in English. R. Scollon asked him if we could record that and he said it would be all right. So the third version of the story (*e*) was then told within a minute or so of the end of the Chipewyan version (*d*) and was also tape-recorded. This version is about 5.5 minutes long. It begins as follows:

> *You know I was going to hunt some beaver.*
> (*uh huh*)
>
> *There's not many beaver that time.*

In this version of the story the formal initial is somewhat different, but it must be remembered that Marcel had already begun to give the English version before the recording was begun. Considering that, we can see that he feels a strong narrative pressure to perform well-structured pieces, because when the recorder was turned on he began again with this general introductory statement.

The close of this story again indicates Marcel's awareness of the frame. He says:

> *I camp there and next day I going back*
> (*uh huh*)
> *That's all right.*
>
> *That's the story.*

Again, the formal final returns him to home. Since R. Scollon did not take that as sufficient reason to stop the recording, Marcel goes on to say, *That's all right.* Finally, he becomes fully explicit and says, *That's the story.* By this time we must have appeared to be very obtuse. It seems, however, that this demonstrates that Marcel was quite aware of the formal narrative frame as well as the performance frame and felt a strong necessity to have only what fell within the narrative frame recorded.

This level of framing is labeled (d. 1) and (e.1). It is well to remember, even though it is obvious, what can and cannot be recorded with audio recording. This recording preserves quite accurately both phonetic detail and prosodic features, such as intonation, pitch, rate of speech, pauses and other silences. It does not record, however, any information about gestures, direction of gaze, or body orientation and movement. To the extent that these are important in constructing a narrative, the audio recording is inadequate.

After Marcel's visit, R. Scollon wrote a short note about this visit of about three pages. The comment regarding these recordings was about a paragraph long. In part it compensates for some of the information not recorded on the audio recording.

> *He was quite shy about recording, saying that he couldn't tell it in English and I think despairing of the idea of telling me a story in Chip. When he did tell the stories he kept them short (in both Chip and in the English paraphrases) and at first looked away but then looked at me as he told them. He used more gesture and hand description in the English versions than in the Chip. I had the feeling that he regarded these versions as trying to tell me something which the gestures would help. The Chip versions—he kept restricting his arms. They were folded mostly and from time to time he would start to move and then stop. There was also more gesture when he was not recording than when he was [Obs. VII: 57, 58].*

This note is the frame labeled (de.1). The two stories were framed as part of a single larger event in the terms of this note. Marcel also told several other stories which are included in this frame but are not specifically considered here.

We can see now a difference between this note and the earlier one. Here, because we knew that the stories themselves had been tape-recorded, there was no need to mention the content or in fact any of the detail which would be preserved by the audio recording. This frame is complementary to the taped frames (d.1) and (e.1). Taken together they give a somewhat fuller view of the narrative performance.

The transcription of these texts formed the next level of framing (d.2) and (e.2). For the Chipewyan version (d.2), a transcription was made which was as phonemically consistent as possible. Where it was impossible to recognize a morpheme, however, it was necessary to write phonetically. Below the Chipewyan transcription we also wrote an interlinear, word-for-word translation. This transcription, which is about 10 pages long, was finished by the day following the recording.

The transcription of the English text was also done the same day. It is mostly in standard English orthography, but there are occasional departures to indicate phonological differences from standard pronunciation. For example, *them* is often written as *'em*. This transcription is also 10 pages long.

Some 2 months or so later, we developed the next level of framing. For the purpose of looking closely at phonetic variation in both Chipewyan and English, we retranscribed the two texts in a narrow phonetic transcription, indicating pauses, breath groups, and sentence prosody. These transcriptions were fully annotated, paying particular attention to structural detail and cross-referencing the notes within the text and to the other text of the pair. The Chipewyan version was given a word-by-word interlinear translation and the English version was given an interlinear orthographic transliteration.

This level of frame we have labeled as (*de*.2). It is important to remember that at the time of making this transcription we had access to the two earlier transcriptions and interlinear translations as well as to the original tapes. So the knowledge we had acquired about these texts in doing steps (*d*.1), (*e*.1), (*d*.2), (*e*.2), and (*de*.1) was incorporated into this transcription, translation, and annotation. And even within this step the work had to be done sequentially. So in making the phonetic transcription of the English text, we had the advantage of having just completed the phonetic transcription of the Chipewyan version.

By this time we understood the stories quite well. At least we were able to "account for" the presence of most of the morphemes, even in cases where these had been very reduced phonetically in the process of performing the stories. With this information at our disposal we then made a normalized, edited version in both Chipewyan and English (*de*.3). The words were written phonemically in Chipewyan (following Li 1933b, 1946, and Li and Scollon 1976) and orthographically in English. We left open the question of a different English phonemic system. These texts were paragraphed by breath groups and punctuated by clause or sentence intonation contours. Hesitations and slips of the tongue were edited out of this version. These texts represented the most fully analyzed and systematized versions of the texts that we could produce while still maintaining them as two separate versions of the story.

Finally, the last framing was produced by combining these two versions of the text into a composite version, translating the Chipewyan and paraphrasing the English into a single, idiomatic English text (*de*.4). This is the text presented above as Marcel's story about his beaver hunt.

It can now be seen that this story has been presented at some 14 removes from the original events which Marcel experienced. Less than half of these transformations were produced by the narrator. Most of them were created by the researchers and carry with them a load of theoretical baggage that must be understood if not unpacked. We would argue that this process of transforming and retransforming events, especially that done by the researcher, must be taken as a serious topic of ethnographic research if we are to make any progress on that elusive issue of what the nature of language is.

We now have the background to see that when we compare Marcel's stories (c), (d), and (e) we are doing so from different positions of knowledge. We know much more about the details of (d) and (e) and our knowledge is better developed at comparable levels. For this reason our study will largely center on those two texts and their subsequent transformations.

We still have some distance to go, however, before we can get to that comparison. First we might ask: Why frame experience at all? We feel the answer to this is, as Goffman (1974) has argued, that that is how our world is created. The ways in which we frame our experience are the ways in which we create our concept of reality. We frame the world because we are human. It is the basic cognitive activity of human beings.

For our purposes, though, we might consider the basic world-creating activity to go on between (a) and (b) and leave open for now the question of the role of language or, more specifically, narrative, in this creation of reality. There is still quite a bit to be found in the further framings of this primary reality.

We have said above that one of the goals of our research was to investigate the place of Chipewyan narratives in contemporary life. We can rephrase this more specifically in the case of this one narrative as investigating the successive framings. What happens when a story that is told casually as part of a visit in the home is later performed more formally on tape? What does it take to produce this change? Is it undertaken willingly as a natural occurrence or is it resisted? What happens when the language in which the story is told changes from English to Chipewyan and then back to English? What motives does the narrator have for these different retellings, and do these affect the linguistic and narrative structure?

A second goal of our research is to reconstruct as much as possible a similar situation for the working relationship between François Mandeville and Fang-Kuei Li. We will need to look at the framing of the narratives that Mandeville told to Li and see to what extent they are analogical to the frames we have studied for Marcel and ourselves. That is, we want to see in what ways the linguist–informant relationship was the same and in what ways it was different for the two situations.

We will also have to look closely at differences in the framings that we have produced and those that Li produced. We will want to consider to what extent we have shared goals and where our goals have differed, and to look at the effects of those goals on framing practices. When we have finished these discussions we will then be able to study in detail the actual language used by Marcel in the texts we are considering.

NARRATIVE DICTATIONS OF BENJAMIN MARCEL

It was quite difficult to make tape recordings of Chipewyan narratives in the speech community of Fort Chipewyan. Although we will defer the discussion of this problem until later, we would now like to discuss this statement in light of the cases in which it was possible. To begin, we found that narratives were being told "sometimes." As an example, we were told by a woman that when her sister came back to town for a visit after being away in Calgary their mother talked to them about the old days. This talk was described as "telling stories." From this report the stories were all about events in the life of this family when the children were young and the family lived in the bush. In other similar cases we were told about old people getting together on Sunday afternoon and telling stories. Again, these were said to be about "the old days." It was quite rare for anyone to tell us about stories that were not about the personal experiences of the narrator.

Stories, it appears, are most frequently narratives of personal experiences, not traditional myths and legends. They are told in gatherings of close family and then usually only on special occasions such as when someone returns after being away, especially when they have been away in a highly modernized environment. The stories, then, seem to be functioning as a means of resocialization to the life at Fort Chipewyan.

The chain of passing traditional narratives from older to younger generation appears to have been broken by the period of residence in the mission school. One older woman who had 12 children had raised none of them herself by her own report. They had all been raised in the mission school. This woman told us a story of the original Chipewyan–European contact, *θa náltθ'eri* (Fallen Marten). Some time later when we had transcribed it and typed it out in large type for use by the school children, this woman's son, a man in his 30s, came to visit. When we showed him the story he became very interested first in trying to read it in Chipewyan and then he became interested in the content. He said he had not heard this story before.

The occasion for this woman's telling the story was the first meeting of the Chipewyan class in the Native American Studies Program in the school. She told us beforehand that she felt children now were not learning anything about their own history and that this story was very important for them to know on those grounds. We find it ironic that she had sent her own son to the mission school, and, at least by his report, had never told him this very important story. It is perhaps hindsight that is leading the older people to become interested in passing on their traditional narratives to children. In any case it is often true (if not always true) that they themselves have not passed on what they know of this tradition to their own children. The narrative lineage appears to have been fully severed.

One further comment about the school program is appropriate here. When the school system was reorganized in 1975, it was argued that the children should have instruction in their "native language and culture." A survey taken by the Athabasca Cree–Chip Band School Advisory Committee showed that the native community universally supported this. When it came down to implementing this program, however, it became very difficult to do so. The storytellers did not want to go to the school. Although they expressed enthusiasm about the principle of the program and said they were willing to tell stories and even tape record them for the schoolchildren, they were too busy during the day with housework and in the evenings they preferred playing cards and bingo to tape-recording stories. This reaction was the same whether the contact was made by us, by the Chipewyan woman who was a teacher aide in the school, or by the schoolchildren themselves. It also made no difference when the schoolchildren left the school to go visit the older people. The reasons why it was not possible "at the moment" were always the same. People were otherwise occupied.

In the long run, even though we were strangers and did not understand Chipeywan well, we had the best success in at least hearing traditional narratives and sometimes even in recording them. We can attribute this only to a persistent interest. Where the sons, daughters, and grandchildren would stop listening and go back to watching television, we would keep listening. Although there were people in the community who remained suspicious of our interest in their past, it was generally recognized that we were interested, and this no doubt was a welcome change for some of the older people with whom we worked.

Fred Marcel, the Chipewyan chief, told us that various other people from the community had tried to make recordings in the past but had been unsuccessful. One difficulty may be that recording narratives redefines the situation too strongly. Several times when people were quite drunk they told us stories, especially about Raven Head (*datsą́tθí*, cf. Li and Scollon 1976) and Sakiscak (cf. Wolfart 1973 for mention of Cree stories of *wīsahkēcāhk*). They said that they could not record in that condition because they would get "all mixed up." Thus we can suggest that there is a set standard for the performance of a narrative which may be relaxed under conditions of drinking, especially when everyone is drinking, but which nevertheless is not relaxed in the recording frame.

Other claims were that though one knew about the story, one did not know how to tell it. Or in some cases one knew only a fragment of the story but could not complete it. Putting these things together, then, we see a seriously eroded narrative tradition. While the memory of the formal characteristics of a well-performed narrative remains, the contents are rapidly being lost. People are willing to perform these narratives that are imperfect in various ways only to intimate audiences. When the performance situation is altered by the inclusion of the impersonal and distant recording, it takes a great deal of goodwill on the part of the narrator to overcome his or her resistance to performing.

Benjamin Marcel is a man with much of this goodwill. We met him the first day we were in Fort Chipewyan when we went to call on his brother, Fred Marcel, who has been the Chipewyan chief since 1954. We showed Fred Marcel the Mandeville texts (Li and Scollon 1976) and described the work we hoped to do in Fort Chipewyan. He was very interested and enthusiastic and asked his brother Ben to come and listen as R. Scollon read several of the stories. At this time we talked little directly with Ben Marcel.

From the next day we began to develop a friendship. When we met him shopping at the Bay (Hudson's Bay Company retail store), Marcel spoke to us in Chipewyan and we struggled to answer. From then on we met almost daily in accidental encounters downtown. Within a week we asked Marcel if he would tell us stories. His only response at that time was to laugh. Later we learned that he felt his English was not good enough to do this.

After being away at Jackfish for a month or so Marcel returned to town. We met once and he asked very indirectly if we could get him some plywood from the school for his boat. His request implied that he had characterized us as being somehow related to the school. We presume he thought us to be teachers. We had no connection with the school at that time, and because we did not share this presupposition, we understood only much later what he had been asking of us or even that he had been asking for something. After this meeting Marcel returned to Jackfish for another few weeks.

When he returned from the bush we met again a few times in town. In each of our meetings we first talked in Chipewyan. We would say all that we could that was relevant to the situation. This consisted mostly of comments about the weather. When we had exhausted our repertoire of small talk, we would then ask about something else, also of relevance to the situation. On occasions where we introduced topics at some distance from the situation, Marcel would quickly excuse himself and go on to speak to someone else. On occasions where we did not press for new words or topics Marcel often volunteered things.

This pattern was very useful for some time in finding ways to talk in the single most common speech situation we had in which we needed or could use Chipewyan. Of course we were always interested in fuller conversation or getting beyond the immediate situation. With few exceptions, however, neither Marcel nor others with whom we developed a similar pattern would tolerate much talk in Chipewyan that moved out of the ongoing context.

One of these exceptions came in the fall when we met Marcel walking outside our house. He was ostensibly on his way to visit someone else but came in for tea. He claimed he was "not doing nothing anyway." While visiting we talked about Chipewyan. He told us various words and finally agreed to let us tape record two short narratives. The first described how he tans moosehide, and the second was the traditional *His Grandmother Raised Him*. Marcel felt it was odd that this story had not been included in Mandeville's collection. As we found out later, Mandeville had arranged for another narrator to tell this story to Li and thus he had considered it included although he did not himself tell it.

On this occasion R. Scollon said he would write out the stories as Marcel had told them and then come to him and let him correct any errors. Although we had made a transcription within several days, this did not take place for nearly 2 months. In the interim we met Marcel many times as before and he often said he'd come "visit" to "help with the stories," but in fact he never came, and when we went to see him he claimed to be very busy. This must be taken partly at face value. During the fall he was quite busy hunting ducks and cleaning them. There were also, of course, times when he would stand chatting in the Post Office for hours. From this we took his busyness to indicate some disinterest in what we were wishing for him to help us do.

Three weeks before Christmas we went to visit Marcel in his home. He had told us his wife had been asking him to see "our stories," that is, the Mandeville stories. This was the visit labeled as (c) above during which Marcel first told the story about the bear and promised to come to our house to record it.

Two weeks later we met Marcel in town in the morning. Again, we asked him if he was going to "visit" us. He said he might because he was "not doing nothing anyway." Notice that this is the way he put it the first time as well. That afternoon he came. That visit is the one during which he told the versions of the bear story, his beaver hunt, labeled (*d*) and (*e*).

Marcel had just returned from trapping to spend Christmas in Fort Chipewyan when we visited him 3 weeks before Christmas. His trapping had been quite successful and he was feeling satisfied. Although we do not have a complete record of what happened during the visit, a number of things can be mentioned which will give a fuller view of one situation in which a narrative was told.

Marcel showed us his family Bible in which the family history was recorded. We had been interested in genealogies, especially in light of several cases we had heard of in which switches between Cree and Chipewyan band registry had occurred. In this case we learned that Marcel's wife was from a Cree family that had begun to consider itself Chipewyan.

During the visit our 2-year-old daughter was displaying her few words of Chipewyan which included *sas* 'bear'. We told Marcel of her fondness for Mandeville's version of the man who hibernated with a bear (Li and Scollon 1976:254). Marcel then began telling the story. The story corresponded detail by detail with the version that Mandeville told. Marcel, of course, was telling it to us in English.

Before going further, we should note here that this indicates that Marcel's knowledge that we knew the story was taken as a reason to tell his version of the story, not to refrain from telling it. This we noticed in other cases. Repetition is relished. A single story may be told two or three times in succession by either the same or different narrators, with or without changes. Thus as an elicitation technique, one does well to display whatever knowledge one has of the stories one wants to hear. Ignorance begets ignorance in this case.

When Marcel got to the part of the story where the man and the bear lie down in their den for the winter, Marcel began to tell of some of his own experiences with sleeping bears. He told of coming back from trapping one time when he drove with his dogs and sleigh directly over a sleeping bear which did not move.

Here we might note that Marcel used a portion of a traditional narrative as a bridge from the current topic to a personal experience. Since this was followed by more narratives of his own experience and since we have observed above that the great majority of stories told appear to be of this type, we can see that the functional role of traditional narratives may have been shifted considerably in recent times. In the way that Kirschenblatt-Gimblett (1974) has observed for East European Jewish narratives, a

Chipewyan narrative may be used in whole or in part as a device for producing a larger structural whole. Here we suggest that the preferred whole is a multilingual, multiparticipant speech event in which through relating personal experience one displays one's own position in the conflict between worldviews in the community.

Several days before this visit with Marcel, R. Scollon had recorded some stories that Marcel's younger brother, Fred, had told. One of those stories was about a time when the younger Marcel had killed a bear with an axe. R. Scollon told the older Marcel, who incidentally is about 20 years older, about this story. He then told us about how he had killed a moose with a butcher knife and then just the next day killed a bear with an axe.

We suppose Marcel anticipated some skepticism because he also told us who the witness was that we could consult about these events. We were reminded of the young Kutchin man in Arctic Village, Alaska, who told us of his ambition to kill a grizzly bear with just a jackknife. It seemed that this might be a genre of bravery-test narratives that would be interesting to record, and so we asked Marcel if he would come to our house to record these stories and to help us with details of the two stories we had recorded some 2 months before. He agreed.

It was after all this talk of bears and bravery that R. Scollon asked Marcel, as we said above, about who he talked to in the bush. He then told the story which we are now seeking to put in context. We can note three details of the story which specifically relate to stories told earlier. In this case he went out alone. This makes the exploits somewhat more daring but also raises the question of verifiability. He not only faced one bear at 8 feet or so before shooting it with only a small caliber rifle, he also killed three others with a butcher knife. Following the killing of a moose with a butcher knife, this killing of the three cubs is more feasible than it might have been without narrative preparation. Finally, in the detail of gathering up all the meat and fat and packing it back, he has shown himself to be aware of the end of the traditional story he did not actually finish earlier. He has, in fact, fully assimilated the traditional story to the narrative performance and displays its conclusion through a narrative of his own experience.

We may now raise the question of why Marcel told us this story. As an answer we would suggest in anticipation of Chapter 4 that it displays his position in the conflict between worldviews. In this story he shows himself to be strongly in sympathy with the reality set we will characterize later as the bush consciousness. In the context of a "quiet" evening of conversation with friends we can see him emphasizing qualities of individuality, nonintervention, and integration. There is no doubt also of an interest in not letting his younger brother get away with all the glory for bravery; and the older Marcel's stories are certainly the equal and perhaps just a bit better in this regard than his brother's.

Finally, we should consider Marcel's appreciation of a sympathetic audience, especially among the younger generation. As we sat and talked on this "quiet" evening, some 10 or 15 Marcels of two generations came in and out while some of the younger ones played. None of them showed the slightest interest in our conversation when they discovered it was about "the old days." There was no attempt to show respect by being quiet even if they had no intention of listening. Marcel frequently asked the younger children to go play in another part of the house, even if just 10 feet away from right in front of us, but these attempts to clear a space for this conversation were largely futile. A television set played loudly about 10 feet in front of where we sat and was the general focus of the room, not the old grandfather telling of the exploits of his youth. In the face of this struggle for attention it is not surprising that many of the older people despair of the younger generation taking any interest in their knowledge and tradition.

When Marcel came to our house 2 weeks later it was tacitly to record the stories he had told during this earlier visit. Yet we did not immediately broach the subject. We chatted for a time first. He said he would record "later."

For some time we had hoped to get his help in clarifying certain parts of the stories he had recorded the first time. We got these out, both tapes and transcriptions. It turned out to be impossible, however, to clarify anything. If we said the unclear portion ourselves from the transcription, he said he could not hear what we said. If we played the tape and asked him to say it again slowly, he would either say something quite different, that is to say, he would paraphrase the original, or he would repeat the same thing at about the same rate of speech and with the same amount of phonological reduction as in the originally recorded text.

In making such attempts at somewhat more traditional informant work, we made sure to ask both about things which were quite clear to us and about things on which we genuinely needed help. From the cases in which we were able to understand quite well what was being said, it became clear that Marcel would not display a citation form of speech which was different from his normal (and quite rapid) speech. The form of the texts he dictated in running speech is substantially the same as the form when he was speaking carefully. This in itself may be a major difference between modern Chipewyan speakers at Fort Chipewyan and Mandeville.

The next thing we worked at on this occasion was the basic noun dictionary we were compiling for school use. Marcel's interest in this was high but he freely admitted not knowing many things. The Chipewyan names for the months is an example of one of the lacunae in Marcel's traditional vocabulary. On the other hand he did know of such traditional cultural objects as bows and arrows. This may be compared with another person, a woman, who was able to give us the names of the months but did not know how to say 'bow' or 'arrow' in Chipewyan, though she did know them in English. Thus we see that a basic traditional vocabulary is not uniformly controlled by even the older generation of speakers.

In this dictionary work as in the texts, Marcel's forms were said quickly, and when they were repeated it was nearly always with some phonological changes. In the cases where we had the same terms from Mandeville we saw that there had often been considerable reduction in the overall length and complexity of the terms.

Finally we asked Marcel if he was willing to record the stories we had asked him about. He said he was willing and so we brought out the tape recorder. As R. Scollon turned it on, Marcel said *wait*, as we have described earlier. He then covered the microphone and said he would tell about hunting beaver. Then, uncovering the microphone, he began with the traditional initial of his beaver hunt.

Following the story of the beaver hunt in Chipewyan and the English version, Marcel reversed the order of the performance at his home and told about killing the moose with a butcher knife and killing the bear with an axe. These were told together as a single narrative and followed by the English version. This time he recorded in English without any hesitation.

When he had finished this he said he was tired and had to go down to the Bay (Hudson's Bay Company retail store) to shop before supper. After he drank his tea he got up to leave. We paid him, and although he protested that it was too much for what he had done, he took the fee and left. On the way out he told us the word for the rubber boots he was putting on.

We can see in this "visit" some of the same goodwill and interest in helping us with our work that Marcel always displayed. We can also see, however, an underlying hesitation and resistance to doing the recording. Because his reasons for not wanting to record were probably much stronger than his reasons for recording, we suggest in this case it was the need for cash in the period preceding Christmas that made him overcome his general resistance. This seems to be supported by the fact that a woman with whom we had also been working went through nearly the same pattern, including coming to dictate stories shortly before Christmas. She more openly said she needed the money.

The two situations we now have before us to compare can be seen to be quite different in certain respects. In the first case the narrator was at home among his family, disinterested as they may have been. He was under no pressure to tell any particular story and very much in control of the flow of the narrative performance. In the second case he was in our home and under some pressure to tell stories for recording. His control over the total narrative performance was limited and shared.

In spite of the situational differences and the differences in the total narrative performance, the narratives themselves are remarkably constant, at least in structural outline. He told the same stories and told them in essentially the same way. Here we can mention again the recordings we had made of Fred Marcel's stories. Very early in our field period he had told us that he wished to record his life story and was happy when we said we would like to help him to do it. At that time he told in very rough outline which things he thought he would tell and how they would be arranged. He emphasized that he could not tell everything because he did not remember it all. He felt that he had remembered just the important details and would therefore include just those.

When we finally prevailed upon Fred Marcel to tell this story we were quite surprised at how closely the story he told followed the outline he had suggested several months earlier. Of course, we had written down the outline. He himself claimed to have no memory of having talked about just what would be in the story before.

We wonder, then, at what level the memory of these events is preserved. Is a narrative structured around certain events and then remembered as a story which is then told and retold? Or are the events structured and remembered at some deeper level from which narratives are constructed according to the dictates of the performance situation? We prefer the latter because of the cases where the "memory" is not held by a single person. We have observed remarkable similarities between a narrative told by Marcel about how he tans a moosehide and Mandeville's narrative on the same topic some 50 years earlier (Li and Scollon 1976:368). Marcel never head Mandeville tell this story. We suggest that it is the similarity in the process of tanning and the structural organization of narratives working in conjunction which produce the overall likeness. We feel it is most reasonable to think that for the individual narrator it is a constant framing of the original events added to the requirements of traditional narrative structure which results in the very great similarities in successive tellings of the same story.

When we compare the three tellings of Marcel's beaver hunt we see, then, that the biggest difference is a result of the language used. The two tellings in English were intended to tell us about the event. The telling in Chipewyan was intended to display this story in Chipewyan. The gestures that Marcel used in the English version and his restriction of gestures in the Chipewyan version indicate that the degree of communicative involvement was quite different. Our own responses to the narrative were also quite different. In the English version R. Scollon responded with *Uh huh* after nearly every breath group. In the Chipewyan version he rarely responded. Thus both narrator and audience thought of the task as quite different in the two cases. As we shall see below, these differences are reflected in a difference in the overall narrative structure and point to an important interaction between the communicative intent of the participants and the structure of narratives.

THE NARRATIVE DICTATIONS
OF FRANÇOIS MANDEVILLE

When we think of the ease with which Fang-Kuei Li plunged into his work with François Mandeville, emerging 6 weeks later with 10 books of texts and 2800 slips of verb paradigms, and compare it with our own fieldwork at Fort Chipewyan, we are not only personally discouraged but we are also made aware that something is very different in the two fieldwork situations. The greatest single difference was in the person of François Mandeville. He was intelligent, articulate, well traveled, at least in the Mackenzie River Basin, and took a considerable interest in developing his own knowledge and the knowledge of others. He came from a family of interpreters, and when Li arrived in Fort Chipewyan everyone directed him to Mandeville.

Mandeville's only son, Philip, is still living as of this writing and was present during the time of the Li–Mandeville collaboration. He was about 25 years old at the time, and his description of the situation as well as his history of his father's life are invaluable records in trying to understand the differences between Li's fieldwork and ours.

According to Philip Mandeville, François Mandeville was not originally from Fort Chipewyan. He was born in 1878 at Fort Resolution, some 250 miles downriver from Fort Chipewyan. His father was Michel Mandeville, the interpreter for the Treaty Eight Commission at Fort Resolution. His grandfather had also been an interpreter. The Mandevilles all spoke Chipewyan in addition to French, which they regarded as their language.

François Mandeville's mother was Marie Fabien. Philip regards his family as being French and, although they all spoke Chipewyan, he considers French to be their "mother tongue." In speaking of his family, Philip does not use the term "Métis" which is commonly in use in Canada for people of mixed native and European blood, even though most of its members in all generations but the first were of mixed blood. He apparently prefers "French."

François Mandeville worked during his youth at Fort Resolution for the Hudson's Bay Company. His son says he was a company man to the end of his life though there were periods when he worked for various competitors. In 1901 when Metis were given script for their share of land, Mandeville sold his share to finance his wedding at the age of 23. He went to Fort Rae where he married Margaret Lafferty, a Metis woman who could speak Dogrib in addition to her French "mother tongue." The new couple soon returned to Fort Resolution and in 1902 their only child, Philip, was born.

In 1908 Mandeville took his family to Hay River where he worked for the independent traders Heslop and Nagle. There he learned to speak Slavey and some Beaver. He then continued using Slavey when he moved to work at Fort Providence in 1910. It was his father's wish for him to work for the Hudson's Bay Company, however, so when his father died in the same year, he returned to Fort Resolution to rejoin the company.

In 1911 the Hudson's Bay Company moved Mandeville to Fort Smith where for 2 years he was in charge of their new trading post there. At Smith he was trading primarily with Chipewyans and thus frequently used that language there.

Two years later in 1913 he was moved again. This time he went to Fort Wrigley down the Mackenzie River. He quickly adjusted the Slavey he had learned at Hay River to the dialect differences at Wrigley. Then in 1915 he went farther down the Mackenzie to Arctic Red River where he learned Hare and Loucheux. According to Philip, he was soon able to speak just like the people who had always lived there.

His next position with the company brought him back into more central Mackenzie Athapaskan with an assignment at his wife's old home town, Fort Rae. When they went there in 1917 Mandeville could probably already speak some Dogrib. His wife spoke Dogrib as well as French and there had been Dogribs at Fort Resolution in his younger years. At any rate, before becoming sick and having to leave the Hudson's Bay Company in 1921, Mandeville had again become able to speak "like the people who had always lived there."

In 1921 Mandeville returned to Chipewyan territory. This time he went to work for an independent trader at Fond du Lac at the far end of Lake Athabasca from Fort Chipewyan. Philip remembers his father at the Fond du Lac store standing by the stove exchanging stories with all the old people of the region. Mandeville in his travels had acquired quite a collection of stories which he told to the people there in Chipewyan, and they in turn told him their stories. Philip regards this as the period in which his father began to truly develop as a storyteller.

After 4 years at Fond du Lac, Mandeville then went into retirement at Fort Chipewyan. There he passed his time building various boats, skiffs, and canoes. He is well remembered today for his exceptional skill and for the great degree of care he took in "everything he did." He was a meticulous craftsman as well as a consummate storyteller. This was the period in Mandeville's life when Fang-Kuei Li met him. He was 50 years old at the time.

Finally after 15 years at Fort Chipewyan, Mandeville went out to trade again. This time he went to a location on the Peace River in Wood Buffalo National Park. He moved out there in 1940 where he traded with Chipewyans and Crees living in that area. Thus it was only near the end of his life that Mandeville began to learn any Cree. His interest in languages had before that time encompassed French, his "mother tongue," English, Chipewyan, Slavey, Beaver, Dogrib, Hare, and Loucheux. As a religious man, Mandeville had spent much time reading Biblical narratives in both French and Chipewyan. He had lived in five different locations in which Chipewyan was used and thus was well aware of much of the range of variation within that language as well.

Mandeville died at Fort Chipewyan in 1952. He was 74 years of age. His reason for spending so much of his time in his later years at Fort Chipewyan was that he had "done well with the Bay." That was its Athabasca–Mackenzie headquarters and had been so for many years. He was not in good health and his sister had settled there. It was also a good place for the hunting and fishing that he loved to do.

The reputation Mandeville has in Fort Chipewyan, the report of his own son, and Fang-Kuei Li's account all confirm that François Mandeville was an unusual person. He was shown "the ABCs" by Father Dupire on one of his visits to Fort Resolution. Otherwise he was entirely self-taught and yet, as Philip Mandeville says, "He had beautiful handwriting," and "He could talk on any subject with the best of them." His interest in language was considerable. He could write in the syllabic system which had been developed by the Wesleyan missionary, James Evans, as well as alphabetically, and in later years he read "everything." He was an excellent mimic and especially enjoyed entertaining people by giving impersonations of oddities of speech whether dialectal or idiosyncratic. Thus we see that not only was Sapir's student Fang-Kuei Li "very able," he had met in François Mandeville an equally able partner. He was a man who had by the accident of his personal experience taken a speaker's course in comparative Mackenzie-drainage Athabaskan. He was very well prepared to abstract and isolate a conservative and, as we will argue in Chapter 6, a partly reconstructed Chipewyan which was just the target of Li's research in the field.

It is not surprising, then, that when Li arrived at Fort Chipewyan he was immediately directed to Mandeville. As they began working Mandeville took quite an interest in Li's phonetic writing since he himself had struggled for many years to find a way to write Chipewyan exactly. Several people have told us that as Li and Mandeville worked, Mandeville kept notes. We have no record, however, of what the content of these notes might have been. It is likely that he was trying his hand at phonetic writing. Perhaps he may have also been making notes about the stories as he told them in his concern to create a coherent narrative performance in the face of the difficulties of slowly dictating his texts.

Li and Mandeville worked at Mandeville's home every day except Sunday for about 6 weeks. In the evenings Mandeville took Li around to visit other storytellers and to hear others speak Chipewyan. Their manner of working was for Mandeville slowly to dictate a text which Li would transcribe phonetically. As they went along Mandeville would ask Li to read it back to be sure he had gotten every detail. When the text was completed they would then return to the beginning and go through it word by word, translating and annotating it. At each stem Li would ask for the fullest paradigm he could elicit, and in this manner the 2800 file slips of verb paradigms were obtained.

We can now return to the question of frame. If we draw a chart showing the narratives as Mandeville and Li framed them we will then have a basis for comparison between those framings and ours (Figure 2.3).

The set of frames we have used here assume the events in (*a*) were real ones from the life of Mandeville which have been framed in (*b*) as narratives. This would only apply to three of the full set (Li and Scollon 1976, Nos. 15, 16, and 18). These three would compare best, however, to the text we are considering for Marcel. For traditional narratives the relationship between (*a*) and (*b*) is somewhat more of a problem in crossing cultural boundaries. Events framed in narratives are understood by many to be real but to have not actually happened either to the current narrator or in the current time period. Others consider them to have not actually occurred. In any event, at least one more frame is introduced between (*a*) and (*b*) for traditional narratives. This is the narrative framing of the narrator from whom the story was learned.

For our purposes we are concerned with the frames labeled (*c*) and (*d*). These are the dictation in Chipewyan (*c*) and the glossing and annotation in English (and French) that followed (*d*). We are also interested in the vertical frames which are those created by the linguist, Li. The first level (*c*.1) and (*d*.1) has been described above. The remaining steps were

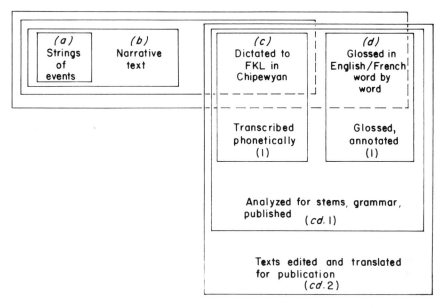

FIGURE 2.3.

taken later. The frame (cd.1) took place in several steps. The stem list and the analysis of the consonants were finished and published in 1933 (Li 1933a,b). The grammatical sketch did not appear until 1946 (Li 1946). Thus this step was really several steps taken over a number of years.

The last frame (cd.2) was the editing and publishing of the texts. This frame, again, was produced in several steps. The first was the publication of the single text in 1964 (Li 1964). Then the full set was edited, translated, and published in 1976 (Li and Scollon 1976).

We can now see more clearly what the differences are between the Marcel frames and the Mandeville frames. The first difference is that there are no informal visits in which stories are told casually without recording. Some of this did occur presumably as Li and Mandeville went about town visiting in the evenings, but no record exists of any of those visits.

A second difference is that whereas Marcel rarely could be induced to give citation forms, Mandeville ultimately gave only citations forms. The texts were dictated slowly and carefully with every tone considered deliberately. Thus there is little phonological reduction or tone sandhi which is produced by sentence prosody. What exists in the Mandeville texts can be considered to be a lexical level of morphophonological processes.

The slowness of the dictation raises the question of how well Mandeville could have maintained the structural organization of the whole text when he was being careful of each morpheme. Philip Mandeville feels that this was no problem. His father had told the stories many times by 1928 and knew them well. Not only that, Philip claims that once his father learned a story he never departed from the form. Of course, Philip had heard his father tell many stories many times so this claim is to be taken seriously. There is indeed a formal regularity in the texts that is striking. Both the general narrative structure and the lower-level syntactic structuring are very regular and highly formal. We take these as marks of a well-developed repertoire. Here it may also be remembered that Mandeville took notes and perhaps in this way he was able to maintain the structural integrity of the narratives, especially those which were dictated over a period of several days.

The transcriptions that Li made were quite narrowly phonetic to begin with but became somewhat less so in the texts dictated later. In one text about midway through the fieldwork there are bracketings of nonsignificant phonetic detail and markings indicating probable word boundaries. Nevertheless Li followed Sapir in never fully phonemicizing as he took dictation. Thus, for example, all [t]s with the strong velar aspiration are still written [t^x] in the last pages of transcription, even though by that time Li was certain that [t^x] did not contrast phonemically with [t'].

The last difference to be considered is that there is no paraphrase or translation of the texts produced in a different language as a narrative performance. Of course Mandeville could have done this in, perhaps, eight languages. The glosses in English were prepared a word at a time. The high degree of cooperation in this frame makes it really a jointly produced frame. In our case this word-at-a-time translation was impossible to achieve with either the original narrator or other native speakers. What we have are full English performances which are, in fact, the real communications between the performer and his audience. In the sections which follow we hope to demonstrate fully the interest and value of these parallel versions of the same text. Here we must admit, however, that at the time of recording there was simply no other way of getting a translation.

In concluding this section on the context in which our material was collected we can emphasize that fieldwork is not unilaterally controlled by the researcher. In Li's case there was an unusually good matching of the goals of the researcher and the talent and experience of the informant. Li has told us (personal communication) recently that of the more than 40 languages he has worked with in the field in both North America and Asia, his field situation with Mandeville was one of the best.

In our own case we were inclined to think at times that we were in one of the worst situations likely. In both cases the material that was collected as well as the means of collecting it were the result of an interaction between the informants and the researchers which could be only partly anticipated. In our case the unanticipated good fruit of what at first seemed to be infertile sowing was a view of languages in contact that we might well have missed had we found an informant such as François Mandeville.

MARCEL'S BEAVER HUNT

We can now return to the story above, the story of *Marcel's Beaver Hunt*. The versions of the text that we will use first will be the texts labeled (*de.*3) in Figure 2.2. This level is phonemic for Chipewyan and orthographic for English. It includes a fair amount of analysis and "reconstruction" on our part. That is to say, in a number of cases the morphemes given were interpreted on the basis of very reduced phonetic forms. This problem will be taken up somewhat later when we compare the narrow phonetic transcriptions with these versions. We feel, however, that it is important to give a view of the larger structural details first, and a narrow phonetic transcription provides too much detail for the discussion which immediately follows.

We have introduced several conventions in writing the texts below which need to be clarified now. For some of these we are indebted to Tedlock's (1972a,b) efforts to develop improved ways of representing texts which have crossed a major linguistic boundary before being presented in written form. In some cases this boundary is translation, in others it is the transition from oral to written texts and in most cases with which Tedlock has been interested, it has been both boundaries at the same time.

The largest divisions are marked with a line of space. This indicates that the narrator paused and took a breath. These divisions have been numbered consecutively for referencing. A pause without a breath is indicated by beginning a new line. Where this pause group is larger than a line of typed text, its continuation is indented. Thus only lines blocked to the left column indicate pause groups. A breath without a pause is indicated with a comma (,). In some cases the overall pitch drops off at the end of a phrase. This falling pitch is marked with a period (.). Where the final pitch rises, a question mark (?) is used. Quotations are marked with a dash (—) and an indentation. Within the quoted piece the preceding conventions remain the same. The Chipewyan phonemic writing is given in Times Roman (the same type used for the text of this volume), and English orthographic writing is in *Univers type*. *Univers light type* indicates a whispered aside. Parentheses ( ) give the speech of the audience which was always R. Scollon in this case. A series of three dots (. . .) indicates a short piece of stammering or self-corrected speech has been deleted from the text. A series of three lowercase *x*s (*xxx*) indicates a piece of wholly uninterpretable speech.

1. Wait

2. I tell you one time
   I going to hunt the beaver.
   So that's what I tell you first.

3. **Well** *ʔi̜łá tsákayaú si θani.*
   θá nɛsdiú

4. yuwé t'ats'én tsá ła nɛsθen łi̜-ni̜ djǎ·sya.
   saskátcuwén-ts'én dɛáłł'ul ʔą́sk'ɛðɛ.

5. kozí tsákayaú

6. kú · tsá ła-híłɛ-ni̜ kú-hú

7. djḁ ots'i̜ hiya ots'i̜
   ta· ɣitḭú dódítθǎ·
   ʔɛyɛr hų́łdų́ · tsá łáłdé-ni̜.

8. ʔɛyɛr ots'i̜ hi·yaú, t'ahu dɛstcoɣ-ni̜
   dɛstcoɣ θá-híłɛ-ni̜-hit'ází
   ʔɛyɛr nî·yaú ʔɛyɛr tθ'i nákɛ tsá łaíθer.

9. ʔɛyɛr ots'i̜ hi·yaú, ʔɛyi dɛstcoɣ-gá nániyaú ʔi̜łáɣɛ céθ·nɛtcá ·
   bɛtɛðiyaú, kúɛyɛr sas ʔi̜łtcuz túé húlyɛ-ni̜.

10. sas ʔi̜łtcuz túé **that's bear lake** *ʔɛyi húlyɛ.*
   ʔɛyɛr hóθiya ʔɛyɛr hų́łdų́· tθ'i tsá łaíłdé nadli.

11. ʔɛyi-tł'á xíłts'én
   ʔałk'éta· tsá łaíθer-ni̜.

12. tθ'i ʔɛyɛr ots'i̜ nɛsdja-hú tθ'i ʔḁnénɛsdai̜
   tsá húlɛ-t'á hoθida.

13. ʔɛyɛr ots'i̜ nɛsdjaú ʔḁnénaɣasdał-t'ŭ·
   ʔi̜łáɣɛ łuwɛtúétcoɣ ʔɛyɛr na·stí̜-ni̜ tsiłɛdjɛr
   tsiłɛdjɛrú ʔɛyɛr ɣitḭú, hɛłts'i k'abi̜ nɛsdja.

14. k'abi̜ nɛsdjaú ʔi̜łáɣɛ tu nɛnéθ θɛʔą́
   kú· ʔɛyɛr łuk'é-dé ʔi̜łasi̜· sas ła bɛk'ɛ.
   łuwɛ-ɣḁ nádé tθɛbḁ xayɛ łuwɛ łą̌·dé.
   ʔɛyi-ɣḁ nádé

15. ʔɛyi tu ots'én ʔanɛsdja-nįú yų̃nésk'ɛðɛ sas náðer k'é
nįðá-tcoγ-hílɛ.

16. Well twenty-two úțį sɛts'į.
twenty-two adaįłáγɛ k'ítcoγ dianátθ'ɛrt'ɛ.

17. ʔɛyɛrʔá
ʔɛyɛr níhoθɛsda-xaú
—kú· úțį sélalʔasolâ·cį·

18. ʔɛyiʔá hû·lk'é—nɛsθén hosk'íθ
hɛsk'íθ básdi-hílɛ-kúlú

19. ts'ínaθé-nįú ts'ínaθé
k'áł bɛts'į nįðá-hílɛ k'ítcoγtą tθ'i ádjaú t'axą ʔɛbahéłgéú
tθ'i θá-hílɛ-t'ŭ· tθ'i tc'anaigé k'ałdané tθ'i.
ʔɛłɛbazínįzéti-xa náðer.
tθ'i nada-xa héłgé

20. kúlú ʔɛdaγa nįðá sįni k'ólyą́ú t'axą si hɛził déstθ'aγ.

21. —θiłk'éðú taú—nɛsθen.

22. kú· tθ'i nɛsdjaú
ʔɛyɛr ts'ínaθé θiyaį tł'ázį́ ʔɛyi túk'ɛ.

23. ʔɛyɛr t'axą sas náðer-nį ʔązasɛhi tųlų ʔįłáγe hoʔą.
ʔɛyi tųlų ɛs nį́nįya.
ʔɛyi-gá nɛsdja tųlų-gá nɛsdja. ʔɛyi céθ-láyɛ káθisdja-nįú t'axą sas-
yaze ts'éłgé
tuts'én hełgé sɛts'éłgé.

24. kú· nįðá-hílɛ
ʔasí ta·
łǫ́·na dɛnɛké ʔaniłθa taú
ʔɛyɛr ots'į
k'énołgé
xxx
k'énołgéú tθ'i sɛts'ɛnałgé sɛts'ɛnałgéú tθ'i nį tθ'i ʔałų́ bórɛt'i-t'ŭ· tθ'i
sɛts'ɛnałgé nadli.

25. tθ'i ʔałų́ nįðá-hílɛ-t'ŭ· tθ'i k'énołgé sɛts'ɛnałgé ʔałų́.
ʔałų́ tθ'i yuwɛ dɛtcįɛ́ héłgéú

26. tθ'i sɛts'énałgé nadli.
taγɛ kú· ʔɛyɛr.
kú· tθɛ taγɛ dɛnɛkétcoγ kwidéθíłozɛta.

27. kú· ʔɛyɛr kú· nįðá-hílɛ
—si θaiká—nįðen—ʔɛyikałi taú—.

28. *ʔɛyer húɬdú· θiɬk'éθ ʔɛyi sas.*

29. *ʔɛyi sas θiɬk'éθú*

30. *nâ·ltθ'er*
    dátθ'i tc'ádiɬ bíyɛ tθí ʔaɬú tθ'i bɛtθí θiɬk'éð nâ· θiɬk'éð

31. *nịú yɛstθi t'a ots'én ots'ị sas bɛya nílgé-nị*
    sasaze tθ'i sɛk'éni sasaze ʔɛtɛʔás-k'é taγɛ.

32. *kú· kwálɛsi.*
    —dɛʔązị́ tθɛ núwéstɛ lɛsi k'ócyạ-dé yɛk'ólyạ—kwadi.
    —djạ nóh bék'ósyạ-dé kwáslé-xa-híle-nị—dɛsi.
    Well.

33. *tθ'i θá daγuná tθ'i-híle-t'á bɛs nɛtcá sɛts'ị-nị ʔɛyi xxx tθ'i sas*
    náit'áðú
    kú· si sɛɬị dɛʔązị́ bɛγɛlé dánɛdáð-híle-nị-t'á

34. *ʔɛyiʔá*
    hodɛlyǔ· sastθén tθ'i nailaú sas tθ'i ɬɛk'á k'é
    bɛk'a tθ'i hodɛlyǔ· híɬtcú ʔɛyi tθ'i si θani bɛk'ésθa.

35. *kwą́t'ǔ· ʔɛyer ʔịɬá naγɛstịú hɛlts'i k'abịú sɛkúẹ nɛsdja.*
    Now *tθ'i ʔɛyer ots'én ʔúɬị* that's all I know

36. Stop it

1. You know I was going to hunt some beaver.
   (Uh huh)

2. There's not many beaver that time.

3. Just I leave here for Jackfish?
   (Uh huh)

4. Well after that
   Well guess about three nights
   didn't find beaver yet.

5. Just about three nights I found it one beaver I killed three.

6. After that you know I know in lots of lakes lots of creek
   all over xxx all over.

7. Well one's at the end river was Wolf River that.

8. I know it's very close I found it that's a beaver.
   I kill two.

9. I went there's a big river here I went across?
   That's it one's a big hill?
   And that's the other side's a big lake?

10. *He call it the bear trap island . . . lake is what he call that.*
    (Uh huh)

11. *There's . . . I know there's beaver there all the time.*

12. *That's a I kill two?*

13. *There's another way*
    I . . . was another lake
    I got another two again.

14. *I kill it just that day I come back it's another two more.*
    Well kill six in there.
    (Uh huh)

15. *I camp in there? Next day can't do nothing now*
    Just go back again.

16. *I just go back so didn't never see . . . never find it beaver?*
    He's called Archer Lake that's my line over there right now?
    It's Archer Lake.
    (Uh huh)

17. *I camp in there*
    Well at night there's a lot of snow

18. *Uh, next morning*
    Just all you going straight

19. *I know one's a big lake*
    A long lake
    It's narrow one anyway.

20. *There's in spring time seen lots of bear all the time in there.*
    (Uh huh)

21. *Lots of bear all the time you know there's fish in there*
    That's dead fish you know?
    He eat 'em that xxx
    In the spring time seen lots of bear all the time.

22. *Just I made it just about that's the end on the lake you know?*
    That's a narrow one like that?
    (Uh huh)

23. *Me I was going this way.*
    (Uh huh)

24. *And all of a sudden just*
    That's a lake that last one see I had to go here.

25. *Well see the bear here they cross.*

26. *Well he was passing there.*

27. *Well I'm scare 'em. I want to just scare 'em. Just only twenty-two.*
    A single shot.
    That's all I got.
    That's a long twenty-two.
    (Uh huh)
    That's it nice one too.

28. *That's it twenty-two's a long this one, eh? That's the one use it.*

29. *I shoot 'em*
    Far away I just want to scare 'em I don't want to kill 'em anyway.
    I just want to shoot 'em.

30. *Well it's close anyways I'll see that just where's that drop that*
    *   metal shells?*
    It's close anyway just he jumping back
    Come back again
    (Uh huh)

31. *Well then*
    Well it's after that I shot shoot 'em after again

32. *There's it getting close it's going back in the bush he's coming*
    *   back again*
    (huh)
    Like that all the time?
    Well the next time then just he went back in the bush didn't come
    *   back*
    I hear that thought he yell or something from the bush—
    *   Maybe—I thought you know*
    *   you hit 'em—Then the bear like that*

33. *Gonna yell 'em you know (Uh huh) he gonna die.*

34.   *—Well maybe I hit 'em I guess—*
    I thought.
    (Uh huh)

35. *Just went xxx and just I went back of the lake*
    There's a road in there.

36. *Just I'll following the road then just on top of the hill?*
    That's a bear he's coming.

37. *There's coming me about ten feet he stop*
    Turn back anyway
    (Uh huh)
    Just he went back in the bush he's just coming coming again.
    (huh)
    Well I didn't shoot 'em yet

38. *Well there's just about the same place as we turn back didn't shoot 'em yet*
    Going back in the bush?
    Was after that he came was coming again
    (Uh huh)
    There's not very far now. About eight feet (laugh)
    Well he's coming close all the time you know?
    Well he's not very far now my dog too just he looking just he stop in the behind me.
    (Uh huh)

39. *All of a sudden I know I gotta shoot 'em there his head.*
    (huh)

40. *I didn't miss don't think not very far?*
    He's fall down?
    (Uh huh)
    And I shot 'em again. Twice? He's dead now.

41. *It was after that the young ones you know they about that big*
    Three of them.
    He's coming.

42. —*I'm sorry (yeah) I guess I know you was stay here I didn't shoot 'em that one.—*
    (Uh huh)

43. *Well I can't do nothing the way he was well he gonna die anyway.*
    (yeah)

44. *And then my butcher knife*
    I take my butcher knife. That's in my backsack.

45. *I got I chase 'em together and butcher knife I hit 'em.*
    That's a gonna kill 'em all of 'em.
    (Uh huh)

46. *Lots of bear anyway you know it's in good shape and fat? (yeah)*
    That's a young ones too a little small ones anyways they good shape then now everyone is fat (Uh huh) I'm doing everything.
    That's my dog xxx not heavy. That's backsack? xxx has it xxx, my dog.

47. *I'm took everything for this bear. (huh)*
    And camp then that's it one's a big lake.

48. *I camp there and next day I going back*
    (Uh huh)
    That's all right
    That's the story.

THE NARRATIVE FRAME

We will begin our discussion of this story by looking first at the Chipewyan version of the text. In our earlier discussion we introduced the idea of the framing of the narrative. If we look now at the text above we can see that there are three levels of framing at the beginning of the story. The first of these we will call the "situation frame." In (1) Marcel says *wait* in a whisper and then pauses. Here the recording is effectively changing the situation from a visit to a performance and Marcel indicates with this one word that he is still not quite ready to go along with this redefinition or reframing of the speech situation.

There are five ways in which this frame is marked. The word is whispered, it is followed by both a pause and a breath, it is said in English and the overt content of the word requests that we refrain from recording. We think that this frame was also marked with a change in the direction gaze and in body posture, but we have no record of these to verify our memories.

The performance frame consists of the next breath group (2) in which Marcel gives a brief abstract of what kind of performance he is going to give. We see this as belonging to a larger frame than the narrative itself because Marcel by saying *first* has implied that the following story will be one of a set. The performance which followed did indeed include several stories. This performance frame is marked by being a single breath group, by being in English, by being whispered, and by its content.

During the second and third lines (pause groups) Marcel covered the microphone with his hand. This was his solution to temporarily stopping the recording. We see this as indicating that Marcel associates recording with the narrative frame, not with the performance frame. We feel this shows a desire to maintain a sharp discontinuity between the narrative structure and the nonnarrative situational structure.

This contrasts with another case we can look at. Marcel's brother Fred told the story of his life. We began with a short bit of tape just to test recording levels. It went like this:

1. *Oh, just to try, eh.*
   You're testing, right?
   (Yeah, right.)
   Um.
   O.K., eh.

2. *Since you asked me to tell you my story about my life*
   I'll I can only tell you
   as I remember. And. I can't remember always. In my young days

> *I can't remember some parts then the other parts they'll be skip-*
> *ping because I don't remember them.*

3. *So*

4. *Well I'll try eh as well as I remember. I'll try me*
   tell my story about myself.
   (O.K.)

(Tape turned off, listened to, turned back on)

5. *(xxx)*
   Uh huh.
   What you first name?
   (Ron)

6. *Well, Ron*
   Since you asked me to tell you
   story about myself

This case is much more elaborate but involves the same kinds of framing. In (1) Fred Marcel is concerned with establishing what kind of speech situation it is, a test rather than a performance. He rehearses the performance frame from (2) through (4) and then, when the tape recorder is turned on, after a brief aside (5), he begins the performance at (6). In this case we can see that Fred Marcel includes the performance frame within the recording, in contrast to his brother, Marcel, who seeks to exclude it. Of course, as Chipewyan chief for 20 years, Fred Marcel has had considerable experience in making recordings and various kinds of speeches. This experience has not been shared by his brother, Marcel.

Returning to Marcel's story, we can see that the narrative frame itself begins with the initial in (3),

> *Well ʔįɬá tsákayaú si θani.*

In our first consideration of this story in its composite form, we suggested that this initial fit nicely into a general pattern for initials of narratives of personal experience. That pattern we saw to be

$$Once + (time) + verb.$$

Here we have no time element and we have an additional *well.*

The postposed *si θani* will also need some explanation. If we look at the initial to the next story Marcel told in the same performance setting, we can see that Marcel seems to be uncomfortable with starting a story with *ʔįɬá.* This initial is,

> *Ah, ʔįłá Raphael tcŭ ɣáit'as łuk'éú*
> 'Once Raphael and I went out in the spring time.'

The *ah* is an English hesitation marker. This may be seen by comparing it to the quite different *yaɣɛ, yawɛ, yaɛ* which Marcel uses in Chipewyan texts. The **well** in one case and the *ah* in the other seem to indicate a somewhat reluctant transition into speaking Chipewyan to an audience which will not be able to follow the story. We will have occasion to look again at this when **well** occurs below in the same text.

In the initial given just above, we can see that Marcel does sometimes include a time element. Here it is *łuk'éú* 'in the spring time'. It is of some interest that this time element follows the verb. We may compare this with Mandeville's preverbal positioning of the time element on the one hand and Marcel's postverbal positioning of the agent in the initial we are now considering.

The form *tsákayaú* is interesting in several ways. Although we have no exact examples with which to compare, we can presume that Mandeville would have said,

> *tsá-ka hiya*
> 'beaver-for I went'

Generally speaking in Mandeville's texts we would analyze *tsá-ka* to be a postpositional phrase and separate from the verb. Marcel, however, appears to have incorporated this phrase into the verb and to have deleted any other verbal prefixes.

There are several kinds of evidence that this is what has occurred here. In (5) below the phrase is repeated. Here we must look more closely at the phonetic detail. This is pronounced [*saxayaú*]. Thus we have the following phonetic changes.

$$ts \rightarrow s$$
$$k \rightarrow x$$
$$\acute{V} \rightarrow \grave{V}$$

We suggest that the phonetic reduction shows that this string of morphemes which would have been analyzed by Mandeville as a full clause has been collapsed into a unit of lexical size. Later on we will suggest that this is likely to be due to the influence of Cree on the one hand and a morphological reduction of Chipewyan on the other. This phrase is undoubtedly used very frequently in just this shape or with substitution of the object of the hunt. Thus one would expect,

> *deníkayaú*
> 'hunting for moose'

'*εtθénkayaú*
'hunting for caribou'

dzenkayaú
'hunting for muskrats''

and so forth.

As evidence that these do occur we can point to a 10-year-old's translation into Chipewyan of a story she wrote originally in English. The initial was,

Once upon a time Ron went to hunt moose

She translated this as,

łásį **Ron** *deníyεkaya*

but then when she read it she said,

Ron hunt *kayaú*

On another occasion an older woman asked our 2-year-old daughter,

nεtá?
'(Where is) your father?'

Our daughter some time before had entertained this woman by saying the names of animals and so on this occasion simply said one of these, *ʔεdjεrε* 'buffalo'. The woman then said,

nεtá ʔεdjεrεkayaų́są́?
'Did your father go hunting for buffalo?'

These cases indicate a meaning of *kaya* as 'go to' or 'go for'. Of course the stem *-ya* is 'one person goes'. *ka* has been incorporated in other verbs as a thematic prefix meaning 'in order to' or 'for' as in,

lakasaxa
'I'm going to work (there).'

This is simply compounded of *la* 'work', *ka* 'for', *sa* 'I go', and *xa* (future suffix).

In another case 'hunt' was translated by one informant as *kálzé*, where Mandeville would have given *nálzé* 'he hunts' and used *ka* only with an overt object as in *ʔεtθén-ka nálzé*.

Finally as evidence that *ka* can be used quite freely now, we have the 10-year-old's,

bebi hεtsa **Suzie** *ka*
baby it cries S. for
'The baby is crying for Suzie'

Putting these together, we can see *tsákaya* as a simple three-morpheme compound, 'beaver' + 'for' + 'go'. There is no marking for person or aspect. The final *-ú* is difficult to analyze, and for now we will suggest only that it has become fossilized here as part of the idiom.

Because the form *tsákayaú* is unmarked for person, however, Marcel needs to introduce person into the clause elsewhere. This he does with the postposed *si θani* 'I alone'. Although his being alone is of some narrative importance there is a possible syntactic motive in following *si* 'I' with another morpheme to disambiguate it. *si* would be homophonous with *si* 'for sure' (<*sî·*) since Marcel often drops the nasalization of vowels when they are not in stem syllables and often neutralizes length distinctions. Without the word *θani* to disambiguate it the clause could be read as,

ʔįłá tsákayaú sî
'Once I sure went for beaver.'

which as an initial would be quite unusual.

Thus we can now see a set of interactions between various levels of structuring. The narrative structure requires at least *ʔįłá* and a verb in that order. On the lexical level, however, a set of changes in the structure of the verb have resulted in the loss of person distinctions in some cases such as this. The compensation for this is a new sentential element, a pronominal agent, which must follow the verb because of the narrative restrictions on this sentence as an initial. This postposed agent must then itself be disambiguated with a further morpheme.

This initial sets the stage not only for this narrative but for our analysis as well. We suggest that in Chipewyan the level of structure which has been most resistant to change is the narrative structure. Following that, where there is a conflict between the structure of words and the structure of clauses, more weight is now given to lexical structure. The result of this is a great deal of flexibility in the structure of clauses. For this reason we feel that an understanding of Chipewyan as it is now being used depends on understanding the interaction between narrative structure on the one hand and lexical structure on the other.

Marcel's story of the beaver hunt is begun with three concentric frames, the situational frame, the performance frame, and the narrative frame. We can now look at the conclusion of the story to see to what extent these frames are closed out in returning to the situation of the visit.

The final which closes the narrative frame begins with *kwát'ŭ·* in (35) and consists of that line or pause group. We have said in our earlier discussion that it is customary to end a narrative of personal experience with a return to home. We can compare Marcel's final with Mandeville's final of his beaver hunt (Li and Scollon 1976:417):

ʔɛkwą́t'ŭ·   sɛkų́ę́   nínɛskį̀
thus   my home   I arrived (in a canoe)

The principal elements are *ʔɛkwą́t'ŭ·* and the return to home. In a more general study of Mandeville's finals, R. Scollon found that the final was often somewhat longer than a single clause (1976b). Thus Marcel's two-clause final is not at variance with Mandeville's final. The markers of this narrative final, then, are the word *kwą́t'ŭ·*, the pause group, the falling intonation, and the content.

Here we may add a note about how resistant this final is to change. A 10-year-old Chipewyan girl wrote many short stories for us in which the final was always a return to home. Then when S. Scollon turned around and dictated a story which the girl wrote out, she tried to conclude it with,

Then Murray and Rachel fought until they killed each other.
The end.

The girl hesitated, then said, "What? I can't even tell what you said!" When the same final was repeated the girl paused a moment and then wrote,

Then Murray and Rachel got home.
The end.

Even when she was not authoring the story, this girl would not accept any other final.

In Marcel's story the performance frame is signaled by a shift to the English *now* in the second line of (35). It is also a pause group and mixes English and Chipewyan. Although there is a breath and a pause at the end, there is no falling off of the pitch level. This lack of complete closure indicates that Marcel is waiting for the audience to take some action. This action is the turning off of the tape recorder. Since this does not happen immediately, he closes out the situation frame by overtly asking that the recorder be stopped.

The close of the performance frame is very similar to that used by other narrators. For example, there are

a. *kú   dų̀hų́   dja—*
   then   now   here
b. *hút'a   ʔɛyɛr   ots'én   úłį·*
   enough   there   to   only
c. *'ɛyɛr ots'én ułį   hút'a*
   there- to only   enough
d. **Well** *kút'a   hodɛlyŭ· ah,*   **everything now**
   well   enough   all   ah   everything now

This performance close may be seen now to consist of some combination of the following elements

1. a shift to the present or situational time reference
2. marking a point in the events, for example 'up to there'
3. a shift to English
4. the word *úłį* ('only')
5. the word *kút'a* ('enough')

Marcel's performance close makes use of (1), (2), (3), (4), and *that's all*, which may well be considered a translation of *kút'a*.

We should mention now the importance here of the concept of closing out the performance up to a point. We noted earlier that in beginning the performance Marcel said that this is the story he would tell first. This closing out up to a point implies that more may follow. That is, it is a partial or temporary closure.

We have now seen that the narrative is framed in a three-layered frame. By degrees the audience is taken from the ongoing situation into the events of the narrative, and by degrees is returned to the ongoing speech situation. This is very much like what Darnell (1974) found in the performance of Cree narratives. There are two points we would now like to make before going on. The first point regards the high perceptual salience of these frames. We have seen above that a 10-year-old had developed very definite ideas about the form of narrative finals. Our 2-year-old daughter was in the habit of going around saying narrative initials whenever we were working on tape recordings of Chipewyan. Somehow she had extracted these without any special instruction by overhearing tape recorded and live performances of Chipewyan narratives.

In some cases we worked almost entirely monolingually. That is, we had tape recordings in Chipewyan of what we presumed to be narratives but were unable to get native speakers to help us with transcribing or translating and interpreting them. We found that we could very quickly isolate the narratives as units and within the narratives, isolate the narrative frame. We suggest this perceptual salience leads to an early induction of narrative structure by children (Halliday 1976) and ultimately to a strong resistance to erosion under the stress of linguistic convergence.

The second point we would like to make is that there are complexes of markers which indicate the frames. We have seen so far the importance of the following markers,

1. breath groups
2. pause groups

3. falling intonation
4. language choice (i.e., shifts between Chipewyan and English)
5. channel shifts (i.e., shifts to whispering or covering the microphone)
6. specific lexical items
   a. *well*
   b. *ʔįłá*
   c. *kwát'ŭ·*
7. clause structures (e.g., *'įłá* + (time) + verb
8. overt content

We can expect, then, that narrative structure may be indicated in any of
these ways. At the same time we should point out that in itself no single
marker is used only as a marker of narrative structure. Thus to be used as
markers of narrative structure, these elements must be combined in
complexes of several or more at a time. It is the conplex or bundle that
marks the narrative structure, not the single element.

THE INTERNAL STRUCTURE OF THE TEXT

We now want to turn to the internal structure of Marcel's beaver hunt
narrative. We will be looking for bundles of elements which may indicate
discontinuities in the narrative structure. There is one major break between (15) and (16). This is marked by a shift to the English form *well*, a
breath group, a pause group, and falling intonation. Of course from our
earlier analysis of the story which was done entirely on the basis of the
content of the narrative, we would expect a boundary between the beaver
hunt and the bear encounter somewhere around this point. The problem is
really just to locate the boundary from the narrator's point of view.

There is one more indication of a narrative boundary here. This is the
postverbal emphatic particle *-k'é*. This is probably the same particle as
that given by Li as *-hik'é* 'it is found out' (Li 1946:421). In modern usage
it seems to function to add emphasis to the preceding clause. We were
never able to get an informant to translate this particle. Indeed, in most
cases it was difficult to get someone to even perceive it as a separate
morpheme. It is in keeping with its emphatic usage that it appears in the
clause in which the bear first appears and gives to the sighting of the bear a
feeling that it appeared "all of a sudden." If we look back through the
narrative to this point we see that *-k'é* has not been used previously and
thus it seems to be one further indication of a major narrative boundary.

We can see, then, that the narrative is divided into two sections. The
boundary between the sections is marked by

1. content
2. emphatic particle -*k'é*
3. *well* (as a lexical marker)
4. *well* (as a shift to English)
5. pause group
6. breath group
7. falling intonation

The first section is the beaver hunt and the second section is the encounter with the bears. In this case we have also added one possible marker to the inventory. This is the emphatic particle -*k'é*.

We may now look at Marcel's use of the English form *well* in marking this major boundary within the narrative and ask why he should prefer this form over a Chipewyan form. The first thing we can see is that it is followed by another English word, *twenty-two.* It may be, then, that the switch to English anticipates the following English word.

There are two reasons why this is unlikely, however. The first is that again at (32) Marcel uses *well* when it is neither preceded by English, as in the initial at (1), nor followed by English as in this case at (16). The second reason is that *twenty-two* may be better considered a Chipewyan word. There is the general word for rifle or gun *tɛlk'iθi*, but for this more specific case *twenty-two* is the normal Chipewyan word.

This finally raises the question of whether *well* itself is a Chipewyan word. On the basis of this story there is probably no way of deciding. In several other stories, though, Marcel uses *well* along with other short phrases in English. In those cases *well* always accompanies a temporary shift into English for a length of about one clause. If we look back at (32) we can see that *well* stands by itself as a full pause group. The fact that it is not preceded or followed by English within the pause group may not be significant since it is not followed or preceded by Chipewyan in the same pause group either.

So we can return to the question of why Marcel switches to English to mark this narrative boundary. We think it may be wrong to say that he switches to English to mark the boundary. We would rather put it this way: In coming to a major boundary, the narrator's attention shifts momentarily to focus on the audience. Since in this case the two members of the audience are probably not understanding in Chipewyan, the narrator temporarily switches codes to accommodate them. The switch, then, is as much a result of the narrative boundary as a marker in itself.

We have established that -*k'é* may be used as a marker of narrative structure. If we look on through the text we find that the next -*k'é* precedes a breath group at (32) and is followed by falling intonation.

These three markers would suggest another narrative break. In addition to these three, there is the word *kú·* and a shift in point of view, that is, Marcel quotes himself. Together, this bundle indicates a subdivision of the section beginning at (16) into two minor sections. Of course the content confirms this subdivision since this is the point at which the three cubs appear in the story.

Although we have added *kú·* to the stock of narrative markers, we will put off the discussion of this form for a while and look instead at the next narrative section. This occurs at the end of (32) where the disjunction is marked by *well*, that is by a shift to English, a pause group, a falling intonation, and a breath group. There is also a shift from the quoted point of view back to the narrator's point of view at this place. Again, the content confirms that there is a narrative unit being marked here.

Now perhaps it will be useful to review the units which we have suggested above before going on to look at the lowest level of structuring, that marked by *kú·*. There is an initial and a final. Between these there is the major division of the story into two parts at (16). The second of these is divided, again in two, at (32). This section itself is divided in two at the end of (32). All of this is set within the performance frame and that within the situation frame as follows

```
┌─Situation frame (1)
│ ┌─Performance frame (2)
│ │ ┌─Narrative frame, initial (3)
│ │ │   ┌─Beaver hunt (3–15)
│ │ │   └─Bear encounter────┌─mother bear (16–31)
│ │ │     (16–34)           └─bear cubs (32–34)──┌─encounters (32)
│ │ │                                            └─kills (33–34)
│ │ └─Narrative frame, final (35)
│ └─Performance frame (35)
└──Situation frame (36)
```

We would now like to focus more closely on the word *kú·*, which has been said to be the most frequently used word in Chipewyan (Richardson 1968). Because it does occur so frequently in narratives and elsewhere, we feel it is worthy of some attention rather than the quick dismissal it sometimes receives.

Li gives the two forms *ʔɛkú·* and *kú·* in his list of "syntactic or adverbial particles" (1946:422). He gives them a gloss of 'so' or 'then' and suggests that they are free variants of the same form. R. Scollon (1977) argued that these two variants were, in fact, discourse markers. Their function was shown to be to segment the narrative into units. Units of major importance are begun with *ʔɛkú·* and those of somewhat lesser importance are begun with *kú·*. The units which result from using these

words as markers have a number of further characteristics such as forming closed information units with regard to anaphoric reference.

In another paper R. Scollon (1976c) found that the discourse markers
?ɛkú· and *kú·* are members of a larger set of particles and words which
occur between clauses in a narrative which have the function of showing
the relationships between the clauses. The two above indicate a disjunction from the point of view of the narrative structure. Another member of
the set is *-ú* or *-hú* which Li lists under "verbal suffixes (or postposed
particles)" (1946:420). This one he calls a "gerundive suffix." Its
functional role is to show that the first of two clauses is grammatically
subordinated to the second clause.

The study of these forms was based on the full set of Mandeville's texts
(Li and Scollon 1976). In those texts with extremely rare exceptions these
forms are mutually exclusive in the position between clauses. This was
taken as further evidence that they belonged to the same set. It is, of
course, rare for a narrator to wish to mark discourse boundaries between
two clauses while at the same time indicating that this boundary occurs
between a subordinated clause and its matrix sentence.

In Marcel's text we can note first of all that *?ɛkú·* does not occur. This
is general in the modern speech community where we rarely heard or
recorded *?ɛkú·*. It still does occur more regularly elsewhere, however, as
we have heard on radio broadcasts. In Fort Chipewyan this fits a general
phonological process of the deletion of initial syllables. Other examples
include *?ɛt'axạ → t'axạ* 'suddenly' and *?ɛts'ínaθé → ts'ínaθé* 'finally'.

To begin looking for examples of *kú·* and *-hú* or *-ú* we have in (5) and
(6)

kozí tsákayaú
①

kú· tsá łạhílɛ-nị kúhú
②   ③ ④

We can see from this that for Marcel *-ú* and *kú·* may occur in sequence.
That is, they are not mutually exclusive in this position. According to our
analysis above the form marked (1) would be syntactic and indicate
subordination, (2) would indicate that a new segment of the narrative
begins here, (3) would be impossible and very problematical, and (4)
would again be syntactic and indicate subordination.

Beginning with (3) we can suggest from this text that *kú·* here is to be
taken quite literally as a time adverbial. It means simply 'then' or 'at that
time', that is, "beavers were not abundant then." Although Mandeville
rarely uses *kú·* in its most transparent meaning, this use does continue in
Fort Chipewyan. It is, in fact, this meaning that originally made *kú·*
eligible for use as a discourse marker.

If we look on at breath groups (12) and (13), we can see the two forms *nɛsdjahú* and *nɛsdjaú*, which leads us to conclude that for Marcel as for Mandeville *-hú* and *-ú* are variants of the same form. If we look at breath group (24)

kú nįðá-hílɛ

and compare it with a phonetic transcription

ʔų́ʔ nįðéílɛ

or if we compare in the same way

      (26)   *kú·   tθɛ   taɣɛ*
             hú   tθɛ   tawɛ

      (28)   *kú·   ʔɛyɛr kú·nįðá-hílɛ*
             húyɛrhúnįðáílɛ

we begin to see that not only does *-hú* vary with *-ú*, but *kú·* varies with *hú* and *ʔų́ʔ*. Finally if we look at

(33)   *kú· si*

úsi

we can see that at least phonetically there is evidence that not only are *kú·* and *-hú* members of the same set, they are, in fact, the same form. Other narratives by other narrators further suggest that *kú·, hú,* and *ú* are possible pronunciations of the same morpheme in both clause-initial position and postverbal position with or without intervening pauses.

There is still another dimension to this, however, which must now be considered, and that is the problem of pitch. Sapir noted in his early and still very important article on Sarcee pitch accent (or tone) that there was a progressive downdrifting of pitch approaching the close of a sentence (Sapir 1925). Because of this downdrifting, absolute pitches will not discriminate high and low tones. The same general phenomenon occurs in Chipewyan as we can illustrate graphically. A series of high tones would be [⁻ ⁻ − −]. A series of low tones would be [− − − _]. A series of alternating high and low tones would be [⁻ − ⁻ _] and a series of alternating low and high tones would be [− ⁻ _ −]. Thus a high tone at the end of an intonation group may actually be lower than a low tone at the beginning of a group, and tone is determined by contrasting pitches rather than by absolute pitch.

In the text we are considering now we can look at the pitches in the following examples:

(5,6) *tsákayaú kú·*
[⁻ − _ ⁻ ⁻]

$$(14) \quad \theta \varepsilon \text{'} \acute{a} \; k\acute{u} \cdot$$
$$[- ^- ^-]$$

$$(23,24) \quad s\varepsilon ts\text{'} \acute{e}tg\acute{e} \; k\acute{u} \cdot$$
$$[\_ ^- ^- ^-]$$

$$(33) \quad n\acute{a}it\text{'}\acute{a}\eth\acute{u} \; k\acute{u} \cdot si$$
$$[^- \_ ^- ^- ^- ^-]$$

In these cases the high tone morpheme following the pause is raised in absolute pitch from the level of the high tone pitch which preceded the pause. It is this difference in pitch which is significant, not the phonetic form which, in fact, varies between *kú·* and *ú*.

Based on this evidence we would now like to suggest that there are not two (or three or four) separate morphemes *kú·* (or *ʔɛkú·*) and *-hú* (or *-ú*) which contrast in serving discourse and syntactic functions. Rather we suggest that there is one morpheme *kú·* (for Mandeville *ʔɛkú·*) which has a literal meaning of 'then' or 'at that time'. This morpheme is also used in position between clauses to indicate temporal sequencing at some level. The level at which this morpheme is to be understood and its phonetic shape, however, are determined by prosodic and paralinguistic factors. The principal prosodic factors are pauses, breaths, rate of speech, and pitch. When the pause is long, a breath is taken, and the unit then begun is a full phrase, then the phonetic shape of the morpheme will normally be in its fullest form and its function will be as a marker of a boundary in the discourse.

To say this in another way, the variation in the forms of *kú·* is a matter of the degree of care taken in speaking. At significant narrative boundaries we suggest that the narrator increases the care he takes in speaking as he directs his attention to the structure of the performance of the story rather than to the structure of the events which are being narrated. Thus, it is careful speech which marks narrative segments, not the particular lexical forms used. These may vary to some extent for different speakers or for the same speaker in different contexts.

If we compare in a general way Marcel's narrative to those of Mandeville, we see that Marcel's is completely oral. That is, it is dictated for tape recording and only subsequently written. On the other hand, Mandeville's texts were written as they were being slowly dictated. This afforded Mandeville a degree of care with narrative units not available to Marcel. Mandeville's choice of three levels of marking and his very consistent use of three different phonetic forms, *ʔɛkú·*, *kú·*, and *-ú*, is consistent with the care and degree of planning he was afforded by the situation.

As a more extreme case we can compare the Biblical and other liturgical texts written in syllabics with the ones above (*nioɫtsi bedilise* 1932). In these Chipewyan texts there are only two levels of structuring and two forms used, *ʔekú ·* ($<\nabla d\ e\ ko$) for segments of the narrative and *-ú* ($< o$) for subordination. Thus in preparing written translations a choice was made to represent only the extremes of the phonetic and structural continuum from *ʔɛkú ·* to *-ú*.

Returning to our version of the text above, we can now see that the choice of *kú ·* or *-ú* in the phonemic version represents an analytical decision, not a simple phonemicization of a phonetic variant. This decision is based on various prosodic and paralinguistic factors. Breath groups, pause groups, and falling intonations are indicated in our transcription above. We can now see that the choice of *kú ·* over *ú* in the phonemic text crucially depends on the accurate marking of these prosodic features in the phonetic text.

Now we can return to the text to see what further segments of the narrative are marked by *kú ·*. In the first main section, the beaver hunt section, there is a minor division at (6). It is a little difficult to characterize the first section, but perhaps we can call it an "orientation." It is interesting to notice that if this version is compared line by line with the following English version, we can see that this orientation has been completely deleted in the English. Of course in telling the English version Marcel was aware of having just told the story and that may have made this orientation superfluous to the narrative structure.

For the purpose of our current analysis, however, it is useful to see that the segment marked off by the form *kú ·* does, in fact, form a whole piece in the cognitive structuring of the narrative which is indicated by its deletability.

The remaining divisions marked by *kú ·* are at (22), (24), and (27). These subdivide the mother bear episode into seeing and shooting the bear, continuing on his trip, the bear's charging him, and finally his killing the bear. If we add these divisions to those charted above we get the structure on page 66.

There are three general points we would now like to make in conclusion to this section on the Chipewyan version of the story. The first is that the structure can now be seen to be the result of an interaction between the quite abstract structuring of the content of the narrative and the actual performance. As the narrator reaches crucial boundaries in the structure of the narrative, his attention is raised to the audience and his degree of care in speaking increases. This shifting of focus in turn affects the prosodic structure and paralinguistic structure, and that in turn affects the phonetic surface structure of the morphemes being used. Thus we would like to suggest that although the cognitive structure of the text may be to

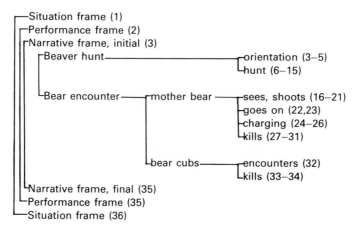

some extent independent of the performance, the actual structure of the text as it is recorded is highly situational.

This brings us to the second point. We saw in our earlier discussion of this story that the structural organization of the narrative could be inferred to some extent without looking at the linguistic details of the original texts. In our analysis here we hope to have demonstrated that a much greater degree of accuracy in marking that structure can be achieved by a close attention to the linguistic detail of the original. The demonstration of this leads to the third point.

We argued from the earlier composite version that there was a complex mixture of Athabaskan four-part structuring and what was perhaps Cree or European three-part structuring. The structure that we have seen in the Chipewyan original, however, is much more purely Athabaskan. There are two-part and four-part divisions throughout the text. Thus our analysis based on the Chipewyan original shows a much clearer relationship between linguistic structuring and cultural patterns of organization.

THE ENGLISH TEXT

We will now turn to look at the structure of the English version of the text. Just after the Chipewyan version was finished and the tape recorder had been turned off, Marcel began to tell the story again in English. He apparently had felt unsatisfied with our understanding of the Chipewyan version and wanted us to hear it then and there in English. This suggests to us that Marcel was always concerned with storytelling above linguistic displays. It is true he had just finished one such display, but his concern for our immediate understanding during that speech situation shows an overriding concern for communication of the narrative content.

We interrupted him to ask if he would let us record the English version, and although he was made a little uncomfortable by the idea of recording in English, he allowed us to do so. He then began again as recorded above with (1). We can see here that the situation frame was not recorded in this case. We still have to consider what level of frame is indicated by (1).

At this time Marcel was still not decided about what kind of a performance this was going to be. He had intended to give not a narrative performance as such but a translation performance. Agreeing to let us record had been tantamount to agreeing to another narrative performance, but Marcel was part way into this breath group before he really decided to go through with it. This is indicated in the phonetic transcription where one can see that (1) begins with a great deal of hesitation and stuttering as follows:

$$\text{ʔyulʔyɔ̃õʔɪʔyaz gwɔt   hã zã bɪvɛr(s)   } \widehat{\downarrow}$$
'you know I was going to hunt some beaver.'

Finally it smooths out into a more confident delivery. We think, then, that (1) represents an unsure amalgamation of the performance frame and the narrative frame and as such is serving both functions without being clearly marked as either.

The closing frames are somewhat clearer. The narrative final in (48) is very much like the final in the Chipewyan version

I camp there and next day I going back.

kwát'ŭ ·	ʔɛyɛr	ʔįłá	naɣɛstʲú	helts'i	k'abʲú	sɛkų́ɛ	nɛsdja
thus	there	once	I sleep	next	day	my home	I return

and therefore can be seen to fit the regular final pattern for Chipewyan narratives. This is followed by the performance frame, but here there is no situation frame. As in the beginning, the situation frame is not recorded at the end. Marcel simply pauses until the tape recorder is turned off.

The absence of the situation frame suggests some negotiation between us over the definition of the situation. In the first story we were inclined to turn on the tape recorder too soon and to turn it off too late to suit Marcel. By the second story an understanding had been reached so that no further overt marking of the situation frame was required. This is further supported by the absence of this frame in any overt form in the other recordings that followed during the same visit. Thus we have the following structure

```
┌─Situation frame (not recorded)
│ ┌─Performance frame──────────────────
│ │ ┌─Narrative frame, initial──────────────amalgamated (1)
│ │ │      story
│ │ └─Narrative frame, final (48)
│ └─Performance frame (48)
└─Situation frame (not recorded)
```

In the following discussion we will not consider again the outermost layer, the situation frame.

Having just completed the analysis of the Chipewyan version of this text we can use that as a heuristic in seeking to understand the internal structure of the English version. We can assume at least tentatively that breath groups, pause groups, and intonation groups will be relevant to the marking of this structure. We can also assume that the narrator will not divide up the content into radically different structural groups. We would expect a fair amount of agreement between the two texts on what the story was about. In the absence of a literature on sequenced translation/paraphrase narrative sets, however, we do not really know just how much conformity to expect.

If we assume that the story consists of two major parts, the beaver hunt and the bear encounter, then we can look for a division of these somewhere between (16), which is the last mention of beaver, and (26), which appears to be the first mention of the mother bear. We suggest that although the boundary appears at first to be less sharply marked in this version than in the Chipewyan version, it occurs at (24). The major lexical marking is provided by *all of a sudden.* This English idiom has about the same impact as the particle -*k'é* in Chipewyan as we suggested above. In that version -*k'é* was followed by a shift to English *well*, and his mention of the .22 rifle. Here we have *all of a sudden*, *well* (in 25) and then in (27) the .22 rifle. Here we can elaborate on the somewhat improbable relationship between -*k'é*, which Li glosses as 'it was found out', and *all of a sudden.* A woman was recorded as saying *I thought it was Kammi. All of a sudden it was Shawna-Leigh.* In this case the meaning is very much like Li's 'it was found out'. What is meant is that she thought it was the girl Kammi but it turned out to be Shawna-Leigh. Thus an English idiom has been given a Chipewyan meaning.

We said above that (26) appears to be the first mention of the mother bear. Actually 'they' in (25) is probably a reference to this bear. Phonetically it is [ðɛ] and this could also be glossed as 'that'. The shift to 'he' in (26) seems to be a correction of the pronominal form in (25).

Given Marcel's initial hesitation to use English and his obvious difficulty in places, it is not surprising that he appears to be less successful in sharply locating narrative boundaries, even this one which is the major discontinuity in the story. There may be another factor at work here, however. We have suggested that the marking of narrative boundaries is accompanied by a heightened awareness of the audience to the performance. In the Chipewyan version this resulted in a shift to English at this point in the story. Here the story is already being narrated in English. What happens is that Marcel begins to draw figures with his hands on the table in front of him. This drawing begins around (22) where *that's* refers to a point drawn on the table. Again, *like that* accompanies a gestural indication. In (23) there is *this way*, in (24) *here*, and in (25) *there*. All of these refer to points which Marcel has indicated on the table. We can see, then, that rather than being less well marked than the Chipewyan version, this text is marked by an increased interaction between the narrator and audience which includes the use of visual as well as linguistic symbolic means. It is the weakness of our purely audio recording that gives the impression that this boundary is not clearly marked.

Having established this here, we can then look to see if there are any other similar boundaries marked. Below at (39) there is another place where Marcel uses *all of a sudden*. This too was accompanied by gesture. When he says, *shoot 'em there* he gestures to his head and then adds by way of clarification *his head.*

This produces an interesting departure from the Chipewyan two-part structure. There appear to be three major sections to the English version. The first is the same as in the Chipewyan version, the beaver hunt. The following section of the bear encounter is treated as two major sections, the encounter with the bear and the killing of the bear. This can be charted as follows:

```
┌Narrative frame, initial (1)
│ ┌Beaver hunt (2–23)
│ ├Bear encounter (24–34)
│ └Bear killing (39–47)
└Narrative frame, final (48)
```

If we look for smaller units of the narrative, we need to establish first how these might be marked. We can assume safely enough that grouping by breaths, pauses, and intonation will be relevant, and so we really are looking now for lexical markings. Of course *well* has been demonstrated in the Chipewyan text as a possible marker, but because of its high frequency in this text it is unlikely that by itself it marks narrative divisions. In this it would correspond functionally to *kú·*. If we look for meaning equivalents, we would consider *then* and *after that* as possibilities as well. *After that* appears to have no other use in the text so may well be considered a marker of narrative units.

Keeping these possibilities in mind we can look back at the structuring of the text. Each of the three major sections is divided into three smaller sections as follows: At (4) there is a break marked by both *well* and *after that*; at (6) another boundary is marked by *after that* and *you know*. It will be recalled that *you know* marks the performance/narrative initial at (1). This is reminiscent of the *well* with which Marcel begins the initial in the Chipewyan version. We can match content to these divisions by considering the first to be orienting, the second to cover the first finding of beaver, and the third to cover the rest of the beaver hunt.

The section of the narrative dealing with the bear encounter is also divided into three units. These are the first segment where he sees and shoots the bear, the second where he shoots it again, and the third where he goes ahead on the trail. The markers are *well then* and *well it's after that* for the first boundary at (31), and *well* followed by a shift in point of view to a quotation of himself for the second boundary at (34). Finally the third section, the killing of the bear, is also segmented into three pieces. The markers are *It was after that* at (41) and *well* following the end of a quotation at (43).

We can now show the full structure of the English version as follows

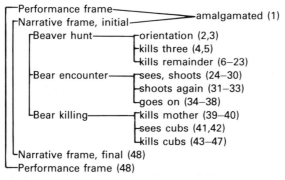

We have seen that the same text as it was told in two different languages differed remarkably in the overt linguistic structural organization. In the Chipewyan version the structure was based on two-part and four-part divisions throughout, and yet in the retelling in English the structure was based on three-part divisions at both higher and lower levels. It would be easy to rush into an assertion that it was something about the structure of the languages producing this difference, but we have not yet considered the crucial difference between the texts.

We have suggested in several places that the overt narrative structure is the result of an interaction between the cognitive content of the narrative and the performance situation. We have suggested that narrative boundaries are marked as part of a general process by which the narrator raises his or her awareness of the audience. It should be recalled that the principal difference between these two texts is that the first was performed as a display of linguistic and narrative form but the second was told to a hearing and understanding audience. The audience was of little importance in the first telling but very active in the second. This is indicated by the frequent interjections transcribed in parentheses in the English text.

We feel that the restructuring of the text in the English version reflects not the narrator's structuring of the performance but the audience's influence on his performance. Unfortunately of all the cues which we used to indicate our responses to the story only the audible ones are recorded. It seems quite plausible to us that in telling us this story Marcel was attending to responses from his audience and structured the story accordingly. Thus it would be our European-based narrative structure that is reflected in the narrative, not Marcel's.

It is unfortunate that we have no access to more complete records of this performance situation. One would like a videotape recording so that inaudible cues could be studied. Given the difficulty of making simple tape recordings with cassette recorders, however, we feel it is unlikely that more complex recording could ever be accomplished without that in itself strongly affecting the performance situation. So we must be content with our rather untested suggestion that Marcel has so radically altered the overt structure of the text on the basis of the reactions of his audience.

To close this section on narrative structure, we can now review our general position. This is that there is much to be gained in the specificity of our understanding of narrative structure by looking closely at the linguistic details of original texts. At the same time, however, we feel we have shown that this narrative structure is quite sensitive to the conditions of the performance. The structural expectations of the audience may be strongly reflected in the narrative structure that is recorded.

We can ask, then: What would be the ideal performance condition for recording? It could be answered that it would be a performance in which the narrator and the audience were all members of the same speech community or other group under study. Of course this would limit the ethnography of speaking to speech communities in which it was an existing academic concern, that is to say, to the ethnographer's own speech community. But this would undercut the cross-cultural foundation of ethnographic work. If we assume first that we want to cross speech community boundaries in our research and that we are seeking to understand the relationship between narrative content and linguistic structure, then the next best situation in some cases may in fact be one in which the narrator performs as a display and openly ignores the contribution of his or her audience. This situation is much like that in which Fang-Kuei Li and François Mandeville worked. Neither had any illusions about Li's understanding the texts as stories while the dictation was proceeding. Thus those texts may be considered to be quite free of the sort of influence from the audience that we have noted above.

Finally, the worst sort of text is a translation or paraphrase into the audience's language where this audience is not a member of the speech community. These texts must be considered to be as strongly influenced by the audience as by the original narrative content and are as a result quite suspect as reflections of the cognitive world of the narrator. It is unfortunate that much of the text on which ethnographic and folkloristic studies have been based is this sort of text. Our findings here argue for a greater involvement of ethnographers of speaking with their own speech communities on the one hand, and on the other hand for increasing the involvement of people in the community under study in the research to the point where they are active participants in the research. Only in that way can the sort of projective bias that we have observed be eliminated in natural narrative performances.

3

LINGUISTIC CONVERGENCE

It is now time to become more specific about what we mean by linguistic convergence at Fort Chipewyan. In the preceding chapter we have presented a narrative in two versions, Chipewyan and English. We have then argued that whereas the overall narrative structure is quite resistant to change, the internal narrative structure is quite sensitive to responses from the audience. In this chapter we will begin by taking the position of Halliday and Hasan (1976) that discourse structure and grammatical structure operate independently of each other; and we will focus here on grammatical structure, beginning with a discussion of the units of analysis. Then we will present the phonetic transcriptions of the Chipewyan and English versions of Marcel's beaver hunt narrative that will serve as the foundation for the remaining discussion.

The phonetic texts will be followed by a discussion of phonological convergence. For this it will be necessary to go quite a bit beyond the material of Marcel's text to include a wider range of speech in the community. After discussing phonological convergence we will return to Marcel's text to look at the structure of words, the structure of the lexicon, and finally clause structure.

This discussion is given in the order of our own discovery. It is, of course, no accident that we encountered phonological problems from the beginning. Our training in Athabaskan had prepared us for the Chipewyan consonant system, and the variation we encountered was immediately striking. As speakers of English we were also struck by a range of variation in that language that closely paralleled the variation we were recording for Chipewyan. It was our attempts to account for the very similar variation in both languages that first suggested the convergence of languages to us.

It was more difficult, at first, to see that there were corresponding changes in the structure of words and, further, in the structure of the lexicon. The phenomenon that we are calling convergence in clause structure only became visible to us after a considerable amount of study and abstraction. We will argue, however, that convergence is taking place at all levels of grammatical structuring, and this chapter presents evidence from the analysis of Marcel's beaver hunt narrative for this convergence.

It is perhaps useful here to expand on our reasons for largely restricting our discussion to one text. In comparing two grammatical forms it is crucial to establish first their meaning relationship. For our purposes, where we wish to argue that a particular form in Chipewyan corresponds to a particular form in English, we would like to have a fair degree of certainty that they mean the same thing. By linguistic convergence we mean that (at least) two languages have come to match closely in form and meaning. Where examples are taken from lists of isolated sentences or clauses, there are considerable methodological problems in relating the meanings out of context. In our example, however, Marcel has told the same story twice. The considerable matching of narrative structure, which we have already discussed, and, as we shall see, of prosodic structure in the two texts argues for these two versions being as closely matched for meaning and contextual structure as it is likely to be possible to achieve in the real world of language in use. We feel by using one text in two versions we have imposed a quite natural control on the contextual variability of meaning, while at the same time limiting our discussion to the study of forms that have a genuine currency in the use of speakers.

A further argument for using connected text will become relevant later in the study of clause structures. There are cases where clauses taken in isolation appear to be used quite conservatively while the demands of convergence are met by the juxtapositioning of conservative structures. Thus the convergence becomes visible only in the study of sequences of clauses, not in the internal clause structure itself.

Unfortunately, the depth of analysis that can be achieved with the careful study of a single translation set, such as Marcel's beaver hunt, requires us to sacrifice the wider scope we might have achieved with a more superficial but broader study of additional texts. Because of the preliminary nature of this report on our fieldwork we have felt it to be of central importance to focus first on material that relates most directly to our original goal of understanding the context of the work of Fang-Kuei Li. We hope in future publications to correct this preliminary narrowing of our focus.

UNITS OF ANALYSIS

Before looking at the linguistic content of these texts below the level of the narrative structure, it is necessary first to look into the question of what the structural units are below the narrative structure. This is necessary for several reasons. In his publications on Chipewyan, Li assumes that words, clauses, and sentences are discrete structural levels, but unfortunately he does not ever discuss the arguments for his analysis. Of course Li's work, fitting into the general Athabaskan framework as it did, could be assumed to share the arguments and assumptions of those who preceded him, especially Sapir, whenever he did not specifically depart from them. And further, Li's work on Chipewyan did not depend crucially on an analysis of units larger than the word.

In the task of editing the Mandeville texts, R. Scollon had to face the problem of punctuation. In doing so he made a number of analytical assumptions about the structure of clauses and sentences. Even in writing some morphemes enclosed between blank spaces and others as connected to other morphemes, he had to make various decisions about word structure. One of our goals in the field, then, was to check to what extent this analysis had been correct, or at least to what extent it corresponded to the intuitions of native speakers.

Another problem derives from the oral nature of Chipewyan texts. Pawley and Syder (n.d.) have suggested that oral text may well be structured differently from written text. The basic principle of oral text, they claim, is that it is constructed one clause at a time. That is, they suggest that complex repositionings of elements, embedding, and reversing of temporal order and so forth will not occur in oral text, or will at least be much rarer because of the much greater load they place on short-term memory processing. If Pawley and Syder are correct in this, as we believe them to be, then it calls into question the theoretical status of the sentence in the analysis of oral text. To some extent it seemed that Mandeville's texts were syntactically organized around the clause, not the sentence, and we wished to check this further if possible in the field.

Perhaps the principal reason we need to consider these problems here, however, is that whatever the syntactic organization of Chipewyan was for Mandeville, it is different for Marcel and others in the modern speech community. The two reasons for the changes appear to be that Chipewyan has been influenced by other languages and that the structure of words has been changed, and this has produced secondary changes in the clause. In this section we will look, then, in a general way at the evidence we have for structural units below the narrative structure before going on to look in detail at lexical structure.

To take the grossest sort of indications first, we can look at breath groups and pause groups and ask to what extent these represent syntactic units. If we simply count them for the two texts we have the following figures,

	Chipewyan	English
Breath groups	36	48
Pause groups	83	103

By this measure we can see that the English text is slightly longer and that there are about twice as many pauses as breaths. In fact, if breaths are divided by pauses, we see that for both texts there are just about the same number of pauses for each breath, 2.3 for Chipewyan and 2.2 for English. The fact that both texts are just about the same in this regard suggests to us that these prosodic divisions relate more to something we might call narrative style than they do to syntax.

It might be thought that this narrative pace of around 2.2 pauses per breath is simply controlled by some physical limits on the length of time one can speak on a single breath. This is unlikely, however, since there is quite a bit of variation in the length of these groups. For example, (1) in the Chipewyan text has a single word which occupies a full breath group whereas in (24) there are seven pause groups within one breath and the last is, in fact, a very long one. The English text varies from (12) which is quite short to (32) which has seven pause groups.

We feel that Marcel's breathing and pausing, although they may be used to mark narrative boundaries and although they may coincide with syntactic boundaries or even be used to reinforce them, do not in themselves tell us much about syntactic boundaries. We feel it is more a matter of the pace of the narrative and, as we will argue, Marcel's narrative style is very much the same for the two texts.

We have observed in our discussion of pitch and the phenomenon called downdrifting that the boundaries of this downdrifting are syntactic units. There we said that these units were sentences. We would now like to reopen this question. First, if we look just at the number of final falling pitch contours which are marked in our texts with a period (.), we see that there are 41 in the Chipewyan text and 54 in the English text. This gives 1.1 for each breath group. It almost, but not quite, comes out to a pitch fall for each breath group. Unfortunately, this is only statistical. There are a number of cases in both texts where the pitch does not fall when a breath and a pause are taken, and also cases where the falling pitch occurs where there is not a breath or even a pause.

Intonation or pitch contour, then, does seem to be operating independently of the two other prosodic features, breathing and pausing, in both texts. It is difficult, however, to go from there to asserting that this falling intonation marks syntactic units, at least not as syntactic units are analyzed by Li.

All of Li's (1946) comments on syntactic structure can be quoted in full here: "The verb which is an essential part of the sentence always stays at the end of the sentence or clause, the other parts of the sentence are placed before it. The order is usually thus: subordinate clause, particle, subject, postposition with its object, object, verb [p. 422]." From this we can extract two points for now. The first is that there are no verbless sentences, and the second is that the verb always comes at the end. A perusal of the Mandeville texts (Li and Scollon 1976) will show that, in fact, there are very rare exceptions to this statement of Li's anywhere in some 220 pages of Chipewyan text.

On the other hand, one does not look for long at Marcel's text without finding problems. For example, in (4) the second pause group is either a postverbal locative or a verbless clause, either of which violates Mandeville's clause structure. Again, the second pause group in (26) seems to be a verbless clause. On the other hand, there are a number of cases of postverbal elements which include agents (3), locatives (15), time adverbials (6), and objects (28). As we can see in (4), there is a period after the verb and then again after the next locative phrase. Thus it is now open to question just what units falling intonation may mark. On the whole this intonation does seem to mark syntactic units of some kind, probably sentences, but it is by no means unproblematical.

Of course for any language we would seek citation forms wherever possible to evaluate the analytical independence of forms. Unfortunately, at Fort Chipewyan it was difficult to do anything like standard elicitation of forms from informants in most cases. We do have information, however, that is relevant to this question, and we would like to look at that evidence now.

In the cases where we could elicit words in citation forms, we found that nouns were said promptly and without question or difficulty as translations of English or Cree words. People had no difficulty with listing names of animals, parts of the body, household objects, or other objects for a basic noun dictionary that we were compiling for school use. On the other hand they would not cite verbs in isolation but only in clauses. One person who had easily given us many nouns said about verbs, "You have to say it with something."

Thus we found that there was a difference between the way nouns and verbs were treated in citation. This is not surprising, of course, since the Chipewyan verb normally includes marking for number, aspect, and mode, and cannot be said without some such marking. A request for an equivalent to an English verb that is much less marked leaves the informant in a quandary over which form to supply since there is none that will match at the same degree of generality. Nouns in Chipewyan, on the other hand, are less specific than in English in not being marked for number, and so translation in that case is felt to be easier.

Our best evidence about the status of verbs as words, then, did not come from direct elicitation but from writing. An older woman wrote out a text in Chipewyan syllabics which was dictated to her by a younger Chipewyan woman. As she wrote, she pronounced the words separately first and then one syllable at a time. In the separate pronouncing of words, her divisions were just those which Li has analyzed. The characters that she wrote were written without spaces between them but all of the line ends were made at word boundaries, even where this required her to crowd several syllables in the margin. From this we can see that the analysis that Li has presented and that we have maintained in the Mandeville texts (Li and Scollon 1976) reflects native speaker's intuitions about words as analytical units, despite the fact that it was very difficult to find situations in which native speakers would display those intuitions.

We still need to consider larger syntactic units. We have said that verbs are cited in clauses if cited at all. This seems to argue for the clause as a unit of grammatical structure. What about larger units? We will return to the writing of the text in syllabics. Lines were ended between words, but other than this there was only one place where both people agreed a new line would have to be started even before the current line was finished, "so people won't get confused." In two other places the writer inserted ʔɛkúˑ where it had not been dictated. We will need to look at these.

The text was an announcement to parents about the Native American Studies Program which was beginning in the school. The first section was a general description of the program and its goals. Following this, the parents were instructed to sign their names and return the announcement with the student to school the next day if they agreed to having their children participate in this program. Finally, they were told that if they had further questions they could talk to their chief. It was this last section about further questions that was clearly set off from the rest. We feel that the motive for this was not syntactic but functional. That is, it constituted a return to the general explanation of the original section and was not to be construed as part of the directives that had just preceded.

The directives are quite interesting as well. There are two directives in the text. The first is for the parent to sign the sheet. The second is for the parent to send the sheet back to school. These two directives were marked with ?εkú · by the writer. In our earlier discussion of kú · we argued that there was a relationship between the degree of care taken in speaking and the phonetic shape of kú ·. We also argued that this degree of care in speaking was related to the structure of the narrative and that narrative structure, in turn, was at least partly a function of the narrator's awareness of his or her audience. That is to say, we argued that the forms of kú · were strongly related to the speech situation. Now in this case we see that ?εkú · has been used to punctuate a change in the speech act function of a text. When the shift is from exposition to directive, this is signaled by ?εkú ·. When the function switches back to exposition again, a line break is required to signal the termination of the directive.

As one more bit of evidence on this score we can observe that when the younger person dictated this text originally, we wrote it in an alphabetic orthography. There are many kú ·s in this text. When she dictated the text to the older woman she deleted all these kú ·s. It seems that the function of the kú ·s in the original situation was to mark speech to be written as text in contrast to speech about the text. This contrast, which is normally signaled in English by various changes in pitch and voice quality, was signaled in Chipewyan with the form kú ·. Thus again, we see that this punctuation is a marking of speech function rather than of syntactic structure.

We can summarize now what we have learned about the intuitions of native speakers on Chipewyan analytical units. Nouns are isolated and understood as free forms. Verbs are felt to be bound in clauses. The next larger level of structure is functional in the speech situation.

Intuitions about English are more difficult to study because there are very few people in the modern speech community who have not had quite specific training in the grammar of the language. For younger speakers, intuitions correspond reasonably well to the teachings of the school. There is an interesting exception to this, however. One 10-year-old was quite informative because she had just arrived in the community from a Chipewyan reserve where she spoke primarily in Chipewyan. In writing stories in English she found it virtually impossible to place periods; she had no idea what they were for. In writing down a story dictated by another person she insisted that that person say where to put periods because she could not tell otherwise. Then after writing a period she would write *and* or *and then* before whatever was dictated next. In this she appeared to be trying to treat the period as a marker of narrative structure rather than of syntactic structure, which is in keeping with what we have observed above for older speakers of Chipewyan.

In Marcel's text in English there are a number of forms which, although they are productive forms for other speakers of English, appear to have become fossilized or idiomaticized for him. **That's it** or **that's a** are used as simple articles or demonstratives, as in

> (8) *I found it **that's a** beaver.*

> (28) ***That's it** twenty-two's a long this one, eh?*

As in (8), there are expressions consisting of a transitive verb and a following **it** which, again, do not appear to be analyzed into two morphemes. (16) and (5) give two more examples:

> (16) *never **find it** beaver.*

> (5) *I **found it** one beaver.*

These forms indicate that in some cases Marcel's analysis of what is a word may differ, if not his intuitions about the general class of words concerned.

The prosodic similarity between Marcel's English and Chipewyan texts may show that the units above the word that are marked match the Chipewyan marking of narrative and functional units more than syntactic ones. Later we will be making a closer comparison of the clause structure of the Chipewyan and English texts. In that analysis we will show that to a great extent Marcel's English and Chipewyan clause structures have converged.

THE PHONETIC TEXTS

In the discussion of Marcel's texts to this point, we have had a number of occasions to refer to phonetic details. In the discussion to follow on lexical structure it will become essential to be able to refer to a phonetic transcription of the texts. Before presenting the texts themselves, however, several comments on format will be necessary.

The same conventions have been used in the phonetic version of the texts—as in the earlier phonemic and orthographic versions—to represent pauses, breaths, and intonations. In the phonetic version, however, there are a number of pauses that have not been represented in the earlier versions. These are caused by various kinds of speech errors and hesitations which were not judged to be significant. The result of their inclusion in these phonetic texts is a greater number of pause groups.

In this version of the texts an interlinear translation has been provided. This is given for each morpheme as much as possible, though in general verbs have been translated as words without further reduction. Because of the coalescence of vowels, in some cases there is not a perfect alignment of the two lines of the transcription. It is felt, however, that these lines are never so long that the reader would be unable to pair the translation to the original reasonably well.

Finally, one difference that there seems to be no satisfactory solution for is that the Chipewyan texts are transcribed using the Li–Sapir phonetic symbols but the English texts are transcribed using IPA symbols. We have stayed with the Li–Sapir symbols for the Chipewyan texts because of our frequent references to Li's Chipewyan publications. It should be noted that in the Chipewyan transcription [d] and [t] represent an unaspirated and an aspirated stop, respectively, as do [g] and [k]. There are no voiced stops. In English [d] and [t] represent a contrast in voicing, as do [g] and [k], and [b] and [p].

PHONETIC TRANSCRIPTION, CHIPEWYAN TEXT

1. *wɛt'*
   wait

2. *ʌzdait'ɛlyu ·wʌnt'aimzæ ·*
   uh, I tell you one time, uh

   a
   uh

   a ʔaigɔnəhʌndðəbivɛrs.
   uh, I going to hunt the beaver

   souēðæswʌ ɾətɛlyufɪrʃ.
   so, uh, that's what I tell you first

3. *wɛl ʔiłá ʔtcákɫayaúsiθani'.*
   well once I went for beaver I alone

   θánɛsdeú
   far I hurried-sub.

4. *yuwéda'*
   there

   t'ats'ɔ́n ʔtcáłanɛsθənłịni'djă ·sya.
   to where beaver are many I thought it was past I went

tsəskátcuwéndjéndɛátɬ'ul'ə́sk'əðə.
Saskatchewan to line across

5. *kozísaxayaú*
toward there I went for beaver

6. *kúsáɬą́ĵlenįkúhú*
then beaver many not past then sub.

7. *djǫ·ts'ihiyauts'i˙*
here from I went since
tci'tˣa·ɣɨt'įúdɔ́dítθǎ·
—three times I slept-sub.˙ nothing I found
'ɛyɛrúɬdú·tsáɬáɨ̂dénį.
there then beaver I killed several past

8. *'ayɛrots'įhi·yaúdɔdɛstconį˙*
there from I went-sub. where river-big past
dɛstcoθáhélinįit'ází
river-big far not past since to
'eyɛrnî·yaúeyetθ'ináketcáɬaîθɛr.
there I arrived-sub. there also two beaver I killed.

9. *ayɛrots'ihi·yaú, 'ɛyidɛstcogánániyaú*
there from I went-sub. that river-big over I crossed-sub.
ɬâ·céθnɛtcá·bɛt'ɛði·yaú,
one hill-big I came to-sub.
kwíyɛrsasįɬtcɛzt'úéhúlyɛnį.
then there bear trap lake it is called past

10. *sazitcɔztwéðǽzbɛrlǽ'ɛyihúlyɛ.*
bear trap lake that's bear lake that it is called
'ɛyɛrúθiya'ɛyɛrkɛyɛrɬdų́tθ'itcáɬaɨ̂dénadli.
there I passed there then also beaver I killed several again

11. *'ayɛtɬ'áxɨ̂ts'ə́n·*
that after in the evening
'ɨtk'ə́t'a·tsə́ɬɔíθərnį.
six beaver I killed past

12. *tθ'iyɛrots'įnasdjahútθ'ɛ̨nínasdjaį*
also there from I went back then also home I went-fut.
tcáúlɛ'áθəda'.
beaver there is none since I stopped

13. *ʔɛyɛrtc'inasdjaúanénaɣasdaɬt'ŭ ·*
    there from I went back-sub. I was going on while
    ɬátuwɛt'úétcoɛyma ·st'įnįtsɛltcɪctsiɬɛdjɛrș
    one fish lake-big there I camped past snow—it snowed
    tciɬɛdjɛriụ'ʔɛwɛit'įú,hɛlts'ik'abįnasdja.
    it snowed-sub. there I camped while next morning I returned

14. *k'abįnasdjaúɬâ ·t'unɛnéθɛʔą́*
    in the morning I returned-sub. one lake long it lay
    kwíyɛɬuk'édéiɬásį̂ ·sasɬąbɛk'ɛ'.
    then there spring when one side bear many on it
    ɬuwaɣanádétθɛbą ·xayɛɬuwɛɬą̌ ·dé'.
    fish on they live rapids winter fish are killed
    ʔɛyəɣanádé'
    that on they live

15. *ʔɛyit'uots'ɛ̧anɛsdjanįúyų́nésk'əðə sasnáðɛrgé'*
    that lake toward I crossed past-sub. the side ahead bear he stayed-
       emp.
    nįðátcóílɛ'.
    far-big not

16. *wɛltwɛnit'ú ·ɬįsɛts'í'.*
    well, twenty-two only I had
    twɛnit'úadaɬágɛtcodianátθ'ɛrt'ɛ.
    twenty-two   single shot   it is

17. *ʔayɛrǎ ·ʔ*
    therefore
    ʔɛyɛrnóθɛsdaxǎ ·
    there ground I sit down-fut.-sub.
       —*kų́tisélalʔasolâ ·cį̧'.*
       then only – – – –

18.   *ʔɛyáhû ·lk'é—nɛsθénosk'íθ ·*
    therefore I'll shoot I thought I shot
    hɛsgíθbásdilɛhúlú
    I shot it I touch not but

19. *ts'ínəθénįuʔts'ínaθéʔ*
    finally past-sub. finally
    k'áɬbɛts'ï ·ðélik'itcot'ą ·tθ'í ·djaút'axą bahéɬgéú
    almost from him far not shell falls also it did suddenly in front he
       jumped

tθ'iθé ·lɛt'utθ'itc'anaikégadanə́ði.
also not long while also he came back already also

ʔiꞇabậ ·sét'ianáðɛr.
in front of me he sits he stays

tθ'ínadaxahéꞇgé
again he moves again-fut. he came

20. *kúlúdɔɣɛn̯ðâ ·smík'olyŭ ·daxɑsíhɛzcshɛziꞇdésθə̽.*
    but crossing was far my mind knows suddenly—he roars I heard

21. *—θiꞇk'áðút'o—nɛsθɛn.*
    I shot it-sub. maybe I thought

22. *kwínasdjaú*
    then also I went on-sub.

    ʔɛyəts'ínaθiyaiꞇ'ází ʔi ·t'úgɛ.
    there finally I pass-fut. behind that lake on

23. *ʔɛyɛrt'axasasná ðɛrn̯ ʔ ɑ́zasɛhit'uluꞇáɣɛ ʔa.*
    there just bear he stayed past – – – trail one it extended

    ʔet'uluɛsnín̯iya.
    that trail I arrived

    ʔeigə́nasdjat'ulugə́nasdja.iséðlaik'aðisdjanú̯
    that along I went trail along I went that hill on top I climbed past-sub.

    daxasasazɛts'éꞇgé
    suddenly bear-small he came

    tuzê ·gɔꞇgésiséꞇgé.
    lake toward he went he came at me

24. *ʔú̯ ʔn̯ðéílɛ'*
    then far not

    ʔasít'a.
    some three

    ꞇú̯ ·nadɛnik'éaniꞇθatŏ ·
    ten man feet it was distant maybe

    ʔeyɛrɛts'
    there from

    génoꞇgé
    he came

    wʌ́zədjɑ́
    – – –

    k'énoꞇgéútθ'icⁿtcainawɛts'ⁿts'anagútθ'ini
    he came-sub. also he came back he came again-sub. also past

tθiątúbórɛt'it'úθisɛzɛnałgénadli'.
still he could be seen while also he came back again.

25. *tθ'iałúnįðárɛt'utθ'igénołgɛsɛts'ɛnałgéału?*
also still far not while also he came he came back at me yet
?ałútθ'iyowɛdɛtcína?dɛtcįéilgú
yet also over there woods, in the woods he went-sub.

26. *tθ'isénałgɛnadli'.*
also he came at me again
t'ahwíyɛr'.
three then there
hútθɛt'áwɛ?gədənɛgítcokwi ·déθłozɛt'a'.
then in front three – – –

27. *húyɛrhúnįðáílɛ'*
then there then far not
—*sįθaikətnįðɛnik'ąłɛto ·—.*
– – – I thought wounded it is maybe

28. *?ayɛrúldú ·θiłk'éθeisas.*
there then I shot that bear

29. *?ɛyisasθiłk'éθú*
that bear I shot-sub.

30. *nâ ·ltθ'ɛr'*
he fell down
dátθ'itc'ódłłbíyɛtθíałútθ'ibɛtθíðiłk'óðnâ ·θiłk'óθ
– – – his head still also his head I shot twice I shot

31. *nú ·?yɛstθit'auts'ónots'isasbəɣanílgénį'*
past-sub. I poked it since from bear to it they were coming past
sasazɛtθ'isɛgénísəsʌzi?ɛłɛ?ásgét'aɣɛ'.
bear small also me behind bear small they came emp. three

32. *kúkólɛsi'.*
then I told them thus
—*dɛ?ósįtθɛnúwést'ɛlɛsik'ócyądéyɛkólyąkódæ'.*
too much you sorrow probably who I know if I know it—I said
—*djanóhbégósyądɛkósléxailɛnįdɛsi.*
here you I know if I do so future not past I said
wɛl.
well

33. *tθ'itθádɛɣunátθ'ileá'bɛsbéscnɛtcásɛts'įnįayí ·bxxx*
also long they live also not since knife knife big I had past that

θisasnáit'áðú
also bear I butchered them

ʔúsiseɬįdɛʔázíɣuleléʔbɛɣelédánɛtáðílenįá
then I my dog too much packs their loads heavy not past since

34. *ʔɛyiʔá*
therefore

horyŭ·sastθéntθ'inailaúsastθ'iɬɛk'ágé
all bear meat also I packed bear also it was fat emp.

bɛk'áθiolyuítcúítθ'įʔθɛnĕ·k'ésða.
its fat also all I took that also I along I put it quickly

35. *hát'ŭ·ɛyerɬánawɛst'ŭ·ɛlts'ik'abŭ·tsɛkúénɛsdja.*
thus there once I slept again next morning-sub. my home I returned

natθ'iyɛruts'ónúɬįǽsólainou
now too there to only that's all I know

36. *stɔpɪt*

PHONETIC TRANSCRIPTION, ENGLISH TEXT

1. *ʔyulʔyōōʔɪʔyazgwōthʌzʌbɪvɛrṣ.*
   you know I was going to hunt some beaver
   (mm̩)

2. *ðɛrsɘnadmɪnipivɛrdæt'āɪn*
   there's not many beaver that time

3. *yuɛsʌʔalɪfhiertʃɘrʒɘdʒækfɪʃ?*
   just I leave here at, for Jackfish
   (mm̩)

4. *wɛlafɪ'ɛrdæt'*
   well after that
   wælgɛzbʌtθrinaits
   well guess about three nights
   dĭfāībivɛryɛt'
   didn't find beaver yet

5. *dʒʌswʌtθrinaitsaifandɪtwʌbivɛr'aik'ɪldtθri.*
   just about three nights I found it one beaver I killed three

6. *æfɪ'ɛrdæt'yērnuzai·nouzīlɔtsuleikslɔtsɘkrɪk*
   after that you know I knows in lots of lakes lots of creek

ɔlovɛr xxx ɔlovɛr.
all over xxx all over

7. *wɛl ʔwãndzætðʌendrɛverṣwʌzæwulfɔreverdæt'.*
well one's at the end river was Wolf River that

8. *ʔainouɪsavɛriklous: a ʔʔafãnɪt' ·ætsʌpbʸæ ·bɛ ·bivɛr'.*
I know it's very close I found it that's a beaver
ak'ɪltu.
I kill two

9. *awɪzɛbɛsbɪvyazɛpɪgrɪverhɪerk'ɪwēnəkrɔs?*
I went there's a . . . there's a big river here I went across
ʔæsɪtwʌntsɛbɪghɪlt'?
that's it one's a big hill
ǣdæziʌðəsaidzabɪgleik'?
and that's the other side's a big lake

10. *hik'ɔlɪdðaʻbɛrtræbðɪlɛnðɛhileik'ɪvʌhik'ɔldæt'.*
he call it the bear trap island . . . lake is what he call that
(mm̩)

11. *ðɛrzʌls ʔæhæhainouzɛbiver ·ðɛrɔlɛt'aim.*
there's . . . I know there's beaver there all the time

12. *ðæsʌ ʔaik'ɪl ·t'u?*
that's a I killed two

13. *ðɛsʌnʌðəwei'*
there's another way
aizwʌzɪnʌðəleik'
I . . . was another lake
aigatnʌðɛt'uəgēī
I got another two again

14. *aik'ɛlɛdʒɪz ·ædei'aizək'ʌmbæksɛnaðɛt'umor.*
I kill it just that day I come back it's another two more
wɛlk'ɪlsɪksīðɛr.
well kill six in there
(mm̩)

15. *aik'ampīnðɛrṣ?ənɛksdei ·k'ædunʌθīnau*
I camp in there next day can't do nothing now
ʒɛʃɛgoubæ ·gɪn.
just go back again.

16. *aizɛgoubæksʌdɪnnɛversɪɪtsəbnɛverfaindɪbivɛr'?*
I just go back so didn't never see it's a b-never find it beaver

hizk'ɔldɛartʃɛleikðɛsəmailainoveðɛrainau?
he's called Archer Lake that's my line over there right now
tsiartʃɛrleik.
it's Archer Lake
(hλ̃)

17. *aik'ambınðɛrṣ*
I camp in there
wɛlætnãĩðɛrznlɔ rɛsnᵘu
well at night there's a lot of snow

18. *anɛksmorni'*
ah, next morning
dʒɛ̣ṣɔlyugɔ̃streit'
just all you going straight

19. *ainouzɛwλ̃sɛbıgleik'*
I know . . . one's a big lake
ɔlɔ̣ŋleik'
a long lake
?ɛznærouwλ̃hɛnɛwɛ'.
it's narrow one anyway

20. *ðɛrzə?ınsprıŋt'aimsēlɔtsəberɔlet'ãĩmĩðɛr'.*
there's in spring time seen lots of bear all the time in there
(mm̩)

21. *lɔtsɛberɔlðet'aimyɔnouðɛrzðɛfiʃınðɛr'*
lots of bear all the time you know there's the fish in there
ɛyɛsætfĭ æzɛdɛdfıʃyənou?
. . . that fi-that's dead fish you know
hii rɛmðætxxx
he eat 'em that *xxx*
nðsprıŋt'aimsēnlɔtsəberɔlət'.
in the spring time seen lots of bear all the t-

22. *dʒıʒaimeidıtðedʒdʒıstamaudʒıstabaud ·ðæsa?ɛtsəɛmitanðɛleik*
just I made it . . just abou- just about that's a *xxx* on the lake
yunou?
you know
ðæsənæruwɔ̄laikðæt'?
that's a narrow one like that
(mm̩)

23. *miaizgōðıswei.*
me, I was going this way
(mm̩)

24. *ǣaləʃʌdndʒɪʃə*
and all of a sudden just
ðǣsʌleikðǣtlǣswʌnʃiaihǣdtʼugohierṣ.
that's a lake that last one see I had to go here

25. *wɛlsiðɛbɛrhierðɛkrɔs.*
well see the bear here they cross

26. *wɛlhiwpʼǣsīðɛr.*
well he was passing there

27. *wɛlaimskɛrɪm.awandʒəskʼɪləskɛrɪm.dʒɛsōnitwɛnitʼuəʼ.*
well I'm scare 'em I want to just kill ah scare 'em just only twenty-two
əʃɪŋglʃɔtʼ.
a single shot
ðǣtsɔlaigatʼ.
that's all I got
ðǣzəlɔ·ŋgs·twɛnitʼu.
that's a long twenty-two
(mm̩)
ðǣsɪtnaiswʌtʼu.
that's it nice one too

28. *ðǣsɛt·wɛnitʼuʒəlɔ·ŋɪʃwʌnei?ǣðǣsðɛwʌnyuʒɪt.*
that's it twenty-two's a long this one, eh? that's the one use it.

29. *aiʃuɾɛm?*
I shoot him
farɛweihaidʒɪswantuskɛrɪmaidōwānəkʼɪlɪmɛnəwei.
far away I just want to scare him I don't want to kill him anyway
aizdʒɪʃwanəʃuɾɪm.
I just want to shoot him

30. *wɛlɪtsəklouʒɛnɛweiʒalsiðǣdʒɪzhwɛrzəpðǣt·*
well it's close anyways I'll see that just where's that
drapðǣtmɛɾɛltʼʃɛlz?
drop that metal shells
ǣzklouʒɛnɛweidʒɪsɛdʒʌmbǣkʼ
it's close anyway just he jumping back
kʼʌməbǣɛge
come back again
(mm̩)

31. *wɛldzɪn*
well then
wɛlɛtsǣftʼɛrdǣ·yʃɔʃudɪmǣftʼɛgein
well it's after that I shot, shoot 'em after again

32. *ðɛzɛgɛdɪklousɪtsgowɪnbækɪnəbuʃhɪzk'ʌmɪnbaiɛgɛn*
    there's it getting close it's going back in the bush he's coming back
    again
    (m̩)
    laik'dæt'ɔlðɛt'aim?
    like that all the time
    wɛlzɛnɛkst'aimzɛn ·dʌshiwē'ʔt'hiwēbækɪnðɛbuʃdīk'ʌ̄bæk'
    well the next time then just he went he went back in the bush didn't
    come back
    aihɛrdæθɔtiyɛlɛrsʌmθīɳfrʌ̄ðɛbuʃ
    I hear that thought he yell or something from the bush
    meibiaiθɔt'yunou
    maybe I thought you know
    —*zɛeiyuhɪɾɛm*—*ðɛnðɛbɛrlaikdæt'*
       he, eh, you hit 'em then, the bear like that

33. *gəyɛlɪmyunou(mm̩)higɔnɛdai.*
    gonna yell 'em you know (uh huh) he gonna die

34. —*hwɛlmeibiaik ·'ɪbᵘæaihɛtɛmɪgɪs ·*—
    well maybe I kil- be I hit 'em I guess
    aθɔt'.
    I thought
    (mm̩)

35. *dʒɪswɛnxxxændʒɪsɛwēbæk'ʌðʌleik'*
    just went xxx and just I went back of the lake
    ðɛrsæ ·ðɛrzərounðɛr'.
    there's, ah, there's a road in there

36. *dʒɪsəlfalɛndəroudðɛndziʒʌt'ɔpðɛhɪl?*
    just I'll following the road then just on top the hill
    ʔæsəbɛrhizk'əmn̩.
    that's a bear he's coming

37. *ðɛrzək'ʌmɪmiəbʌt ·enfit'histɔp*
    there's coming me about ten feet he stop
    t'ɛrnbæʔɛ ·
    turn back anyway
    (m̩)
    dʒiʃhiwēbækɪnðɛbuʃhɪzdʒesk'ʌmɪnt'k'ʌmɪnɛgēīn
    just he went back in the bush he's just coming coming again
    (m̩)

welaidɪʃurɛmyɛtʻ
well I didn't shoot 'em yet

38. *wɛlðɛrzdʒɪstəbautðɛsɛmplesɛzwɛtʻɛrnbæk'dīʃu ɾɛmyɛtʻ*
well there's just about the same place as we turn back didn't shoot
  'em yet

gonbækɪnðɛbuʃ?
going back in the bush

wʌzæftʻɛrdæthik'eimwʌzk'ʌmɪnəgɛn
was after that he came was coming again

(mm̩)

ðɛznouvɛrifarnau.əbauteitʻfit'(laugh)
there's not very far now about eight feet

wɛlizk'ʌminklousɔlɛtʻaimyunou?
well he's coming close all the time you know

əwɛlhɛzənɔtvɛrifarnəmaidɔgtʻudʒeshilʌkwʌndʒeʒhiʂtɔp
well he's not very far now my dog too just he looking just he stop
  ɛnðɛbəhāīmi.
  in the behind me

(mm̩)

39. *ɔlɛsēainouzaiga ɾəʃu ɾɪmðɛrʻhɪzhed.*
all of a sudden I know I gotta shoot 'em there his head

(m̩)

40. *adɪdn̩mɪsdounθīŋnɛrvɛrifar?*
I didn't miss don't think not very far

sfaldaun?
he's fall down

(mm̩)

n̩aiʃa ɾɛməgɛn.twəis?hɪzdɛdnəu.
and I shot 'em again twice he's dead now

41. *ɛwʌzæftʻɛrdætðiyʌŋwʌnzyunouzeəbauðæbɪg*
it was after that the young ones you know they about that big

θriəðəm
three of them

hɪzk'ʌmɪn.
he's coming

42. —*amsɔriʻ(yæʻ)aigɛsainouyuwʌzsteihieræ ·dɪnʃu ɾɛmdætwʌn.*—
  I'm sorry (yeah) I guess I know you was stay here that one
  (mm̩)

43. *wɛləkʾǽtdunʌθīðiəweizwɛgwonədaiɛnɛwei.*
well I can't do nothing the way he was well he gonna die anyway
(yǽʾ)

44. *andɛnmaipʾɛmaiputʃɛrnaif*
and then my bu-my butcher knife
ǽtʾɛmaipʌtʃɛrnaif.ðǽtsnmaibǽksǽkʾ.
I take my butcher knife that's in my back sack

45. *aigatʾaitʃeizɛmtʾəgɛðɛrēpuʃɛrnaifaihɛ*ɾɛm.
I got I chase 'em together and butcher knife I hit 'em
ðǽsəkʾɪgənəkʾɪlɛmɔlʌvɛm.
that's a kil-gonna kill 'em all of 'em
(mm̩)

46. *lɛsēnbɛrɛnɛweiyunouɛsɛntguʃeipn̩tʾfǽtʾ? (yǽʾ)*
lots of bear anyway you know it's in good shape and fat (yeah)
ðǽʃəyʌŋwʌnztʾuəlɪlsmɔlwʌnzɛnɛweiz
that's a young ones too a little small ones anyways
ðɛigudʃeipðɛnauɛvriwʌnɛ ·fǽtə(mm̩)anduīeriθīŋ
they good shape then now everyone is fat I'm doing everything
ðǽsmaidɔgxxxnɔ ·nɔtəhɛvi.ðǽtsbǽksǽk?
that's my dog xxx not not heavy that's backsack
wɛǽzɪtɛ·,maidɔg.
xxx has it xxx my dog

47. *amtʾukɛvriθīʃerðɪsbɛr.*
I'm took everything for this bear. *(hā)*
ānkʾǽmpðɛnðǽsɪtwʌnzəbɪgleikʾ.
and camp then that's it one's a big lake.

48. *amkʾǽmðɛrēnɛksdeiaizgānbǽk*
I camp there and next day I going back
(mm̩)
ðǽtsɔlraitʾ
that's all right
ðǽsðəstori.
that's the story

PHONOLOGY

A comparison of the phonetic and phonemic versions of Marcel's beaver hunt narrative will show a considerable amount of phonological variation. This variation is typical of speech in all languages in the speech community to some extent, and for our purposes here we will begin by treating the community as a more or less homogeneous whole.

The Chipewyan consonantal system is now well known from the publications of Fang-Kuei Li. This system is shown in Table 3.1 (Li 1946:398).

TABLE 3.1   Chipewyan Consonantal System.

	Stops and affricates				Fricatives	
	Intermediates	Aspirated	Glottalized	Nasals	Surds	Sonants
Labials	b			m		
Dentals	d	t	t˙	n		
Gutturals	g	k	k˙		x	γ
Labiogutturals	gw	kw	kw˙		xw	γw
Interdentals	dð	tθ	tθ˙		θ	ð
Dental sibilants	dz	ts	ts˙		s	z
Prepalatal sibilants	dj	tc	tc˙		c	y
Laterals	dl	tɬ	tɬ˙		ɬ	l
Glottals			ʔ		h	
Tongue-tip trill						r

We did not know to what extent this consonantal system represented the source of the present-day consonantal system in Fort Chipewyan, but it was one of the purposes of our research to investigate this question.

We soon began to notice a considerable amount of variation in these consonants. We found changes in the place of articulation:

$$tsá \rightarrow tcá \quad \text{'beaver'}$$
$$dzen \rightarrow djen \quad \text{'muskrat'}$$
$$djǫ \rightarrow dzǫ \quad \text{'here'}$$

We found changes in glottalization:

$$ʔɛrɛtɬ'ís \rightarrow ɛrɛtɬís \quad \text{'he wrote,' 'paper', 'mail'}$$
$$ʔɛt'axǫ \rightarrow daxǫ \quad \text{'suddenly}$$

Some affricates had become stops:

$$deɬtθ'i \rightarrow delt'i \quad \text{'they were sitting'}$$
$$tθɛ \rightarrow tɛ \quad \text{'ahead'}$$

In other cases affricates had become fricatives:

$$tθ'i \rightarrow ði \quad \text{'also}$$
$$tsá \rightarrow sá \quad \text{'beaver'}$$

Finally, some of these changes were combined producing considerable reduction from the "original" forms:

ts'ékwi → tc'ékwi → djékwi   'woman'
kú·tθ'i → kúði   → húdi   'then also'

Although we knew that these changes were not wholly regular—that is, there were also instances of the pronunciations to the left of the arrow—we began to wonder what the phonological system would look like if all of the changes were applied in one person's speech.

We saw first that the dz series consonants and the dj series consonants would be merged. Thus we had examples as follows:

dz → dj	dzįné,	djįné	'day'
	dzen,	djen	'muskrat'
	-dzaɣá,	djaké	'ear'
ts → tc	tsá,	tcá	'beaver'
	-tsił,	-tcil	'wash'
	-tsuné,	-tcuné	'grandmother'
ts' → tc'	ts'i,	tc'i	'canoe'
	-ts'én,	-tc'én	'toward' (pp)
	ts'ékwi,	tc'ékwi	'woman'
s → c	sélot'įnɛ,	célot'įnɛ	'my people'
	?así,	así	'something'
	sni,	cni	'it is said'
	sas,	cac	'bear'
z → j	-goz,	-goj	'jump'
	ts'ékwaze,	ts'ékwaje	'old woman'

For most cases we also had examples of the opposite change of dj series consonants to dz series consonants:

dj → dz	-djen,	-dzen	'sing'
	dją,	dzą	'here'
	-djá,	-dzá	'act', 'become'
tc → ts	tcŭ·,	tsú	'also'
	bɛtciné,	bɛtsiné	'car'
tc' → ts'	(no examples)		
c → s	-cą,	-są	'raises (children)'

This indicated that the contrast between the two series had been completely neutralized, not just that dz had become dj. In the case of the fricatives, the final of 'jump', -goz, -goj, -gos, and -goc, indicated no contrast (at least in that position) for either articulatory position or voicing.

We had also noticed that the interdental series of affricates had at least partly fallen together with the dental stops. We had the following examples:

dð → d	nedðaɣa,	nedaɣa	'it is lightweight'
tθ → t	tθɛ,	tɛ	'ahead'
tθ' → t'	náltθ'er,	nált'er	'she fell'
tθ' → ð → d	kú·tθ'i,	kúði, húdi	'then also'

From the original 39 consonants, we had now seen the system reduced to the following system of 26 consonants.

b			m	
d	t	t'	n	
g	k	k'	x	ɣ
				ɣ^w
			θ	
dj	tc	tc'	c	y
dl	tɬ	tɬ'	ɬ	l
		ʔ	h	
			r	

The vertical series of glottalized consonants had also been affected in various ways. Generally, glottalized consonants were replaced by the unaspirated member of the same series. Thus we had observed,

t' → d	ʔɛt'axạ,	daxạ	'suddenly'
k' → g	-k'é,	-gé	'emphatic verbal suffix'

tc' → dj	ts'ékwi, tc'ɛkwi, djékwi	'woman'
	ts'i, tc'i, dji	'canoe'

But in the case of the lateral ejective tɬ', we had seen it replaced by the aspirated member of the series, tɬ:

ʔɛrɛtɬ'ís, ɛrɛtɬís   'he writes', 'paper'

The glottal stop itself was lost in initial position, as in

ʔɛyi, ɛyi   'that'
ʔasí, así   'something'

or in positions where it resulted from a reduction of a glottalized consonant, as in

ʔɛyit'á→ ʔɛyiʔá→ ɛyiá

We then were left with the 21-consonant system that follows:

b		m		
d	t	n		
g	k		x	γ
				γ^w
			θ	
dj	tc		c	y
dl	tɬ		ɬ	l
			h	
				r

There were still other somewhat less regular changes which further reduced this system:

dj → tc	djạ,	ɛtcạ	'here'
x → h	xéɬ,	hél	'with'
ɬ → l	xéɬ,	hél	'with'
ɬ → sl	ʔįɬáɣɛ,	slagɛ	'one'
γ → g	ʔįɬáɣɛ,	slagɛ	'one'
γ → k	-dzaɣá,	djaké	'ear'
dl → gl	ʔɛdláɣɛ,	glá	'what' (interrogative)
xw → w	súɣwá,	suwa	'good'
	ɣwalí,	walí	'it will be'

The system that results from these changes is now very distant from the original 39-consonant system. This system of 16 consonants has only θ and tɬ to remind us of its Athabaskan origins.

b		m	w	
d	t	n		
g	k			
			θ	
	tc		c	y
	tɬ			l
			h	
				r

As we have suggested all along, we suspected that this Chipewyan system was being strongly influenced by other languages in the community. If we arrange this system and the Cree consonantal system in the same order and superimpose one upon the other, we will see just how similar they have become. The Cree system we use here is that given by Wolfart and Carroll (1973) and may be questioned to a certain extent since there has been no study of Cree in the Fort Chipewyan region with which to compare modern Cree, let alone Chipewyan. Nevertheless, Wolfart's (1973) suggestion that Cree in Northern Alberta is somewhat different from Cree as it is spoken farther south seems to be restricted largely to grammar. In the following chart, Cree consonants are in parentheses and the overlapping areas are enclosed:

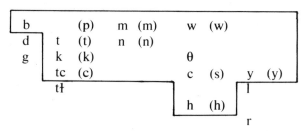

As we collected these examples from different speakers, however, we noticed that these changes were by no means regular in anyone's speech. They were, in a word, variable. One might find a single speaker saying both *tsá* and *tcá* for 'beaver' or, it seemed, using one form, for example, ts, exclusively in one word such as *tcá* but in another such as 'grandmother' using only ts, *betsuné*. We also were observing during this period that English appeared to be undergoing many of the same changes.

We do not know, again, what to consider as the original English consonantal system for Fort Chipewyan. The first English speaker in the area, Peter Pond, was an American. The influence of Scottish English (of various varieties), however, was regular for many years. Recently southern Canadian English has been strongly represented in the schools. The system that follows probably does not seriously misrepresent the sources of the current pronunciations although we acknowledge it to be essentially a guess:

b	p	m		w
d	t	n		
g	k	ŋ		
			f	v
			s	z
dʒ	tʃ		ʃ	ʒ
			θ	ð
				l
				r
			h	
				y

As it is spoken at Fort Chipewyan, there are a number of changes in this system which together result in the loss of contrast between voiced and voiceless stops. We noted for example,

$$b \rightarrow p \quad p'u\int\!\varepsilon r \qquad\qquad \text{'butcher'}$$
$$s\tilde{\jmath}p\jmath d\varepsilon, \; s\tilde{\jmath}b\partial di \qquad \text{'somebody'}$$

but also,

$$p \rightarrow b \quad buk'\varepsilon r \qquad \text{'poker'}$$
$$t \rightarrow d \quad nad \qquad\quad \text{'not'}$$

Most often either /t/ or /d/ was represented by an unaspirated stop [t] as in

$$taim \qquad \text{'time'}$$
$$t\jmath g \qquad \text{'dog'}$$

The voiced velar stop is devoiced in final position, as in

$$doks, \; d\Lambda ks, \; d\jmath k \qquad \text{'dog'}$$

but the voiceless velar stop may be voiced, as in

$$zgul \qquad \text{'school'}$$

These changes indicate a lack of contrast for voicing in the stops which is also found in the alveopalatal affricates, /dʒ/ and /tʃ/. Thus we have the following:

$$\bar{e}ind\!\!_{3}\varepsilon l \qquad \text{'Rachel'}$$

This pronunciation in itself may well appear to be simply a confusion about the name 'Rachel', taking it to be 'Angel', except for another pronunciation of the same name, [rēntsɨ·] which immediately followed the first in calling the child, Rachel. To understand this pronunciation and other developments we need to note that in some other cases,

$$r \rightarrow \emptyset \quad s\Lambda p\Lambda \qquad \text{'supper'}$$
$$k\jmath s \qquad \text{'across'}$$
$$f\varepsilon s \qquad \text{'fresh'}$$

There are also many cases of [tʃ] ~ [ts], as in

$$p'\!\!\textit{æ}tsi, \; p'\!\!\textit{æ}t\int\!i, \; b\!\!\textit{æ}t\int\!i \qquad \text{'Patsy'}$$
$$autsaid, \; aut\int\!aid \qquad\qquad \text{'outside'}$$

There is also a neutralization of voicing, as in

$$sp'eit\int \qquad \text{'spades'}$$

In view of these developments, [ēindʒel] and [rēntsɨ·] for 'Rachel' are in fact possible and are consistent with these other pronunciations.

With these changes considered we can now look at the fricative system of English:

f → v	vɛrz	'first'
v → f.	tʃɔf	'shove'
f → ∅	maisɛl	'myself'
	wul	'wolf'

In some cases /f/ becomes other consonants such, as in

wult, wuld   'wolf'

The net result of these changes if correctly ordered is the loss of both /f/ and /v/.

The interdental fricatives have fared no better. In some cases /θ/ has merged with /t/, as in

hāθī   'hunting'

/ð/ is either changed to [d] or lost, as in

dæts, æts   'that's'

As we have seen in 'hunting' above, /ŋ/ is also lost. To give one more example we can look at,

sʌ̄mθī   'something'

Summarizing to this point, we have the remaining English system as follows:

p	m	w
t	n	
k		
	s	z
tʃ	ʃ	ʒ
		l
	h	
		y

Finally, there is abundant evidence that the set /s/, /z/, /ʃ/, and /ʒ/ has been fully merged to a single consonant, as in Chipewyan. We have, for example, the following:

s → ʃ	sikʃ	'six'
	ðɪʃ	'this'
	ʃei	'say'

ʃ → s	*si*	'she'
	suz	'shoes'
s → z	*əz*	'us'
	zgul	'school'
z → ʒ	*ðoʒ*	'those'
	wənʒ	'ones'
	giʒ	'keys'

Again, if we rearrange the resulting system and match it with Cree, we see a remarkable similarity:

p	(p)	m	(m)	w	(w)	
t	(t)	n	(n)			
k	(k)					
tʃ	(c)		s	(s)	y	(y)
			h	(h)		

1

Only /l/ remains outside of the overlap, and it could easily be argued that /l/ should be considered a Cree consonant as well because of the steadily increasing number of loan words involving this consonant.

As we have said above for Chipewyan, these changes were never applied as categorical rules across the whole lexicon. Individuals varied in their use of these possible phonological alternations. Taking these changes as extreme and categorical as we have here, however, does point to the direction of convergence. It seems quite clear that the phonology of both English and Chipewyan is being strongly affected by the phonological system of Cree.

Here it is necessary to mention that French is likely to have undergone very similar changes. Unfortunately, of the four languages in Fort Chipewyan we found it most difficult to gather direct information about French. Many people reported, however, that French was "all mixed up" and attributed this to the influence of other languages, especially Cree. For this study, then, we are tentatively suggesting that French has also been affected in the same ways.

We will now need to look much more closely at this variation. In order to do so we have chosen to focus on just one set of the changes, the alternations between s-type consonants and ʃ-type consonants. This is both the most regular set of alternations and the most frequent. We feel that an understanding of the variation in this case will lead to a general understanding of the whole phonological system, though it will certainly not exhaust the store of interesting questions.

The set of changes we are interested in is listed below. In this list and in the following discussion all three languages will be written with the same phonetic symbols to avoid confusion:

$$
\begin{array}{ll}
\text{s} \rightarrow \text{ʃ} & \text{ʃ} \rightarrow \text{s} \\
\text{z} \rightarrow \text{ʒ} & \text{ʒ} \rightarrow \text{z} \\
\text{dz} \rightarrow \text{dʒ} & \text{dʒ} \rightarrow \text{dz} \\
\text{ts} \rightarrow \text{tʃ} & \text{tʃ} \rightarrow \text{ts} \\
\text{ts'} \rightarrow \text{tʃ'} & \text{tʃ'} \rightarrow \text{ts'}
\end{array}
$$

The first set of these alternations or substitutions we will refer to as s→ʃ, although later we will indicate in a table a distinction between the fricatives and the affricates. Here this rule will be used as a shorthand for the whole set of alternations. The second set we will refer to as ʃ → s.

The implications of this rule are different, however, for English and Chipewyan on the one hand and Cree on the other. By writing this as a substitution rule (s → ʃ) we are, at least for the moment, assuming that an underlying consonant of the s series has been replaced by a surface consonant of the ʃ series. The other rule (ʃ → s) assumes just the opposite. Since it can be argued that both English and Chipewyan have underlying contrasts for these consonants, this rule may be taken to represent either an assumption about the current phonological systems—that is that they do make these underlying contrasts—or an assumption about the histori-cal developments of the consonants.

For Cree the situation is somewhat different. Wolfart and Carroll (1973) analyze a contrast between /c/ and /s/. The phonetic values which /c/ can have are [ts], [dz], [tʃ], and [dʒ]. The phonetic values /s/ can have are [s], [z], [ʃ], and [ʒ]. Thus the contrast that Cree makes is between an affricate and a fricative. Voicing and point of articulation are variable. When we summarize the use of speakers of Cree with this rule (s → ʃ), the implication of substitution on the one hand or, if one prefers, deep-to-surface change on the other is not at all accurate. For Cree this rule should be considered to mean that /s/ and /c/ have the surface values [ʃ] or [ʒ] and [tʃ] or [dʒ], respectively. In the reverse case (ʃ → s), the rule should be considered to mean that /s/ and /c/ have the surface values [s] or [z] and [ts] or [dz], respectively. That is, for Cree we are assuming no underlying contrast between /s/ and /ʃ/ as we are for Chipewyan and English. Even though we realize that using a single rule format to cover the Cree, the

Chipewyan, and the English discussion is inaccurate, we feel that it is important to be able to informally summarize all of the material within the same table below.

Eleven "speakers" are represented to some extent in Table 3.2. Since some knowledge of their ages, sex, and band affiliation will be useful later on, we will give a brief sketch of the informants here.

The first eight are single speakers.

1. BM. This is Benjamin Marcel, the narrator in whose speech we have the greatest interest in this report. He was 75 years old and a registered Chipewyan. We know him to speak preferably Chipewyan but also Cree, English, and French.

2. VM. Victoria Mercredi. She is the narrator of the legend of the original Chipewyan–European contact in Chapter 5 of this book. She is a

TABLE 3.2 Summary of Alternations of s and ∫

Speaker	s → ∫			∫ → s		
	Chipewyan	English	Cree	Chipewyan	English	Cree
BM (1)	$16.8\,\frac{1.8}{15.0}$	$16.1\,\frac{14.2}{1.9}$	—	$4.6\,\frac{.6}{4.0}$	∅	—
VM (2)	$11.6\,\frac{6.9}{4.7}$	$15.3\,\frac{15.3}{}$	$28.7\,\frac{22.8}{5.9}$	$1.5\,\frac{}{1.5}$	$2.1\,\frac{2.1}{}$	$71.3\,\frac{52.5}{18.8}$
FM (3)	—	$5.2\,\frac{4.5}{.7}$	—	—	$1.0\,\frac{.7}{.3}$	—
PS (4)	—	$24.5\,\frac{17.0}{7.5}$	—	—	∅	—
FC (5)	—	$22.0\,\frac{20.2}{1.8}$	$45.2\,\frac{25.1}{20.1}$	—	$2.7\,\frac{2.7}{}$	$54.8\,\frac{50.3}{4.5}$
LP (6)	—	$6.2\,\frac{6.2}{}$	—	—	$2.5\,\frac{}{2.5}$	—
TF (7)	—	$3.3\,\frac{3.3}{}$	—	—	$4.4\,\frac{4.4}{}$	—
MN (8)	—	$25.2\,\frac{25.2}{}$	—	—	$0.6\,\frac{}{.6}$	—
SG (9)	—	$11.1\,\frac{11.1}{}$	—	—	∅	—
CB (10)	—	$28.6\,\frac{20.4}{8.2}$	—	—	$6.1\,\frac{}{6.1}$	—
PG (11)	—	$29.2\,\frac{29.2}{}$	—	—	∅	—

councilor in the Athabasca Chipewyan Band and is 60 years old. She speaks preferably Chipewyan but we recorded her speaking in Cree to the schoolchildren. She also speaks English and French.

3. FM. Fred Marcel. He has been the Chipewyan chief of the Athabasca Band since 1954. He is BM's younger brother and is about 60 years old. He speaks Chipewyan, Cree, English, and French.

4. PS. This speaker is a woman 62 years old who is registered in the Athabasca Cree Band but characterizes herself as a Chipewyan speaker.

5. FC. This is a man in his 50s who strongly characterizes himself as a Cree and is registered as a Cree. He speaks Cree, English, and some Chipewyan. His wife is a Chipewyan.

6. LP. This is a woman in her mid-30s, a registered Chipewyan, and a Chipewyan teacher-aide in the school.

7. TF. This is a woman in her early 20s who is registered as a Chipewyan. She teaches in the preschool. She is BM's niece.

8. MN. This is a 10-year-old Chipewyan girl who had recently arrived in Fort Chipewyan from Janvier, a Chipewyan reserve near Fort McMurray to the south.

The last three categories are not single speakers. They are small groups of closely related children. Because their voices on tape recordings are so similar, it is quite difficult to isolate individuals. Their samples, however, may be lumped at least initially as a single speaker because of the high degree of uniformity in their speech.

9. SG. These are four girls aged 9 to 12. Two are full sisters, a third has been raised by the same grandmother, and the fourth is also related but at some greater distance. The first three have been raised largely together by their grandmother, PS (No. 4 above), and her husband. The first three are registered as Crees, but the fourth is nontreaty. She is BM's granddaughter. This group will require further discussion later.

10. CB. This is a group of four or five brothers aged 7 to 12. They are registered as Crees.

11. PG. This is a group of two sisters and a cousin who live next door to each other. Their ages range from 8 to 11. Two are registered as Chipewyan and are the daughters of LP (No. 6 above), and the third is registered as a Cree.

The samples that we were able to obtain for these speakers inevitably varied in size. For the first three, BM, VM, and FM, the samples are largest. For the others they are somewhat smaller. The minimum sample, however, was 50 words. For the first three this sample was about 100.

Unfortunately, our method was to get whatever recordings we could of these speakers. The texts for BM, VM, FM, and FC were dictated intentionally as narrative performances. The others were made in the context of informal visits where the focus of the recording was on another speaker and at least sometimes forgotten. From these tapes we selected a consecutive list of words in which a consonant of the s or ʃ series was required. That is, we took every instance out of a continuous stretch of speech where the speaker had to make a choice of one of these consonants for a maximum of 100 words but always for a minimum of 50.

To make the judgments about where a required position was we used three different standards. For English we used our own English as the standard. This is obviously quite arbitrary but, we would argue, no more arbitrary than any other standard. Since we were not considering deletions, epenthetic consonants, or s and ʃ consonants derived from any other source, we feel that we have not severely misrepresented the underlying system to which the rules have been applied.

The Cree analysis was simpler since we did not have to make judgment about the underlying form but had only to note whether a consonant that appeared had an s value or a ʃ value.

The figures in Table 3.2 are given in percentages. This percentage was taken in order to render the tabulation comparable across samples of different sizes. The percentage given represents the number of times the rule was applied out of the total number of instances in which an s or an ʃ consonant was required for English and Chipewyan. For Cree the percentage represents the number of times the surface consonant had the value to the right of the arrow in the summarizing rule.

Thus if we take one example to clarify: BM, in speaking Chipewyan, shifted s → ʃ 16.8% of the time, ʃ → s 4.6% of the time, and the remaining consonants had their "normal" or, if you like, their historical value. By comparison, FC, in speaking Cree, gave the consonants an ʃ value 45.2% of the time and an s value 54.8% of the time.

Finally, by way of explanation, it was thought that perhaps one subset, such as the affricates, might be making the largest contribution to these consonant shifts, and so all of the percentages were recalculated making a distinction throughout between affricates and fricatives. These figures are given in the small box to the right of the total percentage. Fricatives are given above the line and affricates below.

The first thing to be learned from this table is that no speaker applies either of these rules very frequently, though all speakers use the rule s → ʃ some of the time. Because of the quite low percentages for the rule ʃ → s, we would suggest now and leave for more detailed consideration

later that s → ʃ is the basic rule and that ʃ → s represents a hypercorrection. We will, of course, need more situational information to support
this. We will also suggest now that s → ʃ is a surface rule and that the
underlying consonants, at least for Chipewyan and English, are the original or historical ones, that is, the consonants to the left of the arrow.

Before advancing the discussion of the factors that may be involved in
the use of these rules, however, we need to consider the possibility that
they are mechanically motivated. The percentages are low enough that
they might be caused by phonological processes, such as assimilation in
rapid speech. They could also be caused by a few words having changed
consonants but leaving the overall system unaffected. It is also conceiva-
ble that the changes might apply only to consonants in particular positions
or in particular word classes. These possibilities will have to be ruled out
before we seek other explanations.

We may begin by looking at Chipewyan. We might expect that s → ʃ
is a palatalization. Thus we have cases as follows:

$$s \rightarrow ʃ/\underline{\quad}i \qquad ʃi \qquad \text{'I'} \quad \text{(VM)}$$
$$ʃi\cdot \qquad \text{'for sure' (verbal suffix) (VM)}$$
$$ʃni \qquad \text{'it is said'} \quad \text{(VM)}$$

As a counterexample, though, we could suggest BM's

$$si \qquad \text{'I'}$$

and argue that different speakers might apply the rule to different morphemes. If we look back at VM's speech we see, however, that she also
has

$$sî\cdot \qquad \text{'for sure'}$$
$$sni \qquad \text{'it is said'}$$

Looking more closely at these forms we see that VM uses [s] five out
of eight times for sî· and [ʃ] the remaining times. For sni she uses [s] nine
out of sixteen times. This variation indicates two things. The first is that
for VM the variation may apply to a single word. The second is that this
variation for a particular word may not be just the same as the overall
variation which for VM is 11.6%. Looking at another speaker, BM, we
see also that for 'it is said' he has both [sni] and [ʃni].

We can now simply list several more forms to indicate that it is
impossible to maintain that s → ʃ because it is followed by a high front
vowel:

hɛɬ ʃi	(BM)	'make'	
hɛɬsi	(VM)		
naθɛɬ ʃil	(BM)	'soak'	
natsɛl	(BM)		
tʃ'i	(BM)	'boat', 'canoe'	
ts'i	(VM)		

There are several other phonological possibilities, but they are somewhat less likely. If we look at the possible rule

$$s \rightarrow \int /\_\_\_u$$

we can compare the following:

-tsuné	(BM)	2/12	'grandmother'
-tʃuné		10/12	
-tsuné	(VM)	48/53	
-tʃuné		5/53	

And if we consider that there is a rule in Loucheux (Kutchin) that on the surface appears to be (R. Scollon 1975)

$$ts \rightarrow t\int /\_\_\_a$$

then we would want to rule out that possibility here. For the same two speakers we have the following:

tsá	(BM)	2/7	'beaver'
tʃá		5/7	
tsá	(VM)	4/4	
tʃáðéð	(VM)	3/7	'beaver pelt'
tsáðéð		4/7	

Because of the amount of variation within lexical items, we would want to rule out the possibility of this alternation being produced by assimilation for Chipewyan. For English the situation is quite similar. We have both [ʃi] and [si] 'see', [bɔiʒ] and [bɔiz] 'boys', [tsa], [sa], [za], [ɪʃa], [ɪʒa], and [ɪsa] 'it's a', [ðɪs], [ðɪʃ], and [ðɪʒ] 'this', where the varying forms are spoken by the same speaker.

In some cases it appears that

$$s \rightarrow \int /r\_\_\_.$$

Thus we have

bækwɛrtʃ	'backwards'
berʒ	'bears'
yirʒ	'years'

But as counterexamples we have

dirz	'deers'
dirs	
firs	'first'
ðɛrz	'theres'
ðɛrʒ	
tʼors	'towards'
tʼars	

In short, it is probably not possible to demonstrate phonological motivation for the shifts which take place in English either.

There seems to be some slight tendency in Cree for the following assimilation to occur:

$$/s/ \rightarrow s/a\underline{\quad}$$

as the examples below will illustrate:

ni·ʃo	'two'
məwaskiʃu	'reindeer'
mwawaskiso	
mwawaʃkiʃu	

The [s] preceding [o] suggests the rule

$$/s/ \rightarrow s/\underline{\quad}o$$

but of course the first form listed, 'two' [*ni·ʃo*], is a counterexample, as the ones below may be:

mu·sɔ	'moose'
muʃɔ	

The form for 'fox' suggests the following rule:

$$/s/ \rightarrow s/i\underline{\quad}\#$$

magisıs	'fox'
magiʃis	
magiʒis	

But /s/ is [s] in final position after other vowels, as in

wadʒʌs	'muskrat'
mustus	'buffalo'

but not always [s] in final position, as in

muʃtuʃ	'buffalo'

We might suggest /s/ → ʃ between high vowels because of

aiʃinu   'people'
u ·ʃi   'boat'

but there is at least one counterexample in

usi   'boat'

The form for 'fox' above [magɪsɪs] has /s/ between a high vowel [i] and a slightly lowered vowel [ɪ].

Again, we feel that although there is perhaps a tendency in Cree for the choice of [ʃ] over [s] for the surface value of /s/, the evidence is far from convincing. We feel that as of this writing we must consider the variation in Cree to be free variation, at least as far as phonological factors are concerned.

The second possible explanation for this variation is that it is produced by a small group of words having undergone the changes without affecting the whole lexicon. If this were the case, we would expect to find a high degree of agreement across speakers on which words have undergone the changes. It would be a sublexicon that had become specialized for some reason. Our evidence is all to the contrary. In our Chipewyan lists for BM and VM we have a total of 87 different words which occurred spontaneously in the samples taken from both speakers. Of these, 29 words occurred in the texts of both speakers and so tentatively may be presumed to be words of high frequency in the language lacking any other means of establishing frequency. Yet of these only two have shifts of s or ʃ consonants for both speakers. These words are 'grandmother' and 'to say'. They are, of course, words of fairly high currency. Nevertheless, among the remaining 27 there are no others which overlap in having alternations.

From this we can suggest that the shifts of s → ʃ and ʃ → s are not confined to certain lexical items, nor do speakers vary the same words to any appreciable extent. If we look for the explanation in word classes, we can see that the variation is present across Chipewyan grammatical categories as the following examples illustrate:

Monosyllabic noun	*tsá, tʃá*	'beaver'
Postposition	*-tsʼį̃, -tʃʼį̃*	'from'
Polysyllabic noun stem	*-tsuné, -tʃuné*	'grandmother'
Pronoun	*si, ʃi*	'I'
Verb-stem initial	*-tsi, -tʃi*	'make'
Verb-stem final	*-gos, -goʃ*	'jump'
	-goz, -goʒ	

The evidence for English is quite similar. For our purposes here we have used the texts of BM, VM, and FM, since those were more closely comparable in size and situation. Two hundred eighteen different words involving s or ʃ consonants occurred in these texts for these speakers. Forty-five of those were affected by the phonological alternations we are considering. Only nine of the affected words occurred in the texts of all three speakers. These may then be considered words of high frequency. They are listed in Table 3.3.

TABLE 3.3 Words Frequently Used by BM, VM, and FM.

	BM	VM	FM
first	V	—	—
just	V	—	V
say	—	V	—
scare	—	V	—
see	V	V	—
something	—	V	—
stay	—	V	—
that's	V	—	—
this	V	—	—

As Table 3.3 shows, there is little agreement about which of these quite frequent words to vary. Only two words, 'see' and 'just' are varied for two speakers, and none is varied for all three. Since this variation is found across word classes as in Chipewyan, it seems that we should rule out for both languages the possibility of the explanation for this variation being a question of either phonological process or lexical differentiation.

We will not look further at Cree now. We will rely on Wolfart and Carroll's analysis of this variation in Cree being simple allophonic variation and not seek an explanation in lexical factors.

It could be suggested that the shift of s → ʃ or of ʃ → s could be explained as a rapid speech phenomenon. It is also possible that these shifts would occur as a speaker began to take less care in speaking and thus represent a difference between careful and casual speech. It is somewhat more difficult to produce evidence in these cases. Some of our recordings are not strictly comparable for situation, and for most speakers, what we have is from only one situation and thus it is difficult to know what they would do otherwise.

The problem with looking at the variation within a particular setting is that most of our samples are not large enough to select two separate samples, say from the beginning and the middle of a speech event, in order to compare "warmed up" speech with the speech of someone just beginning to tell a story.

These problems, however, are probably not of much consequence in light of the much more serious problem of understanding what counts as careful and casual speech or even what counts as rapid speech in a speech community that is not one's own. In this case we must simply admit our inadequacy and rely for our comments on our considered but untested judgments.

It is our impression that the proportion of shifts from s → ʃ increases in narratives as the narrator "gets into" the story. Although this may well be thought of as an element of narrative style, we think it is not that at all. We feel rather that as the narrator gets more involved in the performance, he or she is less able to monitor the forms of speech. We feel, as we shall suggest later, that the shifts we are considering are motivated by the reality set of the speaker. The loss of the awareness of the immediate situation, that is, the outermost frame, allows a relaxation into an unmonitored speech which in Fort Chipewyan tends toward the set of shifts we are studying.

We would now like to return to Table 3.2 to seek an explanation for the alternations given there. We would like to be very cautious in our approach to this analysis for several reasons. The statistics we have given are unreliable in not being strictly comparable for sample size or situation. Moreover, the total size of the group being studied here, 11 individuals, is far too small to do more than suggest ideas about a speech community of some 1500 people.

The first point we would like to make is that where we have data on speakers for more than one language, that is for BM, VM, and FC, there is not a very great difference in the frequency with which the rule s → ʃ is applied. This is especially true for BM and VM for Chipewyan and English. This suggests to us that the rule is not specific to either of the languages, but rather is a very low-level phonetic rule which is applied to the output of the separate phonologies. We are not accustomed to thinking of phonological rules at the analytical level of the speech community or even at the level of the individual speaker. The current linguistic tradition views phonological rules as belonging to (or in) the analysis of particular languages. We do not feel that it is of any advantage in this case, though, to think of Chipewyan and English as separate analytical systems, each of which has adopted the same phonological rule for independent reasons.

We feel it is more in keeping with the way language is used and conceived of in Fort Chipewyan to associate this phonological rule with speakers rather than languages. Thus we think of speakers who are multilingual as generating the surface output through separate (to some degree) linguistic systems, but then at a very low phonetic level variably applying this rule to undo some of the distinctions created at a deeper level, the lexical level. The overall effect produces a surface phonology that looks more or less like Cree.

This organization of language by speakers rather than by languages is what Grace (1977) refers to as the idiolect. It is his view that at least for some speakers in some situations, especially for multilinguals, language is not organized into discrete systems, each with its own sets of rules, lexicons, and so forth. Rather, in a speech community such as we have described Fort Chipewyan to be, speakers would operate from a single system as much as possible, making only the distinctions between languages that were necessary for communicative and social reasons. There would be no a priori reasons for maintaining separate systems. That is, it is Grace's view that it is not necessarily in the nature of language for it to be organized around discrete symbolic systems. This view of the multilingual's converged system is what Grace has chosen to refer to as the idiolect.

The nearest analogy to this process that we know of is found in various play languages where very low-level phonetic rules are applied to the otherwise more conservative output of the phonological system. To our knowledge, however, this sort of "idiolect rule," in contrast to a language rule, has not been reported before this.

We have suggested that the source of this rule is the free variation in the Cree consonants /c/ and /s/. We would like to be careful now to distinguish between the source of the variation and explanations for it. That is, the fact that Cree varies the phonetic realizations of these consonants tells us nothing of the reasons why in speaking English and Chipewyan people would approximate the Cree system. We so far can only suspect that they might want to "sound like Crees."

We have a full sample only for English and so we will now have to restrict ourselves to an analysis of what this variation indicates in English. If we take the figures for the 11 speakers in Table 3 and rank order them, we get the following order:

1.	PG	29.2
2.	CB	28.6
3.	MN	25.2
4.	PS	24.5
5.	FC	22.0
6.	BM	16.1
7.	VM	15.3
8.	SG	11.1
9.	LP	6.2
10.	FM	5.2
11.	TF	3.5

It is likely that for children the amount of surface variation present in the community could make the learning of underlying forms problematical. We would predict at least a higher percentage of s → ʃ shifts for children than for any other group. The groups in Positions 1, 2, 3, and 8 are the children in this sample. For the highest three we see that they do indeed apply this rule more frequently. Since there is also a considerable age discontinuity between these and the others, we feel that we may fairly eliminate Groups 1, 2, and 3 from further consideration. Group 8, however, will need further discussion.

It will be remembered that this group, SG, consists of three sisters and a cousin. Further study of the individuals in this group made in other situations indicated that all of the shifts of s → ʃ were probably made by one of the four girls, the one related at some distance. The others, in fact, were not observed to make this shift. Thus we could put this girl, Marcel's niece, in the category of children below 12 years of age who have a high percentage of the application of this rule.

We then need to account for the absence of this rule in the group of three sisters. Although these girls are now living in Fort Chipewyan, at the time of making the original recording, they had just returned from Fort Smith where they had been going to school. We have not conducted any formal research at Fort Smith, but our casual observation while visiting there is that this rule does not occur in that community. As further support we have the report of Philip Mandeville who now lives at Fort Smith that people at Fort Chipewyan have a strange way of talking. He used the pronunciation of 'beaver' as [tʃá] rather than [tsá] as an example pointing to the s → ʃ shift. Thus these girls may be expected to behave quite differently from the other children in the speech community.

In contrast to them we could look at MN (No. 3 in the rank ordering) who is also new to the community. Her percentage is very high. The difference is that she came to Fort Chipewyan from the south, from Janvier near Fort McMurray. Again, we have not conducted research in that area, but we do know that the native population is predominantly Cree to the south of Fort Chipewyan and Athabaskan to the north. This girl's alternations may further indicate, as we have suggested above, a Cree source for this rule.

In the remaining cases we see that there is a discontinuity between VM and LP as shown below:

PS	24.5	
FC	22.0	bush subsistence
BM	16.1	
VM	15.3	

LP	6.2	
FM	5.2	regular, salaried employment
TF	3.5	

The one characteristic that separates these two groups is their employment. The three below the line, LP, FM, and TF, have regular salaried employment. The ones above the line receive their subsistence largely from the bush or from native crafts. Since regular employment is likely to be strongly related to worldview, or reality set, we may tentatively consider the discontinuity to be a discontinuity between reality sets.

Age appears to be of no importance in this division of the groups. The four above are all above 50, it is true, but so is FM who is in the employed group. LP is in her mid-30s and TF is in her early 20s. Sex is also probably irrelevant with two women and one man in the employed group and two women and two men in the bush group. FM, who is the oldest of the employed group, may, in fact, have been the first treaty Indian in the speech community to develop a modernized position. As the Chipewyan chief since 1954, he has had more than 20 years of experience in communication with the larger Candian community, especially through contacts with Indian Affairs.

With this distinction in mind we can now look back at the group of children we labeled SG. These girls are, in fact, the most modernized in our sample. Fort Smith's position in the Northwest Territories as one of the most aggressively modern communities may well be reflected in the speech of these girls. Their physical appearance is more Caucasian than any of the others and they may well have worked at "passing" for white in Fort Smith. At any rate their linguistic behavior appears to match their education, experience, and reality set.

We have suggested now that the frequency of the application of the rule s → ʃ may indicate the speaker's worldview or reality set. A frequency below 10% indicates what we will describe as the modern consciousness, and a frequency above 15% (actually 15–25% in these cases) indicates the position we will call the bush consciousness. We would now like to point out several things about the modernized group.

In our table we have given no figures for Chipewyan for LP, FM, and TF. This is because we have been able to collect very little of their Chipewyan speech on tape. This is ironic since FM is the Chipewyan chief and one would think it should not be so hard to get examples of his Chipewyan recorded. As we will point out later, however, his position is that Cree and English are the "high" languages in the community, and if a recording is made it is in one of those two languages, not in Chipewyan.

It is equally ironic that we have little Chipewyan recorded for the other two in this group since they were pointed out to us as likely to be good informants. Nevertheless we have very little of their Chipewyan recorded on tape. In the times we worked with them we always focused on the Chipewyan of some other speaker, especially BM (Marcel) and VM. This is largely because, for these speakers, Chipewyan has been specialized for intimate uses and English for more public and formal uses. As we will discuss later, this specialization of codes further indicates the modern consciousness.

Despite our shortage of tape recorded material, we have for these three speakers a reasonably good estimation of their use of the s → ʃ rule in Chipewyan based on our handwritten field notes. It is in fact very frequently applied. If anything, it is higher than for any other group. Unfortunately, without a running sample of tape recorded text we can establish nothing about the percentages. The point we would like to make is that these people with the modern consciousness have fairly effectively separated their languages into discrete codes and now apply the rule s → ʃ to any great extent only in Chipewyan. For them it is not an idiolect rule so much as a language rule.

Having said this, it is necessary to point out that these three speakers should not be thought of as fully modernized. There are various kinds of evidence that they are somewhat insecure in their suppression of the idiolect rule s → ʃ in English in the same way that from time to time they express doubts about how much longer they intend to remain in their salaried jobs. We notice, for example, in FM's English the following forms:

was·	'was'
pleiscu̧	'place'
ʃsɛventin	'seventeen'
s:æt	'sat'

In each of these cases s has been given an unusual lengthening. In two cases the point of articulation has shifted in "midstream." The tape on which we based our study of FM's speech was perhaps the most self-consciously made of all those we recorded. We feel that these shifts and extra lengths indicate some insecurity with the separation of codes which was caused by FM's awareness that he was recording his life story for posterity.

A different sort of insecurity shows up in TF's speech. We suggested above that shifts in the opposite direction, that is, ʃ → s, may indicate hypercorrection. In the recording used for this sample, TF was speaking to each of us at different times. All of the hypercorrections were made in speaking to R. Scollon, a Caucasian man, none to S. Scollon, a Chinese woman. This distribution seems to indicate some insecurity with the separation of codes that TF may have felt was necessary in speaking to us.

We may add to this observation the fact that TF's salaried employment is in a preschool that is explicitly functioning to prepare Fort

Chipewyan children for integration into the Indian Affairs school system and the larger English-speaking Canadian community. These hypercorrections characterize a preschool style and are even found in the speech of a number of children from white southern Canadian families who have come under the influence of the preschool.

The rule s → ʃ may be seen, then, as an indicator of the speaker's worldview or reality set. A frequency below 10% marks the modern consciousness group. A frequency above 15% marks the bush consciousness group. Shifts of ʃ → s on the other hand may indicate some insecurity, particularly among speakers who are striving to develop a modernized position.

We can close this section on phonology by reviewing the meaning of the shift s → ʃ for our general question of the convergence of languages in Fort Chipewyan. We are now in a position to give more substance to the claim that the original languages have converged to some extent. The evidence that we have from three of the four languages is that, on the surface, the phonologies of English and Chipewyan have come to approximate closely the phonological system of Cree. By looking in more detail at one special instance of this convergence, the shift of s consonants to ʃ consonants, we have seen that this convergence is variable in the community. This variability appears to be used for social purposes, specifically to indicate the speaker's reality set. This alternation is treated as an idiolectal rule for those with the bush consciousness reality set and as a language rule for those with the modern consciousness. Thus the use of variability itself appears to be under the control of the reality set. The evidence we have indicates that the convergence is a low-level phonetic convergence that, at least for adult speakers, does not affect the underlying forms of the lexical item.

WORD STRUCTURE

It is common to think of the effect of one language on another as resulting in the borrowing of words. Although this has happened to some small extent at Fort Chipewyan, the more interesting effect has been on the structure of words where no borrowing has occurred. In order to get an overall view of the changes in word structure that have occurred we need first to get a general idea of how words are structured in the three contributing language families, Athabaskan, Algonkian, and Indo-European. We will, of course, look more specifically at Chipewyan, Cree, and English. Again, we should acknowledge our absence of information on French to be a lacuna in this discussion. It is likely, however, that because of the much greater similarity between French and English than between either of these and Chipewyan and Cree in regard to word structure that this lacuna is not of major importance in this discussion.

Li (1946) describes the Chipewyan word as follows: "A word in Chipewyan may consist of a single stem syllable, with or without prefixes or suffixes. Two or more stems may form compounds. Prefixes, suffixes, consonant alternation, vocalic alternation, and pitch alternation may be employed to express various grammatical functions [p. 401]." He analyzes three word classes, nouns, verbs, and particles. The first of these are rather simple, being inflected only for possession. The last of these are very simple, rarely alternating in form. Verbs, on the other hand, are very complex. They normally are inflected to mark conjugation, aspect, and person and often include a wide range of thematic and adverbial elements. In sum, we can say that Chipewyan lexical complexity is in the verb.

Sapir (1921) said that "single Algonkian words are like tiny imagist poems [p. 228]." In Cree, lexical complexity is distributed equally among nouns and verbs. This is largely due to the verbal quality of Cree nouns. Thus both nouns and verbs are usually inflected for gender, number, person, and direction, as well as for various other case roles and grammatical functions (Wolfart and Carroll 1973). Wolfart and Carroll also point out that there is a general preference in Cree for verbal forms over any others.

English contrasts with both Cree and Chipewyan in the simplicity of its lexical forms. Nouns are marked for number and verbs are marked for tense, number, and person, in some instances. Generally, however, complexity in English is syntactic, not lexical.

Our material in Chipewyan and English indicates that there has been a general reduction in lexical complexity, but at the same time there have been various ways in which lexical forms have been made more complex. The result is that Chipewyan and English have begun to look more like each other by changes that have taken place in both languages. Although our evidence is scant, the Cree preference for polymorphemic verbal lexical forms seems to be the model on which this structural convergence is based at the speech community level.

We will begin to look in more detail now at some of the reductions that have taken place in Chipewyan lexical structure for which we have evidence in Marcel's beaver hunt story. The largest number of these affect the verb prefix system.

In a number of cases the marking of person has either been deleted or confused. We have mentioned this above for the form *tsákayaú* in (3) and (5) where the stem *-ya* 'one person goes' is indefinite for person. The normal prefix would be *hi-* ($<h\varepsilon - i$) as is found in (7) and (8) *hiya* and

hi·ya 'I went' in which *−i* represents the first person singular in the perfective (Li 1946:411).

Again in (7) is the form *dódítθă·* (< *dódítθaú*) 'I found nothing'. Here the reductions are somewhat more complex. The stem *-tθǫ* is given by Li (1933b) as the perfective of " 'to find' (particularly referring to the tracing of a bear in its den) [p. 141]." Marcel uses this stem to refer as well to the finding of beaver. The prefixes given by Mandeville are *hí* (<*hé* + *i* 'perfective first person singular' + *ł* classifier), and so the full form would thus have *híłtθǫ* (Li, n.d.).

The negative form *dódí*, which is sometimes pronounced *dáúdí* by Marcel and always by Mandeville, is used quite differently by Mandeville. He would have in this case,

dáúdí	*t'asî·*	*híłtθǫ*	*híle*
nothing	something	I found	not

That is, a rather fuller construction would have been required including the suffixed negative. For Marcel the form *dáúdí* (or *dódí*) has fully replaced both the sentential indefinite object *t'asî·* and the negative suffix *-híle*. This use of *dódí* is quite general in Fort Chipewyan, where it has become frequent in pidginized uses such as *tsǫ́ba dódí ~ dódí tsǫ́ba* 'no money' (i.e., 'I have no money'). This negative form, then, has been incorporated into the verb at the expense of all the verb prefixes to give a quite literal meaning of 'nothing found'.

This instance demonstrates the same two principles of change in the relationship of clause and word we have mentioned earlier in Chapter 2 with *tsákayaú*. The first is that the verb itself is greatly reduced by comparison with the structure which Mandeville would have used. At the same time, however, the verb structure is expanded by the incorporation of sentential elements. The verbs that result from this process are less well marked for such things as person and aspect, and as a result new sentential elements are produced by way of compensation. These occur mostly in a postverbal position and thus alter the general structure of the Chipewyan clause.

A further example of this is the form in (19.2) *k'ítcotǫ*. The stem here is *-tǫ*, one of the so-called classificatory verb stems. This is one of the set which refers to the states and processes involving a "long, stick-like object [Li 1933b:130]." Again, there are no prefixes. Instead, in the prefix position is the object *k'ítco* 'ammunition' or 'shell'. This form itself may be quite reduced. Campbell (n.d.) has for this form *telk'íðitco* (cf. *telk'íði* 'rifle') *hék'étca* and *ték'étco*. 'Rifle' in Fort Chipewyan is either *telk'íði* or *helk'íði*. Thus we have a meaning composed of the elements 'shell' (in a reduced form) and 'long, stick-like object', but there is no further specification of the verb to tell us just what becomes of this object. This would have been done by Mandeville in the prefix system. Instead Marcel adds on a copular element *tθ'í·djaú* 'also it did'. So again we see that a reduction in one place has had the result of producing further complexities elsewhere.

In other instances, the marking of person is confused, at least by Mandeville's standards. The form *djă·sya* 'I went' in (4.2) is a good example. This may be analyzed as follows. The stem *-ya* is 'one person goes'. The thematic prefix is *tc'a-*, which gives to the whole a meaning of traveling without referring to the means of travel. The phonological shift of *tc'* to *dj* is normal.

The pairing of this prefix and this stem, however, seems unusual. Mandeville uses the prefix *tc'a* with the stem *-ni* 'to travel' (again, not referring definitely to the means of travel) as in *tc'asni* 'I am traveling' and *tc'anasdi* 'I traveled again' (Li, n.d.). In (19.3) Marcel uses the same prefix again in *tc'anaiké* (<*tc'a* + *na* + *hi* + *l* + *gé*) 'he came back', and this indicates greater freedom in his usage of this prefix with various stems for verbs of going.

This may point to a general restructuring of the Chipewyan lexicon into classes of verbs. Formerly, the meaning of the verb was rather delicately balanced on both the thematic prefix and the stem. Now, the stems of the verbs of going appear to be focusing the verbal impact at the loss of finer distinctions. That is, what is important is the process of going, and distinctions concerning the means of going are transferred into the prefix system if these distinctions are mentioned at all. Thus for Mandeville both the prefix and the stem in *tc'asni* mark indefinite means of travel. For Marcel the means of travel is marked in the prefix while the going is indicated in the stem. There is a more definite separation of function. Another class of verbs seems to be losing its verbal force altogether. The classificatory stem *-tą* is keeping its classificatory force but losing its verbal force and so must be compensated with the addition of a copular verb in the same clause.

To return to the question of person marking in *djă·sya*, we can see clearly the first person singular prefix *s*. The problem is to account for its being so clearly marked. In Mandeville's phonology the only way this *s* could be so clearly preserved would be if it was followed by a *d* or an *l* classifier. If there was a *d* classifier, there might also be the iterative prefix *na* which would account for length in the vowel. Normally the *d* classifier and the *y* initial of the stem give *-dja*, however, and we should expect **djă·sdja* here. The forms *nɛsdja* throughout Marcel's text, for example, (12) and (13), indicate that this *dja* is the normal development. The *l* classifier would give the *-sya* we have here, but the problem would be to determine the meaning. For Mandeville this stem (-*ya*) with the *l* classifier means 'to come to a stand'. This seems quite unlikely as a meaning in this context.

If there is no *d* nor *l* classifier, then this verb should fit the virtually pan-Athabaskan pattern and have -*sa* as the imperfective or *i* + *ya* for the perfective in the first person singular. If we assume that the normal narrative pattern of perfective stems is being followed here, then we have to take this verb as a perfective. And the result is that we can only consider person marking as well as aspect marking to be quite confused in this verb.

We could assume a much simpler analysis, however, and account for this verb. If one begins with the surface form *tc'asni* and simply substitutes the stem -*ya* for the stem -*ni*, one gets **tc'asya*, which is reasonably close to the form *djă·sya* given by Marcel. In order to do this one would have to assume a much greater independence of the verb stem and the prefix system than for Mandeville. This independence of the stem -*ya* is just what we are arguing for in our analysis of *tsákayaú* above, and so we feel that the form *djă·sya* gives support to this argument. We feel on the whole that the stems of the verbs of going are moving toward a considerable independence from the regular Chipewyan verb prefix system, and in doing so are beginning to form a separate verb class.

We now need to look more closely at the marking of aspect. In the examples given, we have noted various cases in which aspect was not indicated in the prefix system. We now need to consider if it is ever marked in prefixes, on the one hand, or if, on the other hand, it is marked elsewhere. In (3) there is the form *nɛsdi* 'I hurried'. Mandeville has for this meaning *naúθɛsdi* (Li, n.d.), with an indication that the *ú* may not be necessary. If we take *naθɛsdi* as the closest form for comparison, we can see that Marcel's form is quite similar. If we assume that *na* + *θɛ* → *nɛ*, then we can see that aspect is marked in this form in the vowel *ɛ*.

The form *nɛsdja* 'I went back' occurs throughout this story. In most cases the prefix vowel is low as in (12), (13), (14), and (15), *nasdja*. Only in (35) is the vowel *ɛ* found, *nɛsdja*. This last form, however, is probably the most carefully pronounced. It occurs as part of the narrative final and, as we have argued above, is therefore likely to be pronounced more carefully. If so, then we can assume the vowel *ɛ* to result as a coalescence of *na*, the interative prefix, and *θɛ*, the perfective prefix, as in *nɛsdi* above.

The question remains, though, of whether the perfective *θɛ* is represented in the earlier forms of *nasdja*. It is common in Marcel's speech for *ɛ* and *a* to vary freely. There are *ʔɛyi* [ʔayɛ] 'that' (11) and *ʔɛyɛr* [ʔayɛr] 'there' (8), (9), and (17) in this text, and such forms as *héni* [hanɛ] 'he said' in other texts as examples. Shall we understand *nasdja* as *na* + *θɛ* + *s* + *d*

+ *ya*, with a phonological shift of $\varepsilon \rightarrow a$, or shall we understand it as *na* + *s* + *d* + *ya* with a morphological deletion of the perfective? Obviously the result is the same, and so aspect marking in the prefix system for this verb is neutralized in all but the final example in (35).

Another case in which the marking of aspect is indeterminate is *básdilɛ* 'I am not touching it' in (18.2). Mandeville has *bérésdi* 'I am touching it' and *bédéθesdi* or *bédéɣesdi* 'I have touched it' (Li, n.d.). Again we have the problem of deciding what aspect is represented in Marcel's text. If it is perfective, as we believe it to be, then we have to decide how to analyse Marcel's prefix *bá*. Which of the following is it?

> a. *bédéθɛ*
> b. *bédéɣɛ*
> c. *béθé*
> d. *béɣé*
> e. *bé*

That is, are the reductions morphological as in (e), where both theme and aspect are assumed to be absent, or (c) and (d), where theme is deleted but aspect is represented by *θɛ* or *ɣɛ*, or are the reductions phonological as in (a) and (b), where both theme and aspect are assumed in the underlying form? And if we assume underlying aspect as in (a) through (d), how do we decide which form, *θɛ* or *ɣɛ*, is appropriate? It is obvious at any rate that the amount of reduction involved, whether morphological or phonological, results in a neutralization of aspect in the prefix system for this verb as well.

Finally, there is in (19.5) *nada* 'he moves'. This would be given by Mandeville as *náɣeda*, and so we see one more example in which aspect is neutralized in the verb prefix system.

The reduction of aspect in these forms leads us to look for any examples in which either *θɛ* or *ɣɛ* appear on the surface as a means of deciding if Marcel ever overtly marks aspect with prefixes. In (23) there is

> *t'ụlụłáɣɛ²ą*
> trail one it extended

but this, again, is ambiguous. In this position, Mandeville would probably have

> *tụlụ*   *²iłáɣɛ*   *θɛ²a*
> trail   one it   extended

Unfortunately, we have found no exact examples in Mandeville's texts (Li and Scollon 1976), but in the notes (Li, n.d.) there are some cases in which the *ɣɛ* perfective is used with the stem -*²a*. So we do not know if the $\gamma\varepsilon$ in $\acute{t}\acute{a}\gamma\varepsilon\acute{}\rlap{?}\!a$ belongs to the numeral $\rlap{?}\!\acute{t}\acute{a}\gamma\varepsilon$ or as a prefix of aspect to the verb stem -$\rlap{?}\!a$. What is clear is that here, as elsewhere, there is a much closer relationship between elements of the clause and the verb stem than can be analyzed for Mandeville.

Just below this example in (23.3) there is one of the few instances in this text where the $\theta\varepsilon$ prefix occurs on the surface. Where Marcel says $k\acute{}a\eth isdja$, we may compare it with Mandeville's $hok\acute{a}\theta\varepsilon sdja$ (Li, n.d.). Below we will give further examples of the absorption or deletion of the prefix ho- which is general for Marcel. The stem initial dj is a coalescence of the d classifier and the stem -ya 'one person goes', as in $n\varepsilon sdja$ 'I went back'. The function of the d classifier here is to indicate that the narrator is returning. That is, he has climbed this hill before on his trip out, even though he has not specifically said so in this narrative.

It is interesting to consider how this would be said without the d classifier. Would it be *$ka\theta\varepsilon sya$ with the same analytical problems as for $dj\breve{a}\cdot sya$ 'I went' above? Or would person be deleted, as in 'I went for beaver' $ts\acute{a}kaya$. This latter form may indicate why $\theta\varepsilon$ is present in the form $ka\theta isdja$. If person is also deleted, it would become homophonous with $ka..ya$ of the 'hunting' meaning. In order to maintain a distinction between the $ka..ya$ of hunting and the $ka..ya$ of climbing, the $\theta\varepsilon$ perfective has been retained, not as a perfective, apparently, but as a thematic prefix. This function which it received as a result of the reduction of prefixes elsewhere has apparently now become its central function. In one case a young boy said $hill~la~kaya$ 'he climbed a hill' and eliminated the θ marking altogether. Here, of course, the la 'on' remains to distinguish this from *$hill~kaya$ 'he went for a hill.' So we see that, in fact, aspect is probably not represented in the prefix system in this case either.

We can now look at the verb for killing which occurs in several places and these forms may be compared with Mandeville's as follows:

		Marcel	Gloss	Mandeville
a.	(7.3)	$\acute{t}\acute{a}\acute{t}td\acute{e}$	'I killed several'	$t\varepsilon\gamma\acute{a}ni\acute{t}d\acute{e}$
b.	(8.3)	$\acute{t}ai\theta er$	'I killed two'	$t\varepsilon\gamma\acute{a}ni\acute{t}\theta er$
c.	(10.2)	$\acute{t}ai\acute{t}d\acute{e}$	'I killed several'	$t\varepsilon\gamma\acute{a}ni\acute{t}d\acute{e}$
d.	(11.2)	$\acute{t}\rlap{\jmath}i\theta\partial r$	'I killed several'	$t\varepsilon\gamma\acute{a}ni\acute{t}d\acute{e}$
e.	(14.3)	$\acute{t}\breve{a}\cdot d\acute{e}$	'They are killed' 'They die'	$t\varepsilon\gamma\acute{a}nid\acute{e}$

Although there has been considerable phonological reduction, the form in (e) indicates that an underlying prefix $/t\varepsilon\gamma\acute{a}/$ is not unreasonable for Marcel. Where there are other prefixes, especially the first person singular prefix -*i*, both the medial consonant and the vowel nasalization of the prefix /tɛɣǫ́/ are lost. In (e) the tone rise and length indicate that only the consonant has been lost. Since Marcel in other stories sometimes does pronounce this [ɣ], we can assume /tɛɣǫ́/.

There is no evidence, however, for the prefix *ni* which occurs in all of Mandeville's forms. This *ni* is the "*nɛ*- momentaneous" prefix, a meaning for which has not been given by Li. In this case it acts much like the perfective, and so it is not surprising that it too is deleted from these forms.

It is now useful to recall that Krauss and others (Krauss and Leer, n.d.; Kari 1975) have argued for some time that the so-called *s* and *y* perfectives in Athabaskan ($\theta\varepsilon$ and $\gamma\varepsilon$ in Chipewyan) are not really single morpheme perfectives. Instead they argue that the *s* and *y* are conjugation markers with aspect being represented in the vowel. Marcel's use of θ as a thematic element may argue then for a shift in the use not of the perfective marker, but rather of the conjugation marker. Furthermore, the frequent deletion of the consonantal element θ but some retention of vowel quality (e.g., ε in *nɛsdja*) suggests that Krauss' analysis represents a psychological reality for Marcel.

How then is aspect marked? There are two possibilities beyond the occasional prefix vowels. One lies in the narrative structure and one lies in the stems themselves. To a certain extent, the reduction of verbal prefixes constitutes a reduction in redundancy. Many verbs have varying stems to mark changes in aspect and mode. The markers of these include tone changes, nasalization changes, and stem-final consonants. Li gives a rather full listing of these processes in his grammatical sketch (Li 1946) and the forms also are given in the stem list (Li 1933b). So if we look back at *tsákaya* and *dódítθa* where the prefixes were completely eliminated, we see by comparison with Li's stem list that -*ya* and -*tθa* are perfective forms of the stem. The loss of perfective marking in the prefix system does not constitute a complete loss of marking in the clause.

We have mentioned earlier in this chapter that the normal narrative style is to use perfective forms in narrative clauses (Li 1964; Scollon 1977). Since these verbs occur within a narrative, the marking of perfective may, again, be redundant. Thus where Mandeville marks aspects three ways, with narrative structure, with verb stems, and with verb prefixes, Marcel often marks in only one of these ways. Here again we can mention our chagrin over not being able to obtain citation forms from the same speaker to see what he would do out of the context of a narrative performance.

Besides reductions in marking of person and aspect, other prefixes may also be deleted, at least by comparison with Mandeville. We have mentioned the loss of *hi* in *tsákaya* (<*hi·ya*) and *dódítθa* (<*hiłtθą*), and of *dé* in *básdi*. For Mandeville some prefix would be required in *k'ítcotą*, even if only the 'peg' prefix *hɛ*. There are two other forms we can look at in which there is further evidence for the loss of prefixes.

In (4) 'I thought' is given as *nɛsθən*. Here Mandeville would have *yɛnɛsθen*. Again, in (18) the *yɛ* is missing from the form.

The passage in (20) includes various instances of the verb 'to know' which may be compared to Mandeville as follows:

Marcel	Mandeville
k'olyŭ·	*hɛ*⎫ *k'ódɛlyąú*
k'ócyą	*bɛ*⎭
yɛkǫ́lyą	*k'ódɛsyą*
bɛgósyą	*bɛk'ódɛsyą*

The prefix *dɛ* in Mandeville's forms is one of those for which it is difficult to give a meaning. Lacking a much fuller study of the Mandeville texts and Li's notes, we can say only that it is required for Mandeville as part of the meaning of the verb 'to know'. For Marcel, however, this prefix is quite unnecessary, there being no trace of it in any of his uses of this word.

In summation then, we can say that for Marcel the Chipewyan verb has been considerably reduced in structure. In some cases the reductions are phonological and in others morphological. In any case the result is the same. There is a surface neutralization of person marking in some instances, of aspect marking in most instances, and to some extent thematic and adverbial prefixes have also been lost. The net result of these reductions in the verb structure is a simpler verb structure which is, however, compensated in some instances at least by the incorporation of elements from the clause into the verb and by the production of new elements in the clause primarily in a postverbal position.

Before going on to look at several of the ways in which new elements have been introduced into the verb and clause structure, we will look briefly at various reductions which have taken place in the structure of Chipewyan words of other classes. Generally speaking, words other than active verbs in their reduced forms approximate the stems as listed in Li (1933b) without prefixes. Thus we have as examples:

Marcel		Li (1933b)
(19)	ts'ínaθé ⎤	-ts'į ʔets'ínaθé
(22.2)	ts'ína ⎦	'gradually; finally'
(19.2)	t'axą	-xą 'suddenly', ʔɛt'axą 'suddenly, all of a sudden'
(19.2)	k'áɬ	k'áɬdjįnɛ 'nearly, almost'
(19.3)	θá	-ðá 'to be far (zero)' (usually nįðá)
(13.2)	ɬá ⎤	-ɬá 'one' (usually 'įɬáɣɛ)
(9.2)	ɬâ· ⎟	
(14)	ɬɬâ· ⎬	
(23)	ɬáɣɛ ⎦	
(7.2)	ta·	ta- 'three' (usually taɣɛ)
(11.2)	ʔaɬk'éta·	ʔąɬk'étaɣɛ 'six'
(24.3)	ɬúna	ʔįɬáunéną 'ten'
(16.2)	gɛtco	(Campbell, n.d.) tɛlk'íðitco 'ammunition'
(19.2)	k'ítco	

This reduction has also taken place in forms which only occur as suffixes. Thus we have *-ts'én* (<*hots'én*) 'to there', *kozí* (<*ʔɛkozí*) 'in that direction', *t'á* (<*hotɬ'áɣą*) 'after', *á* or *ʔá* (<*t'á*) 'since', *xa* (<*ixa*) 'in order to', *k'éni* (<*k'éniɛ*) 'behind'.

Perhaps it is worth looking in some detail at two of these to get a fuller understanding of this reduction. In (4) there is the phrase *t'ats'ǝ́n* 'to where'. Since Mandeville would say *t'a hots'ǝ́n*, we need to look for evidence of the prefix *ho* in Marcel's text. This does, in fact, occur in (31) *t'auts'enots'i*. It never occurs with initial aspiration, however, in this text or elsewhere. The similarity of *hots'én* 'to there', 'until' and *hots'i* 'from there', 'since' allows us to include the latter form in this analysis. As the form in (31) above indicates, *a* followed by *ho* is pronounced as *au*. In other instances such as (7) *djǫ·ts'i* (<*dja* 'here' + *hots'i* 'from there'), (7) *dódí* (<*dáúdí* 'nothing'), and (21) *t'o* (<*tau* 'maybe') we can see that the normal development of the sequences [a] + [o] or [a] + [u] is [o]. This suggests that the form above in (4) *t'ats'én* represents a deletion of the prefix since there the vowel has remained [a]. Finally the form *ʔeyɛrets'* (<*ʔɛyɛr hots'i*) 'from there' in (24.4) indicates that even the vowel of the postposition stem may be deleted.

One other form, the suffix *-t'á* 'since', is interesting in the degree of reduction that may take place. In (12.2) for example there is *tcáúlɛʔá* 'since there were no beaver'. Mandeville would have *tsá húlɛ-hit'á*. We have shown above that Marcel deletes initial aspiration. This would give **tsáúleit'á*. Further reductions are *t'* → *ʔ* and the complete loss of the *i* vowel in *hit'á*. In some cases even the glottal stop is lost in this suffix, as in (18) *ʔɛyá* 'therefore' (<*ʔɛyit'á*). We have now looked at several ways in which Chipewyan word structure has been reduced.

Before continuing on with the study of Chipewyan word structure, we would like to briefly consider to what extent similar reductions have taken place in Marcel's English. On the whole there is little reduction in English that is clearly morphological and not just phonological. That is, there are forms such as

(4.2)	*bʌt*	'about'
(5)	*wʌt*	'about'
(40)	*sfaldaun*	'he's fall down'

in which initial syllables are deleted in a way that is quite similar to Marcel's Chipewyan reductions but which does not substantially affect the morphological structure of English words.

Number is marked on English nouns and so the plural morpheme would be a likely candidate for morphological reduction. The forms *naits* 'nights' (42) and *leiks* 'lakes' (6) show that plural is marked at least in some instances. In (6) the word *krɪk* 'creeks', however, indicates that plural is not consistently marked.

Tense is also marked in English, but here it is difficult to know whether tense has been reduced or if a different tense is intended. For example, in (5) Marcel says *aik'ɪldtθri* 'I killed three'. Here tense marking is clearly present in the *d*. Yet in (8.2) *ak'ɪltu* there is no *d* for the past tense and we are left to wonder if its absence is the result of phonological rules reducing the cluster *ldtʿ* or the result of the deletion of tense marking at a deeper level. Of course the effect is the same and so just as with aspect in Chipewyan, in some instances tense marking in English is neutralized. Other than these few examples, however, there is very little morphological reduction in Marcel's English.

To return now to the study of Chipewyan words, a second general way in which lexical structure has been changed is by the amalgamation of forms which were previously analyzable as separate units into units which are larger and more complex morphologically. Three examples of this have been given above in *tsákayaú, k'ítcotǫ*, and *dódítθă·*. In these instances elements from the clause have been incorporated into the verb as prefixes and have thereby displaced the marking of such things as person and aspect. We have suggested that the loss of aspect marking has not been crucial since aspect is marked not only in the verb prefix system but also in the verb stem and in the narrative structure. Another reason why this may not be crucial is that there is a tendency for tense marking to replace aspect marking.

Li gives three suffixes which may be used to mark tense, -ixa 'future purpose or simple future used with the imperfective forms', -i 'future intention used with future forms', and - nį 'past tense' (Li 1946:420). The first two of these are quite rare in Mandeville's texts as well as in this text. This is largely due to the predominance in narrative of a time focus in the past. The third of these forms -nį occurs quite frequently in Marcel's story and so is of considerable interest to us.

The first thing to be noticed is the frequency of the form. Although it is difficult to establish a normal frequency for any morpheme, a search of the three of Mandeville's texts which are most similar to Marcel's beaver hunt covering more than 25 pages of text or about 10 times as much narrative text as Marcel's story turned up only 8 instances of -nį. In Marcel's story there are 18 uses of this morpheme which indicates a frequency of something like 20 times Mandeville's frequency. This much higher frequency may suggest a shift in the use of this morpheme.

In order to understand the change that has taken place, it will be necessary to expand Li's description of this morpheme. Mandeville's normal use of -nį is to subordinate a clause which recapitulates an earlier piece of the narrative action. For example in *My Beaver Hunt* there is the sentence (Li and Scollon 1976:397):

kú· tsá-ʔąγą t'ahi bɛγą 'įgé   -nį ʔɛyɛr ʔą́horígé
then beaver den that which at it they dug through past there I dug at it
'Then at the beaver den where they had dug through, I dug at it to enlarge it.'

This use of -nį is usually translatable, as it is here, with the past perfect, for example, 'had dug through'. In this we can see the general use which Mandeville makes of -nį. This is to produce more complex sentential forms by subordinating an early narrative action and marking this action with the past tense -nį. Petitot (1876) lists -nį as a marker of a relative clause. His analysis can be seen to have been influenced by sentences such as the one given here. -nį is rarely, possibly never, used in sentence final position to produce a simple past tense in Mandeville's texts.

In eight of the clauses in which Marcel uses -nį it is used in a way that is quite similar to Mandeville's usage. These are in (4.2), (8), (9), (15), (23), (24.7), (31), and (32.2). The use in (32.2) is quite interesting in its complexity. The combination of imperfective, the future suffix -xa, and the past tense -nį produces the subjunctive which can be translated as 'I would not have done so'.

Another 10 uses of -nį are quite interesting in relation to the preceding discussion of the neutralization of aspect. In three instances -nį follows a verb which we have discussed above as having lost the marking for aspect in the prefix. These are in (7.3), (11), and (23.3). In (13.2) there is a fourth instance, but one which we did not discuss above. So now we can see that not only is time marking redundant in three ways, as aspect in prefixes, stem, and narrative structure, but also as simple past tense which may be indicated with -ni̜. Although tense and aspect are certainly not interchangeable, these examples seem to indicate that for Marcel tense may be coming to displace aspect, or more specifically past tense as marked by -ni̜ is coming to displace perfective aspect as marked by θε or γε. Given the amount of phonological reduction taking place in Chipewyan, this shift would have the advantage of maintaining the ability to indicate time in the clause while still reducing the complexity of the verb or at least the verb prefix complex.

Six other instances indicate that this marking of simple past tense with -ni̜ is not simply a compensation for the loss of the perfective aspect. In (6) -ni̜ is used with łą 'to be many' which is not normally marked in Chipewyan for either aspect or tense. Again, in (8.2) θá 'to be far' and in (33.2) nεtáðíłε 'it is not heavy' are given tense with -ni̜ where for Mandeveille neither tense nor aspect would be marked. A fourth form in (33) is similar. Here the postpositional form sεts'i̜ (< 'me' + 'from') is used as a full verb meaning 'I have'. It is not marked for aspect, but -ni̜ puts it into the simple past tense, that is, 'I had'.

In these four instances a form which is verbal in quality but not marked for tense or aspect is given tense with the suffix -ni̜. This may indicate that Marcel is concerned with representing time in clauses even where it is not normally marked for Mandeville. Thus it is not just a question of compensating for the loss of aspect marking in prefixes. One further form indicates that, in fact, the frequent use of -ni̜ represents a general shift from the marking of aspect to the marking of tense. In (31) a verb which is not changed from the Mandeville form nevertheless has -ni̜ suffixed to it.

Finally, there is one form which is quite strange. In (19), -ni̜ is suffixed to the adverbial form ts'ínaθé 'finally'.

In beginning this section we noted that the frequency at which Marcel uses -ni̜ is quite high as compared to Mandeville. Now we have suggested that tense marking is coming to replace aspect marking in Chipewyan at Fort Chipewyan. This is further borne out by the very high frequency of the future marker -xa in nonnarrative speech. In Mandeville's texts the form -ixa is used with rare exceptions to sequence two clauses in a narrative. It indicates that the normal temporal order has been reversed (Scollon 1976c). As an example there is (Li and Scollon 1976:370),

dɛníye-ðéð   hɛstsi-ixa   dɛníyɛ-ðéðdɛtciné   náθiłtsi̧
moose hide I make-future   moose hid frame I took
In order to make the moosehide I took the moosehide frame. . . .'

The English translation of 'in order to' plus an infinitive form of the verb captures this reversal of the narrative sequence. So while it is true that *-ixa* is used to mark future purpose as we have said above, it is rarely used in forming simple futures in Mandeville's narratives. In current usage, however, *-xa* is by far the most common way of forming simple futures. Thus with *-xa* as with *-ni̧*, there seems to be a shift to marking simple tenses with suffixed forms in place of marking aspect in the prefixes.

Of course the motive for this shift to the marking of tense must be seen to involve a much greater simplicity in lexical formation. Aspect marking in prefixes is rather complex because of the considerable number of co-occurrences among the prefixes for aspect, person, and the classifiers. The marking of simple past and future tense with the suffixes *-ni̧* and *-xa* allows the speaker to use imperfective forms as the unmarked present tense and then without further modification in the prefix system to create the other tenses through suffixation. It is not surprising to find accommodations of this sort where many people in the speech community are required to learn as many as four languages, especially where the resources for making the shift lie within the existing grammatical system.

To close this section on changes in Chipewyan lexical structure, we need to consider whether these suffixes of tense should be thought of as part of the lexical structure or as part of the clause structure. Of course in speaking of them as suffixes we are implying that they are bound morphemes and we would not expect to find either *-ni̧* or *-xa* separated phonologically from its verb.

If we look through the 18 examples in which *-ni̧* is used by Marcel, we see that the normal suffix order is

VERB + FUTURE + NEGATIVE + PAST + SUBORDINATOR
          (*-xa*)   (*-híle*)   (*-ni̧*)   (*-ú*)

Thus we have

(6)	VERB	+			híle	+ ni̧	+ kúhú
(8.2)	VERB	+			híle	+ ni̧	
(15)	VERB	+				ni̧	+ ú
(19)	ADVERB	+				ni̧	+ ú
(23.3)	VERB	+				ni̧	+ ú
(32.2)	VERB	+	xa +	híle	+ ni̧		
(33.2)	VERB	+			híle	+ ni̧	

We have discussed the problem of *kú·* and *-ú* and suggested that it must be considered to be a single morpheme which receives varying phonetic shapes depending on prosodic factors. As *-ú* it is felt to be strongly related to the preceding clause as a verbal suffix which subordinates that clause to the following clause. The placement of *-nį* to the left of *-ú* then suggests a strong relationship with the preceding verb and suffixes. In some cases the vowels of *-nį* and *-ú* have even coalesced into *-nų̆·*, as in (23.3) and (31).

This latter instance (31) is instructive in that although the vowels have coalesced, it occurs at the beginning of a breath and pause group. This separation from the verb by such a distance might be thought to argue for a certain amount of freedom for these morphemes on the one hand, or on the other hand it might argue for the insignificance of breathing and pauses as markers of grammatical units. We suggest that the second alternative is the right one. There is no fall of the pitch preceding this suffix, and so we feel we may continue to think of it as a suffix on the preceding verb that has been separated for reasons having more to do with narrative style than with grammatical structure.

We have seen, then, that there have been quite a number of changes to the structure of Chipewyan words, especially to verbs, that have resulted in the reduction of the complexity of the prefix system. There has also been a smaller number of changes resulting in some increase in the amount of suffixing in verbs. In English there were very few changes in lexical structure that could be called reductions. On the other hand there are a number of forms which have developed that tend toward an increase in the overall complexity of English words. We would like to turn to these now.

Even in a casual reading of the transcription of Marcel's English version of his beaver hunt narrative one is struck with the number of phrases that are repeated throughout. There are *that's a*, *going to*, *all the time*, *lots of X*, where only the filler for *X* varies, and others. Some of these phrases such as the last three mentioned are regular English idioms, and what is striking is the frequency of their use in this text, not their form. Others such as the first, although they are clearly derived from regular English usage, are used in rather peculiar ways. For example *that's my dog* in itself is not odd, but *I found it that's a beaver* or *that's it one's a big hill* are very unusual. These forms suggest that an idiom has been formed that has then been extended from its original use and also from its original grammatical functioning so that as a whole it is now operating as a word. Thus we take these idioms to be instances of the amalgamation of English morphemes into somewhat more complex structures.

We can begin looking at these idioms by taking one which is common in ordinary English, the idiom *going to*. This is widely reduced to something like [gən], and so it is not surprising that Marcel frequently pronounces it in a similar way. The question we want to ask is: What evidence is there that Marcel recognizes this as made up of two separate words (and three morphemes)?

He uses this idiom six times in the two stories. These six pronunciations are given below. 'C' marks the one occurrence in the frame of the Chipewyan text, the others are in the English text:

a. C(2)	*gɔnə*	'going to'
b. (1)	*gwɔt*	
c. (33)	*gə*	
d. (33)	*gɔnɛ*	
e. (43)	*gwonə*	
f. (45)	*gənə*	

Case (c) is interesting in showing the extent to which this idiom can be reduced. There is one syllable and no nasalization. The two-syllable forms (a), (d), (e), and (f) give evidence for both *going* and *to* in the underlying form. The final [t] in (b) is the only evidence for a /t/ in *to*, however. In none of these forms is there any evidence for the velar nasal /ŋ/. For this we need to look elsewhere.

There are 35 places where an underlying /ɪŋ/ is likely to occur in Marcel's text. In 26 of these the /ɪŋ/ represents the progressive morpheme 'ing'. In the remaining 9 it does not. These remaining cases are,

(15)	*nəθɪ*	'nothing'
(43)	*nʌθɪ*	'nothing'
(18)	*morni*	'morning'
(20)	*sprɪŋ*	'spring'
(21)	*sprɪŋ*	'spring'
(27)	*ʃɪŋgl*	'single'
(32)	*sʌmθɪŋ*	'something'
(46)	*ɛriθɪŋ*	'everything'
(47)	*ɛvriθɪ*	'everything'

The 5 of these which have [ŋ] indicate that Marcel may, indeed, have /ŋ/ where he has [ŋ] on the surface. The evidence for /ŋ/ in the progressive morpheme 'ing', however, indicates that the underlying form is /ɪn/. Although in some cases this morpheme is greatly reduced, in others it is much fuller, as in

(32)	*gowɪn*	'going'
(32)	*kʼʌmɪn*	'coming'
(36)	*falɛn*	'following'

In no instance is there a final [ŋ], even though 13 of the 26 forms have [n]. This suggests, then, that the underlying form for 'ing' is /ɪn/.

In this context it is useful to recall the important contribution of Scottish English in the Fort Chipewyan area because of the presence of the Hudson's Bay Company. It may be this influence which is showing up here in the progressive morpheme 'ing' being pronounced as [ɪn].

Now it will be instructive to compare Marcel's surface forms for the idiom *going to* with those for *going*. We have the six pronunciations of *going to* above, and below are the five pronunciations of *going*:

(18) *gɔ̃*   'going'
(23) *gō*
(32) *gowɪn*
(38) *gon*
(48) *gɔ̃n*

Notice that although both *going to* and *going* may be reduced to a single syllable, a distinction between the two is maintained. In *going* there is some kind of nasalization in every case. In (33) *going to* is reduced to [gə]. We suggest that here the [ə] represents the reduced vowel of *to* which contrasts with the back rounded vowels of *going* in (18) and (23) above.

We have looked at phonological detail in this instance because we want to show that although an idiom may be considerably reduced phonologically in any particular case, there is some evidence that Marcel's underlying forms are somewhat more complex than any one form may indicate.

We can now look at several other idioms which Marcel uses and study one in some detail. There are eight of these which are of some interest. They are

	Idiom	Breath group
a.	*all the time*	11, 20, 21, 32, 38
b.	*lots of X*	6, 20, 21, 46
c.	*all over*	6
d.	*you know*	1, 6, 21, 22, 38, 46
e.	*after that*	4, 6, 31, 38, 41
f.	*all of a sudden*	23, 39
g.	*in there*	17, 20, 21, 35
h.	*that's {it}*	8, 9, 12, 22, 24, 27, 28, 36, 45, 46, 47

The first three (a), (b), and (c) are quite ordinary English idioms even though the frequency of their use becomes unidiomatic at times. Thus we have in (20) and (21) both (a) and (b) occurring three times each. By the third time in (21.4) that we hear *lots of bear all the time* we realize that the use of these idioms has gone quite beyond the normal English frequency, whatever that is. If we look more closely at this third time, we can see that it is not even finished.

lɔtsəberɔlətʰ
lots of bear all the t-

This suggests to us that the rules of phonological reduction are being applied to the whole idiom as a unit rather than to the separate words as in *going to* above. The final syllable 'time' can be reduced to [tʰ] because the lexical unit is /ɔlʌtaim/ with a meaning of 'always'. The surface form [ɔlətʰ] is sufficient to recover the full lexical item, especially given the immediately preceding instances of its use.

The next two idioms (d) and (e) are also common in English. For Marcel both are used in marking the narrative structure as we have indicated above. Here we should note that *after that* may not normally be considered an idiom. We feel that for Marcel it is, however, since we do not find other possibilities such as *after a while* being used productively.

The last three, (f), (g), and (h), are the most interesting because of the ways in which they differ from ordinary English usage. The idiom *all of a sudden* (f) has been mentioned above. It corresponds in use to *-k'é* in Chipewyan. We have been calling this particle an emphatic suffix. Li (1946) lists it in his miscellany of verb suffixes with the meaning 'it is found out'. We noted above a case in which *all of a sudden* was used in English where one would expect *as it turned out* or even *I found out*. We see, then, that although the idiom in form looks very much like the English idiom, and it may even function in a similar way in structuring a narrative, it may be understood as having a very different meaning.

The idiom *in there* (g) is used with a locative meaning. In (14.2) *kill six in there* and (15) *I camp in there* a more idiomatic English would have *I killed six there* and *I camped there*. In order to understand the motive for always giving *there* as a locative within a prepositional phrase with *in* we need to look at the other *there* which occurs in Marcel's story. This is the existential *there* as in (11) *there's beaver*, (13) *there's another way*, or (35) *there's a road in there*. This last one conveniently gives both forms. In each case where the meaning is existential the form Marcel uses is *there's*. When the meaning is locative the form he uses is *in there*. In this way Marcel has added a second morpheme to disambiguate the otherwise homophonous forms. We can at least suggest that the fact that these meanings are represented very differently in Chipewyan with *ʔɛyɛr* (locative = 'in there') on the one hand and a range of verb stems for the existential on the other is influential in Marcel's striving to represent them differently in English.

The last idiom we will look at, *that's* (or *that's a* or *that's it*) (h), is used about 18 times in the text and is therefore of considerable importance in Marcel's English. We have said "about 18 times" because in a few instances it is difficult to be sure it is this form because of hesitations and self-corrections. In places such as in (8) *I found it that's a beaver* or (9) *that's it one's a big hill* we can see that Marcel is not treating this as a three-morpheme phrase (demonstrative + copula + indefinite article or third person pronoun) but rather as a single lexical item.

In some instances this idiom could perhaps be taken as an equivalent to the demonstrative *that*, but in most instances the pronoun *it* would be more idiomatic. For example in (36) *that's a bear he's coming* it would be possible to use a demonstrative and say *that bear was coming*, but in (22.2) *that's a narrow one like that* it would be preferable to say *it was a narrow one like that*. In looking at *all of a sudden* earlier, we suggested that the very English-looking form was misleading since in some cases the meaning was being influenced by the Chipewyan meaning of the corresponding verbal suffix *-k'é*. In this instance we will try to show that in order to understand this idiom, we have to consider it to be a calque on a Chipewyan form.

The form closest to the English demonstrative *that* in Chipewyan is *ʔɛyi*. Marcel's use of *that's* (*a* or *it*) corresponds quite closely to Mandeville's use of *ʔɛyi*, and so we suggest that this idiom in English is a calque on the Chipewyan demonstrative.

In an earlier paper, R. Scollon (1976) found that for Mandeville *ʔɛyi* was a member of the set of morphemes which are used in position between clauses to indicate relationships between the clauses. This set also includes *ʔɛkú·*, *kú·*, *-ú*, and *húɬdú·*. What is interesting for our purposes here is that *ʔɛyi* always appears in clause-initial position. Furthermore, when it is in a transitive clause, this *ʔɛyi* refers anaphorically to the object of the preceding transitive verb. Where the object of the transitive verb is new information, the form *húɬdú* is used. Thus we see that the choice of *ʔɛyi* over *húɬdú·* relates to the information structure of the text and the case roles of objects in the clauses in sequence.

The first thing to be noticed in Marcel's uses of *that's*, then, is that of 18 uses all but 3 are in clause-initial position. The exceptions are

a.   (8)   *I found it **that's a** beaver*
b   (16)   *didn't never see **it's a** b- never find it beaver*
c.   (22)   *just about **that's a** xxx on the lake*

In the second two we can see that Marcel is apparently doubtful about these since he stutters in (b) and in (c) becomes wholly unintelligible for a short time. The changed word order in (a) will have to be taken up more fully. Other than in these instances *that's* is put in clause-initial position in spite of the awkward word order that results, as in

(9) *and **that's** the other side's a big lake*

instead of

*and on the other side of **that's** a big lake*

There are five places where Marcel uses ***that's*** in a clause with a transitive verb, (8), (12), (16), (28), and (45.2). These bear striking similarities to Mandeville's uses. The last one (45.2) refers anaphorically to the objects of the preceding two clauses just as Mandeville uses *ʔɛyi*. We must note, however, that the second of these clauses ***I hit 'em*** does not have ***that's*** as it should if Marcel's use of this idiom were obligatory for all such clauses.

In (28) the anaphoric reference is not to the object of a preceding transitive verb but rather to the current topic, Marcel's .22 rifle. Thus we can see that a topic being focused in the current discourse may be the referent of ***that's*** in Marcel's usage.

With this in mind we can now look at the first three uses of ***that's*** in transitive clauses, (8), (12), and (16). The first of these refers to beavers in general, that is, to the beavers that are the object of the hunt. These have been focused in the discourse since the narrative initial in (1). Again in (12) Marcel refers with ***that's*** to the beavers that he knows of or expects to find, as he has said in (11). And finally in (16) he refers to the same beavers, but now as the ones he did not find, with the idiom ***that's.***

We can see now that Marcel's use of ***that's***, although it is not identical to Mandeville's use of *ʔɛyi*, is close enough to suggest a Chipewyan origin rather than an English origin. The contribution of English has been the surface form.

Finally, we will return to look at (8) where the idiom has been shifted out of initial position. To anticipate our later discussion of clause structure, we can see that generally Marcel seems to have some difficulty producing objects of transitive verbs in a postverbal position, as the following examples indicate:

(5)   *I found it one beaver*
(8)   *I found it **that's** a beaver*
(16)   *didn't never see it's a b- never find it beaver*
(45.2) ***that's** a kil–gonna kill 'em*

This list may be expanded from other texts by the same narrator with

I'm shove it stick in there.
They didn't find it nothing.

To these we could add more examples from other speakers to show that this problem is more general for people who speak both Chipewyan and English (the initials indicate the speaker):

VM	*somebody kill it again too nuni̯yɛ*
VM	*wolf go out and kill it and moose*
VM	*he kill it, you know, for łuwaȝe*
VM	*they come and kill it, eh, caribou*
VM	*now he take it out too fish*
VM	*I kill it for ʔɛtθén łaɣǫ́íθer*
EF	*small, I want small baby*

These will be treated in more detail later. Here we are simply illustrating that the structure of a transitive clause in English is often something like

AGENT + VERB + IT + X + OBJECT

The 'X' represents quite a group of forms, from simple hesitations and stuttering to the idiom that we are considering, ***that's***. In the clearest instances there is at least the double object marking of *it* plus the object, or the object appears both initially and postverbally.

To get a better understanding of the problem, we can now look at how Marcel constructs a transitive clause in Chipewyan. The most instructive two clauses for our purposes are in (28) and (29) of the Chipewyan version.

(28)	ʔɛyɛr	hų́łdų́·	θiłk'éθ	ʔɛyi	sas
	there	then	I shot it	that	bear
(29)	ʔɛyi	sas	θiłk'éθú		
	that	bear	I shot it	-sub.	

The second has the normal Chipewyan structure. *ʔɛyi* refers anaphorically to *sas* in (28) as it would for Mandeville, and the object *sas* precedes the transitive verb. The first of these clauses has the object in a postverbal position. This shift is made in order to give emphasis to the focused noun phrase. Here it is important to notice that the postposed unit is the noun phrase including *ʔɛyi*.

Looking back now at (8) *I found it **that's a beaver***, we see that the noun phrase ***that's a beaver*** corresponds analogically to *ʔɛyi sas* in (28). If Marcel is really following a Chipewyan model, then we would expect at least sometimes to find structures like *that's a beaver I found it*. Or, in fact, since ʔɛyi in Chipewyan may stand as the head of the noun phrase, we might expect to find clauses like *that's I found it*.

If we look now at (45) we see that Marcel does actually begin just such a clause, but then he hesitates and rephrases.

(45)   **that's a kill-gonna kill 'em all of 'em**

Looking a little further afield we find the clause we need in another text told the same day by the same narrator, Marcel:

> That time I kill a moose.
> That
> I shot him.

Here Marcel produces a clear calque of ʔɛyi θiɫk'éθ (**that's I shot him**). It sounds as if he is reading an interlinear translation of his earlier Chipewyan text. In this calquing of the Chipewyan clause, *that* in English is a direct representation of ʔɛyi in Chipewyan.

This idiom, **that's**, brings us to the threshold of a discussion of the structure of clauses. We would like to delay this discussion for a time, however, in order to continue looking at various other forms of convergence at the lexical level. We have suggested calquing as an active process which has produced the idiom **that's** as well as the structure of some transitive clauses. Now we would like to look at several other cases in which Marcel uses words in a way that is different from Mandeville. In at least some of these the source of the difference can be seen to be another language spoken by Marcel.

Li lists *taú...taú* as meaning 'either...or' (1933b). As Marcel use *taú*, however, its meaning is 'maybe'. For example, in (21) *tau* [t'o] follows a verb and indicates Marcel's doubt about whether he shot the bear or not. In (24) *taú* [tŏ·] might be better glossed as 'approximately'. In any event, Marcel uses this form as a postverbal suffix. Of course he is not the only speaker to do this. One child was heard to say *netátŏ·* 'your father maybe' meaning something like *I bet this is your father* and so to give *tŏ·* a full verbal force.

Li gives *t'asî·* as an indefinite pronoun meaning 'anything' or 'something' (1946:421). This form is still used generally with this meaning and informants give **something** as its gloss. In (24), though, Marcel extends its use, apparently basing this extension on the similarity in English of 'some' and 'something'. So for 'some three' (i.e., 'approximately three') he says ʔasíta·.

'Therefore' is normally translated with ʔɛyit'á. ʔɛyi is the demonstrative 'that' and *t'á* is a postposition meaning by means of, with, because of

(Li 1933b:131). We have already discussed the reduction of *t'á* to *ʔá* or even *á*. In one place, however, Marcel gives *ʔɛyɛrʔá* for 'therefore'. He is apparently calquing this form anew, basing his choice of *ʔɛyɛr* 'there' on the first syllable of 'therefore'. This was matched in an interesting way by Marcel's brother in a public speech in English when he said *thatfore* in place of *therefore*. The younger Marcel was clearly basing his English form on the Chipewyan *ʔɛyi* ('that') *t'á*.

Marcel's use of *tɬ'ul* for 'line' in 'Saskatchewan line' (4.3) again appears to be derived from the English metaphorical development of line as "boundary" from line as "rope." There already exists in Chipewyan a word for 'edge' or 'boundary' in *-bąn-ɛ* (Li 1933b).

In Chipewyan a verb of going may have its meaning changed to 'returning' by adding the prefix *na* and the *d* classifier. Thus there is *hiya* 'I went' and *nɛsdja* 'I returned'. This returning is usually marked by Marcel in English by adding the word *back*, sometimes with *again*. So in (14) there is *I come back*, in (5.2) *go back again*, in (16) *I just go back*, in (30.2) *he jumping back*, in (30.3) *come back again*, or in (48) *I going back*. None of these is very unusual in English, except perhaps that the overall frequency of forms with *back* is a little high.

It is a second use of the combined prefix set *na...d* that accounts for the frequency of *back* forms being higher in Marcel's texts than one would expect. In this second use it means that the action of the verb is being repeated or continued. Of course this iterative meaning also covers the meaning of returning mentioned above, and so it is, perhaps, only in translation that we think of these as two different uses. The evidence we have indicates that *back* is used in English in an iterative meaning as well. Thus we have recorded for other speakers *Go to sleep back*, (i.e., *go back to sleep*) which is again only unusual in its word order, and *Roll it back* and *Start it back* (i.e., *roll it again* and *start it up again*), which are less likely in ordinary English. Or our 3-year-old daughter learned from her friends to say, *Then I'm going to eat it back* (i.e., *then I'm going to continue eating it*).

Finally, there is the form which occurs in the break between the two major sections of the beaver hunt story, *nįðátcóílɛ* (15.2) 'not very far'. It should be recalled that this boundary was placed on the basis of the forms *-k'é* (15) and *well* (16), among other things. Given the normal word ordering, there should be nothing following *-k'é* since it is a verbal suffix and verbs should come last in the clause. We saw earlier, however, that in one case the object of a transitive verb was placed in a postverbal position for emphasis (28). Here then we would like to suggest that the placement of this adverbial marks emphasis on the fact that the bear was very close.

We have suggested above that *well* occurs at this point in English because the narrator has raised his attention to his audience in marking this boundary in the narrative. We can now look at this phrase (*nįðátcóíle*) and see that it represents in brief focus the convergence of Chipewyan, Cree, and English. First of all, Mandeville does not modify such forms. This would be *nįðá-híle* 'not far'. *-ðá* has a verbal force and so could not take a modifier of any sort following it and preceding the negative suffix *-híle*. It will be recalled that, even for Marcel, the normal suffix order is

$$VERB + FUTURE + NEGATIVE + PAST$$
$$(-xa) \qquad (-híle) \qquad (-nį)$$

The modification of this form appears to be motivated by the modification in Marcel's normal English equivalent *not very far*. In this text, (38.4) and (40), as in other texts, the idiom always contains the three elements (distance *far*, negative *not*, and quantity *very*). Thus Marcel's *nįðátcóíle* contains all three elements as well (distance *nįðá*, negative *-híle*, and quantity *-tco*).

A problem posed by the absence of modifiers in such forms is to find one which would be appropriate. The choice of *-tco* 'big' seems to have been made by analogy with Cree. In Cree the form *mistahi* is used to mean both 'big' and 'much'. As we have already said, Marcel also speaks Cree, as do most others of his generation, and so the association between 'big' and 'much' or 'very' was already established. All that remained was to choose between the two forms for 'big' in Chipewyan, the neutral verb stem *-tcá* and the noun suffix *-tco*. The latter was apparently chosen since it never requires prefixing while *-tcá* requires the adjectival prefix *ne-*.

We see then in *nįðátcóíle* an English idiomatic concept of distance, negative, and quantity given Chipewyan surface forms by way of Cree adjectival metaphors. It is not surprising to see a form such as this appearing at the central juncture in the structure of Marcel's text.

THE CONVERGED LEXICON

We may think of a word as consisting of a pairing of a sound and a meaning. Of course there is more to it than that since a third element, a function, is also part of the word. For our immediate purposes, though, a somewhat simpler view will do to begin with. In the preceding section we have discussed various ways in which the structure of words, that is the sound, has been changed in both Chipewyan and English. Due to these structural changes, words in the two languages have come to look more and more like each other. Nevertheless, this is true only in a quite abstract way. One would still not mistake a word in Chipewyan for a word in

English. The lexicons, though approximating each other in form, are still distinct in listing separate forms for most words.

At the same time as these structural changes have taken place, however, there have been changes in the meanings as well. These meaning changes have also tended toward a convergence of the lexicons, and so we must now look at these to see to what extent separate forms carry with them separate meanings.

As part of a school program in native languages we began making a basic noun dictionary in three languages, English, Chipewyan and Cree. The first point of interest to our discussion that came out of this work was that it was remarkably easy to elicit nouns in all three languages. We worked with quite a variety of people and checked many forms out with different speakers and although there was in some instances some disagreement about what form was the right one, there were rarely instances in which someone would say that a word could not be said in a certain language. People felt that for any one noun in one of the languages there was another single noun in the other two.

Altogether, then, we collected 494 nouns in English, Chipewyan, and Cree. Of these only 22 overlapped in any obvious way. These overlapping forms are listed in Table 3.4.

TABLE 3.4   Overlapping Nouns in English, Chipewyan, and Cree.

English	Chipewyan	Cree
1. kettle	*tili*	*askik*
2. leaves	*ʔitʼátcāyɛ*	*lipiya*
3. sugar	*súga*	*suinikan*
4. butter	*ʔɛdjɛɾɛtʼúɛ́tɬɛzɛ́*	*batar*
5. parka/parky	*barki*	*parki*
6. papa	*-tá*	*baba*
7. teacher	*skultitcɛr*	*ukiskinawmakiw*
8. baby	*bebi*	*bebisis*
9. mama	*ʔɛné*	*mama*
10. bacon	*gugúskʼa*	*kokosowiyin*
11. tea	*lidi*	*liti*
12. pig	*gugus*	*kokos*
13. table	*lɛtab*	*miconahtik*
14. moose	*dɛníyɛ*	*moswa*
15. muskeg	*nɛ́ʼeli*	*maskiku*
16. saskatoon	*kʼí*	*saskatumna*
17. Chipewyan	*dɛne*	*cipweyanamok*
18. pan	*labwíl*	*lapwil*
19. snowshoes	*ʔaʼ*	*asamak*
20. boat	*tsʼi*	*osi*
21. socks	*libá*	*asikane*
22. canvas	*kɛsabér*	*ladwil*

The first 8 or 9 are most likely borrowings from English. The next 5 or so are from French. Item 9 *mama* may have come from either or both English or French. The next four, 14, 15, 16, and 17, come from Cree. The remaining forms may or may not be borrowings or have been influenced by other languages. For Example, 19 *snowshoes*, is given by Li as *ʔaiʿ*. In Fort Chipewyan the diphthong has become *ʔaʿ* for many people and this may well reflect the influence of the Cree *asamak*. Many of these forms were probably borrowed elsewhere. That is, the borrowing did not originate in the Fort Chipewyan speech community. Thus *moose* (<Cree:*moswa*) was probably borrowed into English much further east, and when English speakers first came to the area of Fort Chipewyan they probably already knew this word. But even including these and the doubtful cases, there is still very little overlapping in the lexicons of English, Chipewyan, and Cree, 4.4%.

On the basis of this noun dictionary, then, one would want to conclude that the three languages are quite distinct at Fort Chipewyan. This view would be misleading, however, for three reasons. As we have indicated above, there is a considerable amount of convergence in form which shows up least in the nouns, most in the verbs, and which would as a result not show up in a noun dictionary to a very great extent. Second, although when specifically asked to give a word in a particular language people do so without difficulty, in actual speech there is much "mixing" of languages. People freely use words that they acknowledge to be from one language in utterances using primarily words which they regard as coming from another language. The third reason is that although the forms are still quite separate in most cases, the meanings have fallen together. This third point is what we will take up now.

There are basically two ways in which the meanings of words have converged, by extension of the meaning of an existing word and by the creation of new forms through calquing. As an example of the first process we can look at the Chipewyan word *tɵlɵ*. Its original meaning was probably closest to English *trail*. It meant a more or less regular route made by people for ease in traveling. Where more complex means of making trails are used, such as surveys, modern equipment, grading and graveling or paving the surface and so forth, an English speaker prefers the word *road*, especially where travel is in vehicles. The original Chipewyan word *tɵlɵ* has now been generalized to include this sort of trail as well. Thus Li gives as a meaning for *tɵlɵ* 'road' or 'trail' (1933b). It is used now to refer to roads, trails, and paths of any sort.

This generalization of meaning, of course, is not unusual within languages. The convergence of meaning comes in here in regards to English in two steps. The first step is to treat the set of English words *road, trail,* and *path* as synonyms since they all translate to the same Chipewyan word, *tⱥlⱥ*. The second step is to choose just one of these, in this case *road*, to represent the Chipewyan meaning in English. Thus *road* in English has become an exact equivalent of *tⱥlⱥ* in Chipewyan (and *miskenaw* in Cree), meaning the same thing. They refer to any road, trail, or path.

This process of meaning convergence, then, works toward the production of word-for-word equivalences across all the languages involved. In some instances, meanings are generalized, while in others, words are lost in preference to a single generalized form. From the speaker's point of view the lexicon becomes a list of meanings that because they are identical for all languages he or she speaks, may be thought of as a single meaning with separate phonetic shapes for the different languages. We could diagram this as follows:

	Original	Converged
English	ROAD→ *road* TRAIL→ *trail* PATH→ *path*	↗English *road* ROAD→ Chipewyan *tⱥlⱥ* ↘Cree *miskenaw*
Chipewyan	TRAIL⎤ PATH ⎦→ '*tⱥlⱥ*'	
Cree	TRAIL⎤ PATH ⎦→ *miskenaw*	

Now when a translation is made, a Chipewyan speaker coming upon the word *tⱥlⱥ* translates it as *road*. In the story of the first Chipewyan contact with Europeans which will be quoted in Chapter 5, the woman, Fallen Marten (θa náltθ'eri), comes upon the trail of her relatives. In the original story, the form for 'trail' is *tⱥlⱥ*. The woman who translated this story said that Fallen Marten came to a *road*. When we asked if this wasn't a *trail* she said, "Yeah, a road." Obviously at the time of the first contact of Chipewyans and Europeans there were no roads in the English sense of the word. Again, in Marcel's story we see in the Chipewyan version he says *t'ulu* (23) and in the English version *road* (35.3) and (36). In cases like this, then, the existence of separate lexical items *tⱥlⱥ* and *road* disguises the degree of semantic convergence which has taken place.

Although there are many words for which this has happened, a few examples here will help to illustrate several further points. There are other instances just like *tⱥlⱥ* and *road*, as in

$$
\left.\begin{array}{l} boss \\ factor \\ president \end{array}\right\} \Rightarrow \quad boss,\ k'\acute{o}\eth eri
$$

and

$$
\left.\begin{array}{l} wood \\ stick \\ board \\ tree \\ frame \end{array}\right\} \Rightarrow \quad wood,\ d\varepsilon tcin
$$

In other instances the same collapsing of English forms and generalization of Chipewyan or Cree forms has occurred, but different speakers have developed their own solutions. The English set *today* and *now* has been collapsed into one meaning which is translated in Chipewyan by *duhú*. Some speakers say *today* meaning both 'today' and 'now', and others say *now* for both meanings.

This is even more extreme with the set *read, write, record, draw,* (verbs) *book, paper, letter* (nouns), which are all translated by *ʔerɛtɬ'ís* in Chipewyan and *masanaikan* in Cree. In any of the contexts where one of these would be used, any of the others are sometimes heard. Pronouns are treated the same. Chipewyan does not mark gender in pronouns but only person, and thus we have recorded in English,

> Once upon a time there was a boy who was lost in the wood. He can't find her house. She was going for a walk in the woods but she was lost. Mom call her too but he didn't hear each other.

Although most of the examples we have relate to convergence between Chipewyan and English, it is not restricted to these two languages. The Cree word *askiy* has a meaning which may be translated into English as 'land' or 'country' and also 'year'. For Chipewyan we now have only one word in these meanings, *nené*. Comparative evidence indicates that the Athabaskan meaning for *nené* is 'land' or 'country' and another form was used for 'year'. Apparently, then, the original Athabaskan form for 'year' has been lost and *nené* has generalized to include this meaning by analogy to Cree *askiy*.

Most of the examples we have given are nouns. This is partly caused by the fact that verb meanings in both Chipewyan and Cree are quite complex, more often translating as clauses into English. Nevertheless we can see that there is considerable meaning convergence in verbs as well. As an example we can look at *camp* which now has a range of meanings from temporary lodging overnight along the trail to quite permanent settlement. *Camp* in English has come to have the meaning of Chipewyan *ná..θer* ('to stay', 'to live', etc.).

Finally, we can return to the question of the third aspect of word structure, the function. There is at least tendency for the same meanings to be treated as the same grammatical classes in all the languages. Earlier we suggested that the classificatory verbs are losing their verbal status and taking on the appearance of prefixes to copular verbs. Now we can suggest that one motivation for this is to approximate the other languages that do not represent the classification of objects by shape or other properties in the verb, at least not to as great an extent as in Athabaskan.

Another example is the negative *dódí*. Also earlier we noted that *dódí* for Mandeville co-occurred with an indefinite pronoun and a negative suffix on the verb. For Marcel and others in the modern community, *dódí* is an extremely general negative form that can be used with a verb or alone in a range of meanings centering around 'nothing'. But *nothing* in English is also quite generalized. Thus we have recorded the following exchange.

> ***Where is your hat?*** $\left(\text{i.e.,} \left\{ \begin{array}{l} \text{'I don't have one.'} \\ \text{'I didn't bring one.'} \end{array} \right\} \right)$
> ***Nothing.***

Had this exchange been in Chipewyan, *dódí* would have been the answer, and in Cree, *makikwei*.

In this instance, as with the classificatory verbs and with the idiom *that's* (<*ʔɛyi*), there is not only a convergence of meaning but a convergence of function as well. The whole lexical system is tending toward a goal of one grammar with three (four?) lexifications (Grace 1977). This process is far from complete but it is very definitely occurring.

Up to this point we have discussed ways in which near equivalents in the various languages are adjusted by generalization until there is a central meaning and function with separate phonetic shapes to represent the different languages. In some instances, however, there is no form in one language that may be generalized to match another. In these instances calquing produces new forms in which borrowed meanings may be clothed.

Chipewyans had relatively little to do with Americans, at least by comparison with the Crees to the south. Thus we can suggest that the Chipewyan name for Americans, *bestcoγ* ('big knife'), was derived by calquing from the Cree *kicimukuman* (cf. Wolfart 1973, *kihci-mōhkomān*). As an interesting aside here we can look back at the Chipewyan text (33) where Marcel says he took out his butcher knife:

(33) *besbéscnɛtcá*   'knife big—big'

This is usually *bestcoγ*. In this instance, however, he stutters a bit and finally says in an alternate way *bes nɛtcá* ('knife it is big'). The double pronunciation of *bes* and the isolated *c* suggest that he had nearly said *bestcoγ* and then thought better of it and corrected himself. We suggest that it was because of his audience of Americans (i.e., *bestcoγ*) that he hesitated here. Generally people at Fort Chipewyan resist homophony, polysemy, and synonymy, preferring the relationship of one form to one meaning. Here, where the double meaning of *bestcoγ* threatens to surface, Marcel shifts to another form to provide an unambiguous meaning.

This raises an interesting point in regard to calquing. These forms seem to be much less firmly established as lexical items. They are more like descriptive statements made up on the spot but open to reformulation in other contexts. The names of places and groups of people are all of this type. Osgood (1975) has observed that "One of the marvelous qualities of the complex Athapaskan languages is that names can be engendered at a moment's notice by synthesizing descriptive and accessory particles [p. 524]." So, for example, when the CBC began broadcasting from Yellowknife in Chipewyan and other Athabaskan languages, there was quite a profusion of 'names' for the town of Yellowknife. Finally, a meeting was held involving people from much of the area to decide on one term that would be treated as ***the*** way of saying "Yellowknife" in Chipewyan.

The subgroup of Chipewyans known in English as the Caribou-Eaters have been called in Chipewyan *ʔɛtθéndeli* or *ʔɛtθénhɛdɫ* ('caribou—they eat') as well as *ʔɛtθéntθéné célyi dɛne* ('caribou meat—they eat—people'). What is preserved in these is the meaning, even where the surface lexicalization is changed. In this case the varying forms are in the same language. In the case of the Loucheux (Kutchin), the Chipewyan word *degeði* carries the same meaning as the French, 'the squint-eyed ones'.

In these cases the calquing is based on the referential meaning of the word in the source language. It is not far from there to the simple descriptions which come to have the status of nouns and work as equivalents in the one-word–one-meaning structuring of the total lexicon. Thus we have for 'school' *ʔɛrɛtɫ'ískų́ɛ* (<'paper', 'book', etc.—'house') but also *sɛkwi xáunɛltonkų́ɛ* (<'children—they teach—house') from two different people. The first of these conflicts with 'post office' (<*ʔɛrɛtɫ'ískų́ɛ* 'mail-house'). The two people giving these forms lined them up as follows:

	English	Chipewyan
Speaker 1	*post office*	*post office*
	school	*ʔɛrɛtɫ'ískų́ɛ*
Speaker 2	*post office*	*ʔɛrɛtɫ'ískų́ɛ*
	school	*sɛkwi xáunɛltonkų́ɛ*

So we see that there is considerable individual freedom in the production of calques. It is the principle of organizing the lexicon around a central core of meanings with separate language-specific equivalents that is shared, not necessarily the forms that are used in particular instances.

We can now put together a quite general view of the lexicon on the basis of this and our earlier discussion. In the first place we want to view the system as quite individualistic. That is, the lexicon we are describing is the lexicon of an individual. It is one speaker's solution to the understanding of the complex of languages he or she speaks within the experience of a lifetime. There are many similarities, of course, between the solutions different speakers arrive at, but less than would be assumed if we assumed we were describing the lexicon of a language or of a speech community.

This lexicon consists of a core of meanings that are not specific to any one language. Here, again, we need to emphasize that because the lexicon represents the system of a person rather than a community, for any one person this core of meanings may be more closely centered on one language (as it is spoken elsewhere) than another. In Marcel's case, the meaning core appears to be quite Athabaskan on the whole.

To this meaning core are related a set of underlying forms tending toward one for each language that the speaker will claim to know. Although these underlying forms are distinctly descended from the more conservative forms of the discrete historical varieties that are their ancestors, there is some structural convergence at this level as well. In Chipewyan, verbal structures are reduced by the elimination of prefixes and, at the same time, expanded somewhat by the incorporation of new elements. Suffixes are also added to produce tense marking. In English, morphemes are amalgamated into new idioms that are then treated functionally and phonologically as lexical units.

At the lowest level of phonetic surface rules the separation of languages maintained in the underlying forms is neutralized to some extent by various rules of which the shift of s-consonants to ʃ-consonants is an important example. Thus at the most superficial level and at the deepest level of meaning the convergence is greatest. At the intermediate level, a separation of the languages is maintained in the underlying forms of words. These forms, however, are also undergoing changes that move in the direction of convergence.

CLAUSE STRUCTURE

Our study of Marcel's lexical structure has led us to view a word as having a central meaning core with separate surface representations in several languages. We would now like to look at the structure of clauses to see to what extent Marcel is also converging these higher level structures. Marcel's beaver hunt narrative is particularly well suited to this study since it can be reasonably thought of as saying the same thing in two different languages. We will first look at how he structures clauses in Chipewyan, then in English, and finally we will develop a comparison of those structures to see to what extent Marcel uses one structural organization for both languages at the clause level.

Our first problem in approaching this study was in the definition of a clause. In editing the Mandeville texts (Li and Scollon 1976) we had arrived at a general definition of the Chipewyan clause that we used in punctuating. R. Scollon has also done further work on the elements which occur between clauses to indicate relationships between clauses (1976c), and so in approaching this study we were more concerned with checking the analysis we had already done than with developing a new view of the Chipewyan clause.

The Chipewyan clause is structured around a verbal nucleus. This verb may be either an active verb or a neuter verb as defined by Li (1946). In addition to the verb, there are various other nominal and adverbial forms depending on the type of clause. These other possibilities will be discussed on pages 147–154. The boundaries of the clause are frequently marked by a set of forms which we have called discourse markers. We have discussed *ʔɛkú·* and its variant forms earlier. Others such as the demonstrative pronouns *ʔɛyi* 'that' and *ʔɛyɛr* 'there', which with rare exceptions occur in clause-initial position, serve as initial boundaries. In clause-final position there is the reduced version of *ʔɛkú·, -ú*, and the past tense suffix *-nį*, among others, which again with rare exceptions mark the final boundary of the clause.

Using these forms and the assumption that there is one clause for each verb, we marked the clauses throughout the narrative. In most instances the three major paralinguistic and prosodic features which we have marked, pausing, breathing, and falling final pitch, came at boundaries in the clause structure. Thus we feel that there is good evidence that the clause structure that we have assumed for analytical reasons corresponds to the structure which Marcel himself perceives. That is, the prosodic markings give evidence for the psychological reality of the clause as an analytical unit.

There were several problematical phrases. For example in (4.2) there is a phrase without any verb:

> (4.2) *saskátcuwén-ts'én dɛátɫ'ul ʔą́sk'ɛðɛ.*
> Saskatchewan-to   line   across

The preceding line which is rather complex ends with a clause boundary. This is marked by a pause and a falling pitch. To anticipate our discussion somewhat, we can also note that the verb *djă·sya* as a verb of going requires a locative. This locative is supplied in the preceding embedded clause. Line (4.2), then, is superfluous to the structure of the preceding clause. This line itself is set off with a falling pitch, a pause, and a breath. The following clause begins with the anaphoric locative *kozį́*, and thus line (4.2) is superfluous to the following clause as well.

A phrase like this is a problem since it can be neither defined as a clause in itself nor analyzed as a part of either the preceding or the following clause. There are relatively few of these problematic phrases in the whole text, however, so we will discuss them later in more detail in relation to other clauses.

There are five basic types of clauses in Marcel's Chipewyan text; active, process, stative, copula, and laminating. The active clauses are clauses in which the nuclear verb is an active verb as analyzed by Li (1946). There are two types of active verbs, transitive and intransitive. The transitive verbs are those that require an agent or experiencer and a patient. We will informally refer to both agents and experiencers as agents. The transitive verbs that Marcel uses in this text are given below with their stems and simple glosses. Fuller detail on the structure of these verbs may be found in Li's stem list (Li 1933b) and grammatical sketch (Li 1946). These verbs are *-tθa* 'find', *łɛɣá...ɛłɛ/θer* 'kill', *-k'íθ, k'éð* 'shoot', *-di* 'touch', *-tθ'aɣ* 'hear', *-tį* 'see', *-tθį* 'poke', *-t'áð* 'cut', *-la* 'handle several objects', *-tcú* 'take', *-θa* 'handle quickly'.

The structure of Marcel's transitive clauses may be summarized as follows,

$$\text{Conj–Loc–Time–Adv–Agt–Pat—Adv—V—Suf}$$
$$1 \quad 2 \quad 3 \quad 4 \quad 5 \quad 6 \quad 7 \quad 8 \quad 9$$

There are nine positions or slots which may be filled out, but only position (8), the verb, is required. Position (1) is a conjunction (Conj). This is *ʔeyiʔá* 'therefore' in each instance in which this position has (Conj).

Positions (2) and (3) locative (Loc) and time are filled with the coalesced form *ʔeyerų́łdų·* 'there then'. In a fuller analysis of Marcel's narrative structure, especially involving other texts, these may well be better analyzed as a single form discourse marker. The form *ʔeyer* is usually quite empty of locative content in these transitive clauses.

The adverbial forms (Adv) in (4) and (7) appear to be quite free here and in other clauses and may, in fact, occur virtually anywhere in the clause. *tθ'i* 'also' is by far the most common of these adverbials.

Positions (5) and (6) are invariable in their order. The agent (Agt) must precede the patient (Pat) of the transitive verb. The patient, however, may be postposed into position (9) for emphasis, as in

(28)   *θiłk'éθ ʔɛyi sas*
         'I shot that bear.'

Both agent and patient may be marked on either the verb with prefixes or in the clause in Chipewyan, (at least in Mandeville's use) with some restriction on the co-occurrence of these case roles. In Marcel's Chipewyan, double marking of the patient never occurs. That is, it is marked either on the verb or in the clause but not both. The agent in a few instances is present in both the verb and the clause. The normal arrangement is for the agent to be marked with a verbal prefix and for the patient to be present in the clause as a full noun or noun phrase.

There are several exceptions to this, however, in that either the agent or the patient may be completely absent where there is a clear reference in the preceding context. As an example there is

(7.2)   *dódítθa*
         'didn't find anything'

There is no agent marked in this clause. The agent has been clearly marked in the preceding two clauses, however, as well as in the following clause, all of which together make up a single segment of the narrative. There could be no mistaking of the first person singular agent in this instance, and it has been deleted in both the clause and the verb.

In 30.2 *nâ ·θiłk'éð* 'I shot (it) twice' there is no patient, but this patient has been clearly indicated in the preceding clause.

There are two groups of intransitive clauses, those with verbs of going and the remainder. The verbs of going which Marcel uses are -*di* 'hurry', -*ya* 'one goes', -*dja* 'one goes' (*d* classifier), -*dał* 'one goes', -*gé* 'an animal goes', -*'ás* 'animals crawl'. These all require both an agent– patient (AP), as the one who is the instigator of the going as well as the one who goes, and a locative (Loc). It is the latter requirement which distinguishes these verbs from the other intransitives which may take a locative but for which a locative is not obligatory.

This requirement that the verbs of going take a locative is rather interesting in light of an observation that we made early in our fieldwork. Of course we often walked around the town with no specific destination in mind. When we talked to people they always asked where we were going or where we were coming from. We found that members of the speech community would not accept any statement about going that did not include a locative. At first we interpreted this as ranging from curiosity to rudeness, but then found that in most cases a simple locative eliminated the curiosity. In answer to "Where are you going?" it was enough to say "I'm going down" (i.e., "downtown") to satisfy the questioner in most cases. In this we see an interesting relationship between the structure of a type of clause and a much more general feeling that when people go they go somewhere. The sort of relationship between linguistic structure and thought that Whorf was interested in seems to be manifested in this instance.

The structure of the intransitive clause of going may be summarized as follows:

$$\text{DM—Time—}\begin{Bmatrix}\text{Loc—Adv}\\\text{Adv—Loc}\end{Bmatrix}\text{—AP—V—}\begin{Bmatrix}\text{Adv}\\\text{Suf}\end{Bmatrix}$$
$$\quad 1 \qquad 2 \qquad\quad 3 \qquad\quad 4 \quad 5 \quad\; 6$$

The elements of this clause type are much like those of the transitive clause. Discourse markers (DM) include *kú·*, the most common of them. The two elements in (3) are not ordered, since as we have said, the adverbial elements may occur quite freely in the clause. Although we have shown the suffixes and the adverbials to be mutually exclusive in the postverbal position (6), this may just be an accidental result of the examples we have.

With this clause type as with the transitive clause, there is some latitude in the placement of two of the essential elements, the agent–patient (AP) and the locative (Loc). They may appear in the clause or in the verb. There is a co-occurrence restriction, however, since they may be marked in only one of these places. In a few instances the locative is deleted completely. This is where there is a sequence of verbs of going or where the locative is otherwise clearly implied by the context.

Intransitive clauses that do not have a verb of going may or may not have a locative and do not have a patient. They normally have an agent–patient (AP) as their central case role. The verbs which Marcel uses are *-k'é* 'fire' (a gun), *-tí* 'sleep' or 'camp', *-da* 'sit', *-dé* (or *-θer*) 'live' or 'stay', *-tθ'er* 'fall', *-tą* 'fall' (a long, slender object), *-ti* 'sit', *-da* 'move', *-ził* 'roar', *-ná* 'live'.

The structure of these clauses is as follows:

$$\begin{Bmatrix}\text{DM}\\\text{Conj}\end{Bmatrix}\text{—}\begin{Bmatrix}\text{Loc—Time—Adv}\\\text{Adv—Loc}\end{Bmatrix}\text{—}\begin{Bmatrix}\text{AP}\\\text{Means}\end{Bmatrix}\text{—V—Suf}$$
$$\quad 1 \qquad\qquad 2 \qquad\qquad\quad 3 \qquad 4 \quad 5$$

This structure requires little comment because of its similarity with the other active clauses. The elements in (2) are most likely not ordered in the way we have suggested above. The agent–patient (AP) may be represented either in the clause or in the verb by a verbal prefix, but not in both places. It is not deleted in any example we have.

We have used the term "Means" to describe the relationship of *ɬuwɛ* 'fish' and *ʔɛyi* 'that' to *nádé* 'they live' in (14.3) *ɬuwɛ-ɣɑ nádé* 'they live on fish' and (14.4) *ʔɛyi-ɣɑ nádé* 'they live on that'. We have no evidence for a separate position for "means" either preceding or following the agent–patient (AP).

The active clauses, then, are quite similar in structure. The verbs are distinguished on the basis of the case roles they require. These may be summarized as follows:

Active transitive	Active intransitive [+going]	Active intransitive [−going]
V $\begin{bmatrix} + \text{Agt} \\ + \text{Pat} \end{bmatrix}$	V $\begin{bmatrix} + \text{AP} \\ + \text{Loc} \end{bmatrix}$	V $[\, + \text{AP} \,]$

In all of these the case roles may be marked either on the verb or in the clause, but only agent may be marked in both places. This, however, is quite rare. By far the most common form is to have agent or agent–patient marked on the verb with other case roles marked in the clause.

If we summarize the clause structures of all of these active clauses, we have the following structure:

$$\begin{Bmatrix} \text{DM} \\ \text{Conj} \end{Bmatrix} - \begin{Bmatrix} \text{Loc} - \\ \text{Time} \end{Bmatrix} \begin{matrix} \text{Time—Adv} \\ \begin{Bmatrix} \text{Adv—Loc} \\ \text{Loc—Adv} \end{Bmatrix} \end{matrix} \Bigg\} \; \text{Agt} - \begin{Bmatrix} \text{AP} \\ \text{Pat} \\ \text{Means} \end{Bmatrix} \text{Adv—V—} \begin{Bmatrix} \text{Adv} \\ \text{Suf} \end{Bmatrix}$$

1		2	3	4	5	6	7

The first position is invariable, as is the last, position 7. The forms which occur in these positions relate most directly to the discourse structure and thus are both boundaries on the clause and the means of grounding the clause in the text. The ordering given for position 2 summarizes Marcel's use, but it is quite likely that there are, in fact, no ordering restrictions among the elements that may appear in the second position 2. In several instances a patient or an agent–patient is postposed. These postposed nominals appear in position 7. There are no verbal suffixes when postpositioning occurs.

The cases in position 4 just preceding the verb have in common that they are the physical bodies that participate in the action of the verb. It might be well to consider this position to be the **patient** position as a way of summarizing the various case roles that can occur in it.

There is very little that can be said about process clauses, since there are only two of these and they are the same form. In (13.2) and (13.3) there is *tsiłedjɛr* 'it snowed'. We prefer to analyze this as

patient—V

but must admit that there is no principled way to distinguish between this analysis and one which would treat *tsił* 'snow' as an incorporated patient and thus be written structurally as

V

[+patient]

We are using Goffman's (1974) term "laminating" for a set of verbs which are used to frame a piece of the narrative as spoken or thought by a character in the narrative, not necessarily the narrator. In this instance the narrator and the original speaker or thinker are the same biological person, but of course Marcel the narrator and Marcel the hunter are separated by a distance of some 50 years.

The stems of the three laminating verbs are *-θen* 'think', *-di* (or *si*) 'say', and *-yǫ* 'know'. The clause structure associated with these verbs is,

DM	[quoted]		V	[quoted]
	[known]	knower	V	
1	2	3	4	5

The brackets [ ] indicate that a full clause is embedded at this position as what was said, thought, or known. What is quoted may appear either before or after the verb but not in both places within a single clause. What is known, however, may only appear in position 2. The clause in brackets must have a verb in the first person for 'think' and 'say' but not for 'know'. 'Knowing', then, appears to be treated differently from the other two verbs and much more like a transitive verb. The knower, of course, is in the patient position we have suggested above.

Generally speaking, the clause structure of all the laminating verbs is much simpler than that of the active verbs. This may be explained by the fact that they require an embedded clause as part of their structure.

The small group of stative verbs suggest a somewhat different clause structure. The verbs Marcel uses are *-łǫ* 'many', *θá* 'long time', *-ðá* 'far', *-dáð* 'heavy', and *-k'á* 'fat'. As neuter verbs they take only at most a simple adjectival prefix, which suggests that a structural distinction could be analyzed between the active verbs and the stative verbs as follows,

Active   Prefix—V

Stative   V

The clause structure of the stative clause is as follows,

$$\begin{Bmatrix}DM \\ Conj\end{Bmatrix} \begin{bmatrix}Loc & Time & Loc \\ Poss & Adv & Quan\end{bmatrix} \quad Entity \quad V \quad Suf \quad \begin{Bmatrix}Time \\ Loc \\ Conj\end{Bmatrix}$$

$$\begin{array}{ccccccc} 1 & & 2 & & 3 & 4 & 5 & 6 \end{array}$$

The elements in position 1 are the same as for active verbs. Again, the elements in position 2 are probably not ordered. There is some greater freedom in the elements that may be found in a postverbal position, and these may follow the verbal suffixes. In this aspect stative verbs are treated quite differently from active verbs by Marcel.

There are a few copular verbs in Marcel's text. We have included several of the so-called classificatory verbs in this category. He uses *-łi* and *-lɛ* 'be', *-ʔą́* 'extend', *-dja* 'do', *-ʔą* 'be' (a round solid object). The structure of the clauses with these verbs is:

$$DM \quad Loc\begin{Bmatrix}entity \\ [condition]\end{Bmatrix} \quad \begin{Bmatrix}Pron \\ Adv \\ Quan\end{Bmatrix} \quad V \quad Suf$$

$$\begin{array}{cccccc} 1 & 2 & 3 & 4 & 5 & 6 \end{array}$$

The overall structure appears to be simpler than for active clauses but this may be a result of the small number of examples. The element we have termed "condition" in position 3 is in brackets to indicate that a clause is embedded in this position. There is a greater variety of elements in the preverbal position, 4, but at the same time without more examples it is difficult to argue that this corresponds to position 5 in the active verbs. It may well correspond to position 4, where in active verbs one finds agent–patients, patients, and means.

We can now summarize all the clause types found in Marcel's beaver hunt narrative in Table 3.5.

Although the initial position is empty in some instances, it is probably possible for any type of clause. This would depend on the narrative structure. It is most likely that the unfilled first position represents only the small size of our sample in this instance.

As we have said before, we suspect that there are really no order restrictions on the elements that occur in the second position. The only restriction that relates to this position is the co-occurrence restriction on locatives. A locative may not appear in position 2 if it is represented in the verb.

The third position is the most restricted allowing only agents.

The fourth position may be described as the patient position since all of the elements that occur in this position are the patients of the action of

TABLE 3.5 Summary of Clause Types in the Beaver Hunt Narrative.

	1	2	3	4	5	6	7	8	9
Active ⎡Transitive ⎣In- Transitive ⎡+Going ⎣−Going	{DM / Conj}	Loc-Time-Adv {Loc-Adv / Time Adv-Loc}	Agt	{Pat / AP / Means}	Adv	Pref	V	{Adv / Suf}	
Process ⎡Speaking	DM			Patient		Pref	V		
Laminating ⎣Knowing				[Quote]		Pref	V	[Quote]	
	{DM / Conj}	[Known]		Knower		Pref	V		
Stative		Loc-Time-Loc / Poss-Adv-Quan		Entity	{Pron / Adv / Quan}		V	Suf	Time
Copular		Loc		Entity			V	Suf	

153

the verb. For stative verbs, the entity which appears here is the entity about which the state is predicated. For the copular verbs, the entity is that about which existence or some state of existence is being asserted.

The prefixes in position 6 distinguish the active and laminating verbs from the others. These verbal prefixes were the grounds on which Li (1946) established the two general classes of active and neuter verbs.

Positions 8 and 9 may need considerable revision in the light of more examples. It seems likely as of this writing that there is essentially one position following the verb, with some internal order constraints especially among verbal suffixes.

In our discussion of the laminating verbs we pointed out that clauses with these verbs require an embedded clause as part of their structure. Other than these there are very few places where we are inclined to analyze a clause as embedded within another. The two clearest of these are in (4.1) and breath group (7). The group of clauses in (4.1) includes a laminating verb and may be bracketed as follows:

[yuwé t'ats'én	[[tsá łǫ	nɛsθen]	łį-nį]	djǎ·sya]
there to where	beaver are many	I thought	it was	I went

In (7) there are

[[[djǫ ots'į hiya]	ots'į	ta·γitįú]	dódítθǎ·]
here from I went	since	thrice I slept	nothing found

These indicate that although embedding of clauses is possible for Marcel, on the whole he does not choose to use complex syntactic structures in performing a narrative. In (4.2) where there is a verbless locative phrase, we would like to suggest now that it is the complexity of the preceding sentence that precludes the full incorporation of this locative.

There are two quite general processes that tend to complicate the structure of clauses. The first is the use of postpositioning for emphasis. Nouns in at least two case roles, patient and agent–patient, may be placed in a postverbal position. We will leave open for future analysis the question of whether this should be treated analytically with transformations. The second process we have described as deletions of such obligatory case roles as agents, agent–patients, and locatives where these are clear in the discourse. Since both of these processes are related to the discourse or narrative structure, we may want to think of the clause structures we have given in the chart above as fairly context-free structures which are subject to considerable alternation under the constraints of being grounded in text.

In the English version of this story Marcel uses a very similar range of verbs and clause types. As active transitive verbs he uses *hunt, find, kill, see, eat, scare, want, use, shoot, hear, hit, take, chase*. The clause structure with which these verbs are used is as follows:

$$
\begin{Bmatrix} DM \\ Conj \end{Bmatrix} - \begin{Bmatrix} Adv \\ Time \end{Bmatrix} - \begin{Bmatrix} Inst \\ Pat \end{Bmatrix} - \begin{Bmatrix} Agt \\ AP \end{Bmatrix} - Adv - V - \begin{Bmatrix} Pat \\ Quan \\ IC \end{Bmatrix} - \begin{Bmatrix} NM \\ Adv \\ Loc \\ Source \\ Time \end{Bmatrix}
$$

$$
\begin{array}{cccccccc}
1 & \quad 2 & \quad 3 & \quad 4 & \quad 5 & 6 & 7 & \quad 8
\end{array}
$$

For transitive verbs positions 4, 6, and 7 are required. The other positions are optionally filled. As in Chipewyan, the adverbial forms in (2), (5), and (8) appear to occur quite freely in nearly every position. NM in position 8 is the narrative marker *you know*. IC in position 7 is an embedded infinitive clause.

Position 4 is obligatory, but in some instances it may be deleted where the agent or agent–patient is clearly given in the discourse. As an example, there is in (4.3) *didn't find beaver yet*, where the first person singular is clearly given in (3).

The case role of instrument (Inst) always occurs in position 3, even where this produces somewhat awkward clauses, as in (28).

That's the one use it.

Intransitive verbs may be divided into two classes, verbs of going and the remainder, on the basis of the fact that as in Chipewyan, verbs of going require a locative. Marcel uses the verbs *go, went, come back, made it, cross, was passing, jumping, went back, following, turn back*, and several others clearly derived from these. The clause structure in which these verbs is used is as follows:

$$
\begin{Bmatrix} DM \\ Conj \\ Inter \end{Bmatrix} - Time - Adv - AP - Adv - V - Adv - \begin{Bmatrix} Loc \\ IC \end{Bmatrix} - \begin{Bmatrix} Adv \\ Time \end{Bmatrix}
$$

$$
\begin{array}{ccccccccc}
1 & \quad 2 & 3 & 4 & 5 & 6 & 7 & 8 & \quad 9
\end{array}
$$

The adverbials in positions 3, 5, 7, and 9 probably do not indicate positions in the clause so much as the great freedom with which adverbials may occur nearly anywhere in the clause. "Inter" in position 1 indicates the interjection *see*.

The other intransitive verbs are *live, camp, drop, got, yell, die, looking, miss, fall, stay*, and *stop*. These have a structure very similar to the clauses with verbs of going except that the locative in position 6 is optional, not required:

$$\begin{Bmatrix} DM \\ Conj \end{Bmatrix} - Poss - Adv - \begin{Bmatrix} AP \\ Agt \\ Pat \end{Bmatrix} - V - \begin{Bmatrix} Time-Loc \\ Adv \end{Bmatrix} - NM$$

$$\begin{array}{ccccccc} 1 & 2 & 3 & 4 & 5 & 6 & 7 \end{array}$$

We can now summarize the structure of the clauses which have active verbs. This structure is as follows:

$$\begin{Bmatrix} DM \\ Conj \\ Inter \end{Bmatrix} - \begin{Bmatrix} Time \\ Poss \end{Bmatrix} - \begin{Bmatrix} Inst \\ Pat \end{Bmatrix} - \begin{Bmatrix} Agt \\ AP \end{Bmatrix} - V - \begin{Bmatrix} Pat \\ Quan \\ IC \\ Loc \\ Time-Loc \end{Bmatrix} - \begin{Bmatrix} NM \\ Loc \\ Source \\ Time \end{Bmatrix}$$

$$\begin{array}{ccccccc} 1 & 2 & 3 & 4 \quad 5 & 6 & 7 \end{array}$$

Adverbs have been disregarded since, as we have already said, they do not appear to be restricted in the positions in which they can occur.

There is another set of clause types that have in common the fact that they correspond to clauses in standard English which have the verb *to be* in one of its forms. There are three of these which we will call existential clauses, predicative clauses, and identity clauses. Existential clauses have the forms *there's*, *was*, *is*, and *that's*; predicative clauses have *it's* and *is*; and identity clauses have *it's*. The structures of these clauses are as follows:

Exist: $\begin{Bmatrix} DM \\ NM \end{Bmatrix} - Time - \begin{Bmatrix} Loc \\ Dem \end{Bmatrix} - V - Entity - Loc - Time - Adv - NM$

Pred: $\begin{Bmatrix} DM \\ NM \end{Bmatrix} - Adv - Entity - V - State - \begin{Bmatrix} Time \\ Adv \end{Bmatrix} \quad NM$

Ident: $\qquad\qquad\qquad Entity - V - Entity$

$$\begin{array}{ccccccccc} 1 & 2 & 3 & 4 & 5 & 6 & 7 & 8 & 9 \end{array}$$

The central position of the verb in these clauses is in contrast to its placement very much farther to the right in active clauses. This in itself is enough to distinguish this group from the active clauses. The narrative markers (NM) *you know* or *eh*? occur more frequently in these clauses, and at least *you know* may appear in both initial and final positions. This suggests a framing of these clauses within the narrative as operating on a somewhat different level from the active clauses. Labov (1972b) has proposed a distinction between narrative clauses and free clauses where narrative clauses are those which advance the action being narrated. These clauses are free clauses in that they do not relate directly to the narrative action but serve more to orient to that action or to evaluate it. This secondary function may be what is marked with the NM boundaries.

The essential difference between these three clause types is in the position of the entity about which existence is asserted or a state is predicated, or to which another entity is equated. This essential property may be extracted and represented as follows:

Existential: V   Entity
Predicative: Entity   V   State
Identity: Entity   V   Entity

One further consideration can be mentioned here. Any of these may have either the verb or the entity deleted when either can be assumed from the context.

We are distinguishing this set of existential, predicative, and identity clauses from another clause type which we are calling indexicals. These are clauses with the verb *do* or, in some instances, clauses in which *do* has been replaced with a gesture. Structurally they are more like the active verbs and thus are indexical in that the active verb has been replaced with an "empty" form that "stands for" or indicates the active verb.

The structure of these clauses is as follows:

$$DM—Time—Agt—\begin{Bmatrix} V \\ G \end{Bmatrix}—Adv—Time$$

An example of a clause in which a gesture (G) replaces the verb may be found in (32.6)

Then the bear like that.

In this instance there is no active verb, and a gesture of the bear pawing himself is substituted for it. The gesture can be thought of as standing for a verb like 'pawed himself'. Since this type of clause occurs quite infrequently we will not consider it further.

The two laminating verbs which Marcel uses are *thought* and *know*. It is interesting to notice that although he does quote himself as in the Chipewyan version, the embedding verb is absent. As in Chipewyan, there is a difference between the structure of clauses with *thinking* and clauses with *knowing*. The former allow the quoted speech either to precede or to follow the verb, but the latter allow what is known only to follow the verb. In both instances the quoted or known are given as embedded clauses. For *thinking*, the quoted thinking may either precede or follow the verb but may not occur in both places. As the structure below shows, clauses with knowing are very similar to transitive clauses with the knower in the agent–patient position and the known in the patient position. The structure is as follows:

$$[quoted] \text{ —quoter—V—}[quoted]$$

$$DM \text{ -NM- Adv—knower—V—}[known]$$

The clause structures used in Marcel's English text may now be summarized as shown in Table 3.6.

Now that we have a somewhat more detailed understanding of the structure of clauses in Marcel's Chipewyan and his English, we would like to begin a comparison of these structures. At a glance we can see that there is a considerable similarity among active clauses in both languages. The first position is similar. To discourse marker and conjunction, English adds an interjection (Inter). It is of course not surprising to find these discourse-governed forms as initial boundaries of the clause in both languages.

The difference between the two languages in the second position is the presence of locatives here in Chipewyan.

The next two positions need to be clarified now. We have given the following orders in our summaries for the two languages:

English		Chipewyan	
$\begin{Bmatrix} \text{Inst} \\ \text{Pat} \end{Bmatrix}$	$\begin{Bmatrix} \text{Agt} \\ \text{AP} \end{Bmatrix}$	Agt	$\begin{Bmatrix} \text{Pat} \\ \text{AP} \\ \text{Means} \end{Bmatrix}$

The English ordering is misleading since it implies that a patient (Pat) may precede an agent–patient (AP). These, however, are mutually exclusive. Instruments (Inst) do not cooccur with other case roles in a preverbal position, nor do agent–patient (AP), and so we see that for these the ordering is irrelevant. These positions for English would be better written as,

$$\begin{Bmatrix} \text{Pat—Agt} \\ \text{Inst} \\ \text{AP} \end{Bmatrix}$$

which indicates that ordering is significant only for patients and agents.

The same considerations hold for Chipewyan as well; so for that language it would be preferable to write,

$$\begin{Bmatrix} \text{Agt—Pat} \\ \text{AP} \\ \text{Means} \end{Bmatrix}$$

TABLE 3.6 Clause Structures Used in Marcel's English Text.

Active ⌐Trans. Intrans.⌐[+Go] 　　　　└[−Go]	⌐DM⌐ Conj └Inter┘	⌐Time⌐ └Poss┘	⌐Inst⌐ └Pat┘	⌐Agt⌐ └AP┘	V		⌐Pat Quan IC Loc Time-Loc┘	⌐Loc Source Time┘	NM
Laminating			[Qtd]	Quoter	V		[Quoted]		
⌐Thought⌐Know	DM	NM		Knower	V		[Known]		NM
Existential	DM	Time		Loc	V	Entity	Loc	Time	NM
	NM			Dem	V				
Predicative	DM			Entity	V		State	Time	NM
	NM								
Identity				Entity	V	Entity			
Indexical	DM	Time		Agt	⌐V⌐ └G┘			Time	
	1	2	3	4	5	6	7	8	9

If these two are compared, then, we can see that the only difference between the two languages in this position is in the relative positions of agent and patient.

For English the patient must precede the agent, and in Chipewyan it must follow.

The placement of the verb is the same for both languages, with the exception that Chipewyan, in some cases, has a complex verbal prefix system. Where this prefix system has been reduced or eliminated and where objects have been incorporated into the verb itself, the clause structure that results looks very much like English. This may well be one of the motivations, then, for the reductions that have taken place in the prefix system and for the incorporation of sentential objects. These two processes may be shown schematically as follows:

a.	Chipewyan:	Agt–Pat–Pref	V	
b.		Agt–Pat	V	Prefix reduction
c.		Agt	V	(Object incorporation)
			[+pat]	
d.	English:	Agt	V	Pat

The preverbal Chipewyan clause structure in (c) has become identical to the preverbal English clause structure in (d). All that remains is to put the patient in a postverbal position in Chipewyan or to incorporate the patient in English to get a full convergence in the transitive clause structure.

The clause structures are different to a greater extent in the portion that follows the verb in that English allows much more in these positions. Chipewyan allows the rare postposed patient or agent–patient, but normally only adverbials and suffixes occur following the verb. English requires patients to follow the verb and for these to be ordered preceding source. So for English there are two positions which may take full nominals with an ordering constraint.

We are now able to write out a chart comparing the structures of active clauses in Chipewyan and in English as Marcel uses them:

Chipewyan:		Loc	Agt–Pat	Pref	Suf			
Both:	$\begin{bmatrix} DM \\ Conj \end{bmatrix}$	Time	$\begin{bmatrix} Inst \\ AP \end{bmatrix}$	V				
English:	Inter	Poss	Pat–Agt		$\left\{ \begin{array}{c} Time\text{-}Loc \\ Loc \\ Pat \\ Quan \\ IC \end{array} \right\}$	$\left\{ \begin{array}{c} Loc \\ Source \\ Time \end{array} \right\}$	NM

There are three crucial differences between the Chipewyan active clause and the English active clause. The first is the relative position of agent and patient; the second is the case roles allowed in a postverbal position; and the third is the position of locative which occurs early in the Chipewyan clause and postverbally in the English clause. Otherwise these clauses structures are very similar.

The three active clause types in both languages may be given in prototypical forms using A for agent, P for the patient of a transitive verb, AP for the agent–patient of an intransitive verb, and X for any other elements:

	Chipewyan	English
Transitive	X A P V	X A V P
Intransitive [+Go]	X Loc AP V	X AP V Loc
[−Go]	X AP V	X AP V

The differences between the clause types are the same in both languages. That is, transitive clauses require both agents and patients; intransitive clauses with verbs of going require locatives whereas the other intransitives do not. The differences between the languages lie in the positioning of these case roles. The structural similarity is greatest for intransitives which do not have verbs of going.

Clauses with laminating verbs can be classed as two separate groups. The first has verbs of speaking and thinking. The structure of these clauses is very similar in the two languages:

English: [quoted] Quoter V [Quoted]
Chipewyan: [quoted] Pref   V [Quoted]

For both languages either a preverbal or a postverbal [quoted] is chosen, but not both. In the instances we have in Marcel's text, the English *I* corresponds in position to *nes* (<*ne*—thematic prefix, *s*—first person singular) in Chipewyan.

As a group these contrast with clauses with the verb *know*. The structures of these clauses are different in the two languages, but in each language more strongly resemble the normal transitive clause.

English: DM—NM—Adv—Knower V [Known]
Chipewyan: [Known] Knower Pref V

The known element in Chipewyan occupies the position of the locative, however, not the patient. This is consistent with the English postverbal positioning of the known.

It is interesting that thinking and speaking are structurally different from knowing, since there is also a difference between these clauses in point of view. The embedded clauses in speaking and thinking require a verb in the first person, whereas the embedded clause in knowing does not. It seems then that we may want to consider knowing to belong to a different group, perhaps to the active group of clauses with the knower as an agent–patient.

Other clause types differ more between the two languages in both structure and in function. In the English clauses there are as many elements to the right of the verb as to the left, but in Chipewyan there is very little to the right of the verb and the clauses have relatively less material to the left than do active clauses in Chipewyan.

From a functional point of view, what is done with predication in English is done with stative verbs in Chipewyan. In order to compare the uses of the clauses of different types in the two versions of Marcel's story we have enumerated all of the clauses by type in Table 3.7. The number given in the list is the breath group and pause group in which the clause occurs. The Chipewyan clauses are on the left and the English on the right. A double line (===) divides the narrative frame from the story proper. A single line (__) separates the beaver hunt section of the narrative from the bear encounter section. At the bottom of each column in parentheses is the total number of times that each clause type occurred in the story. Table 3.8 gives the totals from the columns of Table 3.7.

We would now like to compare the two stories on the basis of Marcel's use of active clauses. Table 3.9 gives the percentages of these clauses used in the two versions of the story and in the two sections of the story.

The first thing we can note is that the two versions are very similar in the use of transitive clauses in the two parts of the story. One-fourth are in the beaver hunt prelude and three-fourths are in the bear encounter section. Since the latter is the center of the narrative action, this concentration of transitive clauses there is not surprising.

The two languages are quite different, however, in the distribution of intransitive clauses (verbs of going, and the others are the same in this respect). For Chipewyan they are almost evenly distributed, but for English 20% appear in the first section and 70% appear in the second section. Furthermore the percentage of intransitives out of the total number of clauses is smaller for English (30%) than for Chipewyan (44.6%).

If we look for other differences of this magnitude in the totals in Table 3.8, we see that English has some 11.6% more existentials than Chipewyan, and this is just about the difference we need to account for. This suggests that what is done with an intransitive clause in Chipewyan is done with an existential clause in English.

TABLE 3.7 Types of Causes in the Two Versions of Marcel's Story.

| Transitive | | Active — Intransitive | | | | Laminating | | Existential | |
| Transitive | | Going | | −Going | | Laminating | | Existential | |
Chip.	Eng.	Chip.	Eng.	Chip.	Eng.	Chip.	Eng.	Chip.	Eng.
	1	3.1	1	7.1	3	4.2	6	4.2	2
7.2	4	3.2	9	12.2	15	18.1	8	14.1	7
7.3	5	4.1	9	13.2	17	20.1	11	23	9
8.3	5	5	14	13.3	30	21	19	(3)	9.2
10.2	8	7	15.2	14.3	32.4	27.2	32.4		9.3
11.1	13	8.1	16	14.3	33	32.1	32.5		11
18.1	14	8.3	18	14.4	33	32.2	34.2		11
18.1	14.2	9.1	22	15.1	38.6	32.2	39		13
20.1	16	9.1	23	16.2	40	32.2	42		13.2
21.1	21.3	9.1	24.2	17.1	40.2	32.2	(9)		14
24.7	21.4	10.2	25	18.2	42	32.2			16.2
28.1	27	12.1	26	19.1	43	(11)			17.2
29	27	12.1	30.2	19.4	47.2				19
30.2	27	13.1	30.3	19.4	48				21
30.2	28	13.1	32	19.4					21
31	29	13.3	32	20.1	(14)				21.2
33.1	29.2	14.1	32.3	23					22.2
34	29.2	15.1	32.3	30.1					24.2
34.3	29.2	19.2	35	33					27.4
34.3	29.2	19.3	35	35.1					35.2
(20)	29.3	19.4	36	(20)					44.2
	29.3	22	36.2						46
	30	22.2	37						(22)
	31	23.2	37						
	32.4	23.2	37.2						
	32.5	23.3	37.3						
	34	23.3	37.3						
	37.4	23.4	38						
	38	23.4	38.2						
	40.3	24.4	38.3						
	42	24.7	38.5						
	44.2	24.7	38.6						
	45	24.7	41.3						
	45	24.7	48						
	45.2	25	(34)						
	47	25.1							
	(37)	25.2							
		26.1							
		31.1							
		31.2							
		35.1							
		(42)							

| Stative/Pred. | | Copula | |
Chip.	Eng.	Chip.	Eng.
4.2	8	19.2	15
6	19.3	32.2	32.2
8.2	27.5	(2)	32.6
12.2	28		43
14.2	30		46
15.2	30.2		(5)
20.1	32		
24.1	38.4		
24.2	38.6		
25	40.4		
27.1	41		
33.2	42		
34.2	46		
(14)	46		
	46		
	46		
	(16)		

163

TABLE 3.8   Totals for Marcel's Types of Clauses.

Totals	Numerical		Percentages	
	Chip.	Eng.	Chip.	Eng.
Transitive	20	37	14.4	23.1
Intransitive (Go)	42	34		
Intransitive (other)	20	14	44.6	30
Laminating	11	9		
Process	2	—		
Stative/Predicative	14	16		
Existential	3	22	2.2	13.8
Copula	2	5		
Identity	—	1		
Miscellaneous	25	22		
Total	139	160		

Looking at specific cases, we can point to:

English: (9.2)   *That's it one's a big hill?*
Chipewyan: (9.1)   *ʔiɫáɣɛ céθ nɛtcá· bɛtɛðiyaú*
                         one   hill big   I climbed up—sub.

as an example of an existential clause in English and a clause with a verb
of going in Chipewyan. There are also English existentials that compare
with Chipewyan intransitive clauses that do not have a verb of going, as in

English: (21)   *you know there's fish in there.*
Chipewyan: (14.3) *ɫuwɛ-ɣa nádé*
                          fish on they live

Thus where existence is asserted in English, it is presupposed in Chipewyan. There are other instances, however, where English existentials
correspond to Chipewyan statives,

English: (2)   *There's not many beaver that time*
Chipewyan: (6)   *kú· tsá ɫa-híle-ni̧ kú-hú*
                         then beaver many not past then-sub.

TABLE 3.9   Percentages of Transitive and Intransitive Clauses Used by Marcel.

	Transitive		Intransitive			
			Going		Others	
	Chip.	Eng.	Chip.	Eng.	Chip.	Eng.
Beaver hunt	25	73	40.5	23.5	40	21.4
Bear encounter	75	73	54.8	70.6	55	71.4

to Chipewyan process,

English:	(17.2)	*Well at night there's a lot of snow*
Chipewyan:	(13.2)	*ʔɛyɛr na·stí-nį tsiɫɛdjɛr*
		there I camped past it snowed

and, in fact, to Chipewyan existentials,

English:	(19)	*one's a big lake*
Chipewyan:	(14.1)	*ʔiɫáγɛ tu nɛnéθ θɛʔá*
		one lake long it extended

So we see that the statistical suggestion is misleading if we take it to mean simply that English existentials are represented in Chipewyan in clauses with intransitive verbs. The statistic is useful, however, to point up the fact that clause types may function differently in the two languages and a single narrator telling the same story in the two languages may exercise considerable freedom in choosing among ways of expressing basic grammatical functions.

To summarize now: This comparison of the structures of Marcel's clauses in Chipewyan and English points out that on the whole Marcel preserves prototypical distinctions between Chipewyan and English, at least in clauses with active verbs which make up the largest share of the total. Nevertheless, by various adjustments such as postpositioning of objects or incorporating them into the verb in Chipewyan, or in English placing many of the freely ordered elements such as adverbials and time elements to the left of the verb, Marcel gets the two systems to approximate each other to a considerable extent. These choices were always possible to some extent in the two languages, and so Marcel has taken advantage of the stylistic or idiomatic resources of the two languages to produce these similarities. In English he prefers those structures most like Chipewyan, and in Chipewyan he prefers those most like English. This allows one basic clause type with minor differentiations to represent the two languages. What has converged then is not the structure of clauses at the prototypical level, but the structure of clauses at the idiomatic or stylistic level.

Although we have now said we feel that convergence is taking place at the stylistic or idiomatic level, we would like to consider further just how this might take place. We can compare two very similar verbs in the Chipewyan and the English versions to begin with:

Chipewyan:	(7.2)	*dódítθǎ*	'nothing found'
English:	(4.3)	didn't find	

In both cases there is no agent but the problem is to determine where it has been deleted.

We can imagine three possible models. In the first, we would assume an underlying semantic structure (represented below by capital letters) which has separate realizations in the two languages. Then these realizations are reduced by the operation of language specific discourse rules including the deletion of agents where these are present in the preceding context. We have observed this rule separately in our analysis above for both languages. This model could be sketched as follows:

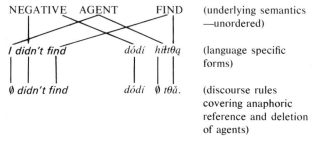

NEGATIVE AGENT FIND	(underlying semantics —unordered)
I didn't find *dódí* *hı̀tɬθq*	(language specific forms)
∅ *didn't find* *dódí* ∅ *tθǎ.*	(discourse rules covering anaphoric reference and deletion of agents)

A second model we could imagine would place these reductions at a deeper level. We could assume the AGENT to be deleted before language specific realizations are determined. This model would compare more closely with the lexical model we have developed above. There we have argued for a single semantic representation for lexical items which is realized on the surface with forms from the different languages. Here we would be assuming that there is a single semantic representation of the clause as well as the discourse relations and that lexicalizations into separate languages occur at a very superficial level. This model could be sketched as follows:

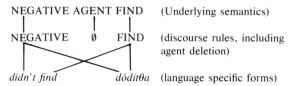

NEGATIVE AGENT FIND	(Underlying semantics)
NEGATIVE ∅ FIND	(discourse rules, including agent deletion)
didn't find *dódítθa*	(language specific forms)

Although we have assumed an unordered deep semantic structure, it is obvious that the surface orders that result for both Chipewyan and English are the same, Negative—Find. This convergence of the surface orders may, in fact, be a motive for the deletion of the agent since it was the one element preventing the full convergence of these forms in surface structure. Thus we would argue from this model that the convergence which shows at the surface level is, in fact, a deeper convergence at a prelexical level. We would also be arguing that discourse-governed deletions would operate on an unordered, prelexical form.

Finally, we could suggest a third model which would assume that the form was generated in one language, in this case Chipewyan, and then simply translated at the surface into the other language. In this model it would not matter where the agent was deleted. This model would be as follows:

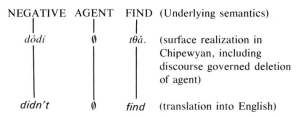

NEGATIVE AGENT FIND (Underlying semantics)

dódí   Ø   tθǎ. (surface realization in Chipewyan, including discourse governed deletion of agent)

didn't   Ø   find (translation into English)

It is difficult to find much evidence that would argue for any of these models. We can look now more closely at some of the evidence that we do have, however, and see that the third model is unlikely because Marcel does not always sustain a morpheme-by-morpheme translation over a longer period than a single word. Thus the full clauses from which we have extracted our examples are:

Chipewyan: (7.2)   [X]   dódítθǎ.
English: (4.3)   [X]   didn't find beaver yet

The presupposed 'beaver' is deleted from the Chipewyan but not the English.

There is another case in which through a series of stutterings we can see that Marcel has some difficulty in lexicalizing what he intends to say. Although the evidence is not strong or unambiguous, we feel it does clearly point out a conflict between two surface lexicalizations:

Chipewyan: (9.1)   ʔeyer ots' i̯ | hi ʯyaú | ʔeyi | destcoɣ |-gá | nániyaú

English: (9.1)   I | went | there's a | big river | here | I went across?

The forms may be lined up as above to indicate that for the whole line Marcel uses very parallel structures. The only serious reorderings are in *big river—destcoɣ* ('river'—'big') and *I went across—nániyaú* ('across' —'I'—'one goes').

If we look closer now at the phonetic transcription, we can see that Marcel has major problems just at those points. First we can compare *there's a big river* and *ʔeyi destcoɣ* as follows. Line (*a*) is the Chipewyan phonetic transcription, (*b*) is the Chipewyan hesitation filler *yaɣe*, (*c*) is the English phonetic transcription, and (*d*) is what we assume to be the English target form. This latter is based on Marcel's normal pronunciation:

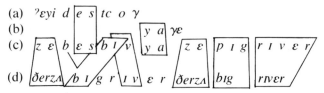

(a) ʔɛyi d e s tc o γ
(b)
(c) z ɛ b ɛ s b ɪ v   y a   z ɛ   p ɪ g   r ɪ v ɛ r
(d) ðerzʌ b ɪ g r ɪ v ɛ r ðerzʌ big   rɪvɛr

Marcel obviously is having difficulty in line (c), the English version. This leads us to believe that it is the English form that is more difficult for him. The first attempt at *big* results in a blend with the element that comes first in the Chipewyan, *des* ('river'). He shifts then to the second part of the form *river*, but at the same time he repeats the initial of *big* and gets [bɪv]. It is interesting that he then pauses altogether with the Chipewyan filler *yaγɛ*. This contrasts with Marcel's normal English hesitation [æ], [hæ] (cf. 11) or [a] (18). This seems to reflect that here Marcel is being rather more strongly influenced by the Chipewyan forms than in other cases of hesitation. After the hesitation Marcel then begins again at the start of the phrase and has little difficulty. The use of [p] for /b/ is a normal alternation in Marcel's speech.

The second place where orders are different in the two lines is in *I went across* and *nániyaú*. These can be given as above in phonetic transcriptions to be compared:

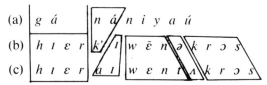

(a) g á   n á n i y a ú
(b) h ɪ ɛ r k ʼ ɪ w ē n ə k r ɔ s
(c) h ɪ ɛ r a ɪ w ɛ n t ʌ k r ɔ s

In the Chipewyan verb the prefix *ná* is a locative prefix indicating the meaning which is translated as *across*. Marcel's [kʼ] shows a momentary blend of the position of the Chipewyan verbal prefix and the English surface form. This sort of false start, incidentally, is not unusual for people who speak both languages and occurs both at the lexical level and at the clause level. Thus for *I want small baby* one person was quoted as saying *small, I want small baby*.

As we have said above, we do not feel this evidence to be unambiguous. It may suggest either the second or the third of the models that we have proposed above. That is, the sort of interference in which phonetic evidence of the lexical forms in both languages appears may suggest that the clauses are structured without reference to the language specific realizations and at the last moment, so to speak, a choice is made between the form in one language or the other. On the other hand it may suggest that the text is generated in one language and then translated as it is performed. The difficulties with reorderings at the lexical level that we have observed here may give some weight to the latter model since they appear to cause low-level hesitations and word replacements more than wholesale reorderings at the clause level.

As we have said above, however, a comparison of longer stretches of the narrative indicates that the similarity of the structures is probably not produced on the spot, as it were, because of translation, but rather through a general convergence throughout the system. This convergence begins at the lexical level but extends through idiom and stylistic choice.

To look at this latter sort of convergence we can compare the two versions for a somewhat larger piece of the narrative. The piece we have chosen to look at includes the verbs with which we began this discussion of convergence in clause structures.

Chipewyan (7)	English (3)
a. *djǫ ots'į*	Just I leave
b. *hiya*	here for Jacfish?
c. *ots'į*	Well after that
d. *ta·γitįú*	Well guess about three nights
e. *dódítθä.*	didn't find beaver yet.
f. *ʔɛyɛr húɬdų́*	Just about three nights
g. *tsá ɬáɬdé-nį.*	I found it one beaver I killed three.

As can be seen from this arrangement, there is considerable parallelism in the general structure of this section of the narrative. The rising intonation which we have indicated with the question mark (?) indicates not a question but that the first clause is subordinated to the following clauses. In this the intonation corresponds to *ots'į* ('since') in Chipewyan.

In group (d) the English *nights* corresponds to the Chipewyan verb *γitį* 'I slept'. In this instance, however, the verb does not mean literally to 'sleep' or 'camp'. The normal way of counting days of travel in Chipewyan is to count sleeps. Thus this form, though verbal in structure, is nominal in function. By using no verb in the English version, Marcel shows that he is not translating literally from the surface forms of Chipewyan into English; if he is translating at all, it is at a deeper, metaphorical level.

In both versions the agent is deleted in the clause in (e). In both instances we can now see that this agent is present in the first clause (a–b). This indicates a sentential group as the unit across which the rule of agent deletion may operate. Unfortunately, it also argues against the narrative boundary which we have analyzed in Chapter 2 between (3) and (4) (b–c) in the English version.

This must now be considered more closely. We argued for a narrative boundary between (3) and (4) on the basis of the pause, breath, and the forms *well* and *after that*. We are now wishing to consider (3) and (4) to comprise a single sentence. What must be explained is the presence of the narrative markers in the middle of a sentence. To explain this we need to recall that we have argued that the structure of the English narrative was the result of an interaction between the narrator and his audience. Now we have a good example of the mechanics of this interaction.

The rising intonation marks subordination for Marcel, not a question. As English speakers, however, we took this rising intonation as indicating a question or, more accurately, a request to respond and, as the transcription shows, answered with *Uh huh*. This unexpected response, in turn, appears to have made Marcel mark a division in the narrative where he had probably not actually prepared to mark one. The unexpected nature of this marking shows up in a pause and a breath in the middle of a sentence unit as well as in a repetition of the marker *well* in (4.1) and (4.2) and perhaps in the form *guess*. Thus we see how the intervention of the audience can produce a narrative structure, even where this structure places narrative boundaries within sentential structures and goes against the original intentions of the narrator.

The closing part of this section (g) is quite interesting in showing the problems Marcel has in representing in English ideas that are structured differently in Chipewyan. The abstract structure of (g) may be seen as

PATIENT   + AGENT + VERB + QUANTITY + TIME
(beaver)   (I)   (kill)   (three)   (past)

In Chipewyan the patient precedes the verb as the nominal *tsá* which is not marked for number. The agent is marked with a verbal prefix *-i*. The quantity is marked in the stem *-dé* which is a quite general stem meaning something like 'to act' (or be acted upon) for plural patients. The meaning 'kill' is represented with the thematic prefix *tɛɣá-*. Aspect is marked in the verb prefix or, as we have already discussed, tense is marked with a suffix on the verb. This is the choice Marcel has made here in marking 'past' with *-nį*. This may be sketched as follows:

BEAVER   I   KILL   THREE   PAST

tsá   táɬdé   nį

The differences between Chipewyan and English are problematical for Marcel and others who speak both languages. In English number is normally marked on the patient or in the noun phrase of which the patient is the head. Person is marked with a free pronoun that precedes the verb.

The meaning 'kill' is represented with a single verb. Tense is marked on the verb with a suffix. Thus the usual way of saying this could be sketched as follows:

The production of these forms becomes a problem only where the speaker uses an underlying form ordered for one language in speaking the other. Thus if we line up Marcel's Chipewyan order and his English form we get

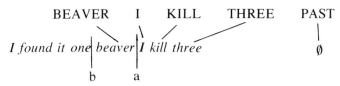

In a line by line comparison of the Chipewyan and English versions, the first clause, *I found it one beaver*, is gratuitous. He does not say he found beaver in the Chipewyan but only implies it. The motive for saying it in the English version appears to be in order to get the word *beaver* into the preagent position for the following clause. If we consider the clauses to be broken at (a), then the English clause structure looks like the prototypical transitive clause structure, AVP. The first clause is strange in having a double patient *it* and *one beaver*. This disagreement in number between the two clauses, however, is not a problem if a clause-at-a-time view of clause structure is taken.

If we consider the clause break to be at (b), we also have a possible English clause to the left of the break, with the exception of the double patient marking. The second clause looks very much like the Chipewyan clause, however, and has the prototypical Chipewyan transitive clause structure PV if we think of the pronoun *I* as a verbal prefix rather than as a sentential form. So we see that at least in some cases by juxtaposing two clauses a speaker can create out of separate standard structures in one language a structural reflection of the analogous structures in another language.

We have argued earlier that people who speak both languages often have a problem producing patients in a postverbal position in English. For Marcel this shows up in the double patient marking of forms with VERB + *it*. Another narrator who had even more difficulty than Marcel showed both this problem and the juxtapositioning of clauses to produce converged structures. As an example we can begin with the following:

he kill it, you know, for ɬuwaze.
kill it. ʔɛyi nunịyaze ɬuwaze ɬagá̧ɬdé.

ɬuwaze	'small fish'
ʔɛyi	'that'
nunịyaze	'wolf pup'
ɬagá̧ɬdé	'he killed it'

The meaning here may be translated as, *The wolf pup killed some small fish.* From the point of view of English structure, *it, you know,* and *for* are all superfluous. The object form is given in Chipewyan, which may indicate that the cognitive load is too great to produce this form in English as well as to put it in a postverbal position. The *kill it* that follows a short pause puts a verb in English after the patient and thus gives the normal Chipewyan position. Finally, the whole is repeated in Chipewyan in an almost classical conservative form, complete with a sentential agent. This undoubtedly reflects the narrator's dissatisfaction with her preceding attempts to produce a coherent structure in English.

Again, for the same speaker we have a similar form:

Somebody kill it again too nuniyɛ
'Again someone killed the wolf'

Then in one case we have both an overlapping of clause structures and a shift in language.

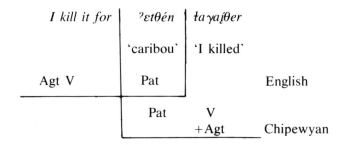

The patient is given in Chipewyan as in the sentences above, but in this instance it is followed by the Chipewyan verb. Thus in one sentence without pause or hesitation this speaker produces both clause structures.

In one other instance this speaker juxtaposed two Chipewyan clauses in the context of a Chipewyan story to produce an English clause structure. This was done as follows:

dɛne ɬaị·θer k'é | nuniyɛ |ɬaị·θer k'é
                a   b

The meaning is 'someone killed the wolf'. This is, in fact, the sentence which the same speaker paraphrased as *Somebody kill it again too nuniyɛ*, given just above. Since in Chipewyan a single noun preceding a transitive verb in the third person could be either an agent or a patient, each of these clauses taken separately is ambiguous. They could mean,

$$\left\{ \begin{array}{l} \textit{Someone killed the man.} \\ \textit{The man killed something.} \end{array} \right\} \quad \left\{ \begin{array}{l} \textit{Someone killed the wolf.} \\ \textit{The wolf killed someone.} \end{array} \right\}$$

In this instance the second clause is said more rapidly and with a lower pitch and volume, and the verb is quite faintly pronounced. Again, if we take the clause break as being at (a), we have two conservative but ambiguous Chipewyan transitive clauses. If we take the clause break as being at (b), however, we have one clear, unambiguous transitive clause but with the prototypical English transitive clause form AVP as well as a superfluous repetition of the verb. We feel that the paralinguistic marking, in fact, indicates that this is the correct analysis. Thus for this speaker, there is evidence that not only is her English transitive clause structure being affected by Chipewyan structure, but her Chipewyan structure is being affected by the structure of the English transitive clause.

For this speaker, as for Marcel, the grounds on which the convergence is being negotiated is not only in the internal structure of the clause but also in the parallels that can be achieved by the juxtaposition of quite conservative clause structures. Thus it is at the level of idiomatic or stylistic structure that the convergence of clause structures become most apparent. As with lexical convergence, changes are taking place where there is a range of possibilities. Where there is freedom in the English clauses to put an element in a preverbal or a postverbal position, a consistent placement before the verb gives the clause a Chipewyan structure. In Chipewyan the postposing of patients for emphasis and the deletion of verbal prefixes gives an English "look" to the transitive clause. At the higher level of stylistic structuring, the sequencing of very conservative clauses may produce highly converged structures.

We have now discussed five ways in which linguistic convergence is evident at Fort Chipewyan. The shift of s-consonants to ʃ-consonants has indicated the phonological convergence that has occurred. There are three points we might now make about this phonological process. The first is that by shifting s-consonants to ʃ-consonants, underlying contrasts in Chipewyan and English are neutralized on the surface. This neutralization, in turn, can be seen as mirroring the Cree consonantal system and thus may be thought of as having Cree as its source. The third point is that this phonological process may occur in all of the languages of a speaker. That is, it may be applied as a speaker's rule rather than as a language rule.

Convergence has also occurred in the structure of words. There have been considerable reductions in the complexity of the Chipewyan verb prefix system. As aspect marking has been lost, in many instances there has been a compensating shift to marking of tense with verb suffixes. This shift may be seen as producing Chipewyan structures which are analogous to English structures. At the same time, through the process of idiomatization, an increase in English morphological complexity has developed: the English forms have approximated the Chipewyan (and Cree). Chipewyan verb stems sometimes appear to be changing their verbal status. The so-called classificatory stems may be losing their verbal force, while the verb stems of going seem to be gaining independence from the verb prefix complex. Each of these changes brings Chipewyan closer to English, in which verbs have a greater independence on the one hand and in which the classification of objects is not strongly represented on the other.

There has been relatively little borrowing which may disguise the degree to which the languages have affected each other lexically. Through two processes, meaning convergence and calquing, there is a tendency to develop a single lexical meaning with separate surface forms in the different languages. The view of the lexicon that emerges, then, is of a common core of word meanings which are undifferentiated for specific languages. Each language, then, has a lexical form which, although it is distinctly related to a unique historical source, has been structurally altered to approximate the other languages in the community. At the surface level, the underlying distinctions which have remained are then neutralized to some extent by a set of merging rules of which the shift of s-consonants to ʃ-consonants is one example. At the deepest level of meaning, there is little to differentiate languages; and at the surface there is also considerable merging of distinctions. At the intermediate level, the distinctions between languages are greatest, but, again, these distinctions are being affected by changes in the structure of words.

Clause structures, like word structures, are maintained as distinct for the different languages only at some prototypical level. Thus in some sense it is still fair to characterize Chipewyan as an SOV language and English as an SVO language. Nevertheless, various discourse-governed deletions of required elements, as well as order changes for the purposes of focus or emphasis, may neutralize this prototypical distinction between languages. Optional elements in the clause structures of Chipewyan and English are ordered so that both structures will be the same. This occurs largely in the preverbal portion of the clause, where, through the deletion of prefixes and the incorporation of objects into the verb in Chipewyan, its preverbal structure has come to closely resemble English.

Larger structures of Marcel's narrative have been seen to match in some instances clause for clause, and within clauses there is often a word-for-word matching of structures. This argues for a very similar overall idiomatic or stylistic structuring of narratives. Within this stylistic convergence, the juxtapositioning of quite conservative clause structures is used to produce at least partial mirroring in one language of clause structures in another language.

4

BUSH CONSCIOUSNESS
AND MODERNIZATION

Although the linguistic convergence at Fort Chipewyan is not complete, as we have seen in the study of Marcel's beaver hunt narrative it is a pervasive tendency that affects his language at all levels. The Chipewyan version and the English version are certainly to be described as being in two different languages. At the same time, much of the structure of each text mirrors the structure of the other. In this chapter our interest will be in describing the worldview or reality set that provides the cognitive context in which this linguistic convergence has developed.

Discussions of worldview, however, are frequently hampered by a descriptive problem. We lack a specialized vocabulary for speaking of such things. The terms available to us are highly charged with worldview in themselves and, therefore, tend to reduce the writer to an endless regression of qualification. Bateson (1958) lamented this problem in his work of four decades ago and yet in the ensuing years there has been relatively little development toward a less highly charged vocabulary. To a certain extent we must use the same solution as Bateson did and give a fairly loose, even informal sketch of worldview to begin with and then seek to tighten up the terminology and concepts after some agreement between the writers and the reader has been reached at a general descriptive level. We will begin this discussion of the bush consciousness, then, with an excerpt from R. Scollon's notebook for September 2, 1977.

BROKEN WINDOWS AND NEW BASEMENTS:
THE ENTROPIC ASPECT

Fixing the stove: Ethnographers of speaking don't have a union to define hours of work, coffee breaks, off time and so forth and so it is easy to begin to work all the time without taking any distance from the work. You think about your material all the time you aren't actually collecting. Then the stove has to be fixed.

You are a regular person in a regular household. If the stove doesn't work everyone gets cold but when do you do it? Shouldn't you be out visiting with someone? or listening to tapes? or writing notes?

Well the point of this note is paradoxical. One can't be working at research all the time—you have to fix the stove and eat and even just fool around sometimes. The paradox comes from this stuff then becoming grist for the mill. By fixing my stove I have my first occasion to talk to my neighbor who seemed to put a little different value on me for doing it. This gives content to my "common sense" knowledge that I need to live in a cold climate. And to the extent this content becomes visible to others I look more and more like a regular person.

This is real visibility too. My hands now have black deep in the creases and under the nails. It is the kind of deep soiling that comes of mechanical work and there are very few men around here without it.

A final aspect of this is that I have a means of evaluating other people's knowledge on common grounds. I discover for example that the former tenant in this house has very poor understanding of how mechanical things work. He had carefully covered over the air intake on the stove fan—presumably so that there would be no escape of air. He has also adjusted the stove carburetor so that it was in a state of permanent overflow then tied down the overflow cut off and then as far as I can tell regulated the flow with the valves from the outside source. That is, he had systematically eliminated the carburetor.

The previous tenant's handling of the stove problem strikes me as magical. He did things here and there which together resulted in a partial operation of the stove but without apparent understanding of his manipulations and without understanding the whole and the carburetor's place in it.

Now to close this note on stoves. This same man, Ed Ladouceur came to see me early in our stay here. His conversation then was full of references to the past and the old way of life. This material recorded as a conversation finds support in my observations made while fixing the stove he fixed. Perhaps his dislike of settlement life comes out of his despair at such things as oil stoves. As a man and a head of a household he probably feels he has to fix his own stove (I don't know of any stove repairmen anyway). At the same time he feels incompetent to do it (I didn't feel much better when I started out) and his traditional ways of thinking do not follow closely "cause and effect" mechanical lines.

Of course R. Scollon took his own handling of the same problem to be reasonable and efficient. Within several hours and starting with no knowledge at all about stoves he had learned how the stove worked by dismantling all of the relevant parts and studying their functions. When he had finished he had three things, a stove that worked, a new knowledge of carburetors, and an awareness that our way of thinking was quite different from the former tenant's.

The evidence in Fort Chipewyan for a worldview different from the prevailing Euro-Canadian worldview is abundant. Outsiders react most strongly to things that are seen as oddities. For example, in a recent socioeconomic study of Fort Chipewyan, Moncrieff, Montgomery, and Associates (1971) observed that

> The general condition and external appearance of many Fort Chipewyan homes does leave much to be desired, particularly from the standpoint of improving the general attractiveness of the town itself. Car bodies, furniture and general waste is evident in many yards and a clean-up program could provide jobs for several young people next spring [pp. B92–94].

Their comment could be expanded to include many other things.

- There is broken glass from bottles scattered in the town, on the rocks surrounding the town, and along the roads.
- Glass in windows is broken whenever buildings are left unoccupied for more than a few days.
- Unoccupied houses are broken into and wrecked internally.
- Broken down cars and snowmobiles are found not only in yards but along roads and trails and in the bush, presumably at the place where they last stopped running.
- Dead ravens fill up trash cans at the beach.

As the sixth spring approached since Moncrieff, Montgomery, and Associates made their report and suggested their clean-up and no clean-up program was mounted, it became clearer that the "mess" may be in the eyes of the beholder. And as the list of "unaccountable" things is extended it is more difficult to think of it all as wastefulness.

One sees, for example, that in the summer the town is crisscrossed by a network of footpaths and in the winter by a similar network of snowmobile paths. These paths are followed in clear disrespect for lines laid down by the town survey. The attitude underlying this behavior then begins to look like a disrespect for order that would include the earlier examples as well.

Still one can look further. We have observed, for example, that before someone sits down in a chair the chair is moved to another position. This movement may only be very slight but exceptions are rare. To this may be added the frequency with which people rearrange the furniture in their homes. It is unusual to visit a house twice in the same month and find everything still located in the same place. And even more extreme are the frequent major alterations in the internal structure of houses, where even walls are moved and, exceeding that, where the house itself is moved.

These latter examples escaped us at first. They appeared to be evidence for a taste for orderliness that contradicted the smashed bottles, broken windows, and footpaths. As the examples piled up though, we began to get a feeling of a community-wide flux which indicated a disdain for planning, design, or order, especially where these resulted in a feeling of permanence or stability. While the construction of new basements for old homes looked like community improvement at first, it later began to look like a good excuse to move a whole house to a slightly new position. This was very much like the slight shift in the chair one makes before sitting down. Then in the next summer when all of these basements were filled in again and abandoned and the one house which had stood above a new basement was returned to its original position, we began to see a general antipathy to planning and ordering.

On a small warehouse there was a padlock. The key had been lost so a screwdriver was used to take the hasp off. This hasp had been positioned in the first place so that no more than a screwdriver was required to open the warehouse. The lock and key were superfluous. In this case as in the case of the carburetor, a more complex system had been functionally bypassed.

In another case, someone reported that a furnace in a trailer did not work. It was found that the outside door to the trailer had been left open when the outside temperature was −40°C. The thermostat was set as high as possible and the furnace was still off. What had happened was that the furnace had been working constantly but had not been able to maintain the temperature set on the thermostat because of the constant flow of outside air through the door. It finally shut off automatically because of overheating of the furnace. In this case the occupants did not succeed in overriding the self-regulating properties of the furnace but had tried to use the thermostat setting as an off-and-on switch.

The characteristic of the bush consciousness that can be seen in these cases we are calling **entropic**. If we take "entropy" to refer to the principle that in closed systems disorder increases as energy decreases, we can then use "entropic" to refer to an attitude that places a high value on the general rundown of systematicity in closed systems or, by extension, the opening of closed systems to energy leakage. As a negative characteristic it can be seen as simple destruction of design, plan, or order. Viewed more favorably it can be seen as a preference for lower-order structures over higher-order structures as requiring less energy to maintain. The bypassing of self-regulating structures such as carburetors and thermostats to produce simpler stoves and furnaces is an example of entropic behavior. The moving of a chair or a house from its position is also entropic in its disruption of an existing order. In some cases, of course, the term is somewhat inappropriate where energy is invested in speeding up the internal rundown of systems.

It is not difficult to multiply examples within the community. Although the townsite has been fully surveyed and mapped with all of the lots numbered and all of the streets named, it is a rare person who knows any of these names, and those few who do know them prefer not to use them. The chaos in the giving of directions that results seems to be enjoyed rather than avoided. Of course people who live in the community know where everything is anyway.

The very widespread use of nicknames is probably also related to this entropic aspect of bush consciousness. It openly subverts the identification of person and family so strongly urged by the government, mission, and school. In one case several boys in the same family have switched names. That is, each has as his nickname the "real" name of one of the others.

Another practice is called "jewing." This amounts to any lie or practical joke that dupes another person. Sometimes this term is used for serious cases, that is, where the intent is personal gain or the other person's loss. Our most frequent experience of "jewing," however, is in practical jokes played on us by children. The pleasure is derived from the degree of disruption in someone's thoughts, plans, or activities that is achieved. Again, both the practice and the pleasure taken in it indicate a consciousness of the world in which the disruption of order is highly valued.

We can look now at two examples to see both that this entropic aspect of bush consciousness is widespread and that members of the community are aware of it. There now is a newspaper in Fort Chipewyan, *The Moccasin Telegram*. It was established because of a need felt by some to overcome what was described as a lack of communication in the community. This lack of communication in itself may well be an expression of the same entropic aspect of consciousness. In a recent issue there was an editorial reprinted from *The Native People*. This editorial dealt with what the editor, Danny Littlechild, calls the "Drag-um down attitude." He says in part,

> Why is it people, particularly Native people, have this "Drag-um down" attitude whenever one of their own is making a "Go" of a business venture? . . . . We as Native people must see the importance of divorcing ourselves from this "Drag-um down" attitude that many of us are married to.

The attitude labeled "Drag-um down" by Littlechild is essentially what we are calling the entropic aspect of bush consciousness, with the exception that we are extending the term to include any case where the subversion of design and order are highly valued. By the act of reprinting this editorial, the editor of the *Moccasin Telegram* is also expressing Littlechild's disapproval and tacitly acknowledging the widespread holding of this attitude in Fort Chipewyan.

In the second example we can mention the concept of "home." An attitude toward home was expressed by a young girl when she said, "That's where you usually go." This implies a frequent movement away from there as well. This is borne out in fact by observing the population of Fort Chipewyan. Our first observations were made during the summer. People left the community for many reasons, including holidays, band business, hunting, fishing, berry picking, and religious retreats. Of the people we had contacted during the first 3 months, well over 200, we knew of only several who had stayed at Fort Chipewyan without interruption for the whole time.

We started becoming aware of this as a problem in communication and as a problem in one's sense of reality when several white people who are employed by the government told us that they were leaving for a short time. Their reason for going was because they were "starting to do funny things." This of course we can take as a lighthearted way of saying that they felt they needed to get some distance from Fort Chipewyan in order to restore a sense of balance or reality. Thus our first view of the frequent travel out of the community was that it was caused by various pragmatic concerns, and we assumed that otherwise people would stay. The second view we began to develop was that people felt they had to leave to get relief from a sense of unreality. We attributed this to the generally chaotic state of community communication which we will discuss in the next chapter. Since it was mostly Euro-Canadians who were expressing this view to us, we were probably correct in this conclusion.

The largest amount of travel in and out, however, was in the non-European population. In many cases this travel could be explained by pragmatic concerns. People went out to hunt, trap, fish, and so forth. In many cases, though, there was no obvious explanation.

A partial explanation can be achieved just by reversing assumptions. We assumed as people who had been raised in cities that explanations were needed for people leaving the settlement but not for people returning. If we assume the opposite, then what needs to be explained is why people come into the settlement at all. That is why this approach was too simplistic. People both came in and went out with such frequency that the only solution was that for some reason people wanted to change places frequently.

Although some of this movement can be related to the relief of stress (Honigmann 1946, Savishinsky 1971), this, of course, also fits the entropic consciousness. One moves a chair before sitting down. One changes the furniture around. One remodels the house. One moves the house from one foundation to another. Ultimately one moves oneself to another location. Home is where you usually go but you leave whenever you feel you are getting stuck, whenever the ordering of your life begins to look stable or threatening.

With this frequent disruption of location comes communicative disruption as well. A message does not get passed because someone left town. A meeting has to be canceled because someone has not come back from the bush. A promise is made to speak to a class of students and then the speaker decides to go hunting instead. To anticipate the discussion somewhat, we can suggest now that Euro-Canadians sense this disruption of communication as chaos and need to leave to recover a sense of balance. The entropic aspect of bush consciousness would place a high value on this same disruption in communication, and it is not unlikely that this disruption itself may be a motive for leaving the community.

To round out this sketch of entropic behavior, we only have to mention alcoholism. We do not mean to suggest here a cure for this pervasive disease. It is important to point out, however, that the behavior of the alcoholic as well as that of the nonalcoholic drunkard is a fine example of entropic consciousness. We can suggest here that wherever this aspect of consciousness becomes part of the worldview there can be expected an increased susceptibility to such entropic behavior as excessive drinking.

PRAGMATIC, HOLISTIC KNOWLEDGE:
THE INTEGRATIVE ASPECT

We began with the entropic aspect of the bush consciousness for two reasons. It is by far the most visible aspect and at the same time to the modern consciousness of Euro-Canadians it is the most difficult to understand (Honigmann 1975). To anticipate our discussion a bit we can point out that perhaps the essential characteristic of the modern consciousness is its belief in progress (Berger, Berger, and Kellner 1973), by which is meant the establishment and maintenance of order. The modern consciousness in approaching the bush consciousness at first sees only the entropic aspect and soon wonders if there is any place where order is possible within it. The integrative aspect of the bush consciousness is its aspect of order.

There have been many attempts in recent years to describe this aspect of consciousness in relation to what have been called "native," "natural," "tribal," "oral," or "nonliterate" cultures. Many of these descriptions are so romantic and fanciful that they are little more than projections of the wishful thinking of the writers. On the other hand, there is a group of people who have been working at a deeper, personal understanding of the process of communication between cultures and have produced rather insightful work. The ethnopoet Hedden (1975:57) contrasts nonliterate and literate societies in several ways, three of which are relevant to the concept we are developing here:

Nonliterate	Literate
self-contained: a sense of a world center and correct order of things restricted within tribal borders/the further from the immediate in both space and time, the closer to chaos	*uncontained*: no sense of ceremonial center except through the individual. The world a continuum in time and space. Border extends to the limits of reported world with a sense of similar unreported worlds beyond
particularistic in names for things, states of being, different conditions of things or relationships	*generalistic*, seeking the ultimate law, the irreducible substance, the atom
concepts implicit, "This is the way it always was," in language, art, myth and ritual. Knowledge transmitted orally, by rote, by reenactment	*concepts explicit*, developed to withstand critical analysis, in history, religion, philosophy, science. Learning through texts or lecture based on texts

We have chosen to speak of the "integrative" aspect of bush consciousness in preference to the terms nonliterate, oral, and tribal. The bush culture we are describing is, in fact, partially literate, which makes the first two terms inappropriate. At the same time it cannot be called tribal because at its fullest expression tribal identification is unclear or even nonexistent. We prefer to focus on the attitude toward reality that sees the world as an integrated whole. It is this holistic perception of the world that Hedden captures.

Our own approach to this aspect of consciousness was through trying to understand our own work in light of community reactions to it. We felt, as others must have before us, that we were unable to explain our presence with any conviction except to other Euro-Canadians. The difference at first seemed to be a distinction between literate and nonliterate thinking, but with time that was found to be only a secondary result. The dimension that came to be important had to do with how much people felt they needed to encode knowledge for storage but not for immediate use.

Our own work was at times near one extreme. We were working at recording texts and observations and, although we were trying to understand it as we went along, in principle we felt as if we were a hired sensory apparatus for a knowledge organism. It was primarily our goal to record, encode, and arrange for storage. Later someone else, even though it would probably be us in another capacity, would find a use for the material. Of course, writing greatly facilitates this kind of decontextualized storage, and that may be its main function, but this could be done in other nonliterate ways. For example, the memorization of genealogies practiced in some societies (Goody and Watt 1963) was not done to our knowledge for the sake of the person who did the memorization. It served as a storage system for the society.

Now it seemed that these decontextualized forms of knowledge (Gumperz 1977) could be contrasted at least theoretically with an approach to knowledge in which what is learned is thought of as being for one's own immediate use. A high value would be placed on knowledge that could be readily assimilated to one's existing knowledge. What this would mean is that everyone in the society would have to know all that was considered essential to the maintenance of life and a sense of reality, and that would include a great deal of what was known. Everyone would have to be able to hunt, prepare skins, make fire, make shelter, and so forth. A division of labor and a consequent division of knowledge would endanger the whole group, since the loss of an individual could jeopardize the whole.

We can now describe the integrative aspect of the bush consciousness in these terms as accepting only fully assimilable experience. Far from rejecting order, it seeks a fully integrated view of world order in which there are no elements felt as foreign. What cannot be assimilated to its worldview is rejected as irrelevant or useless knowledge.

There are many ways in which this integrative aspect of bush consciousness is expressed. One expression which we frequently encountered was in the absolute mistrust of hearsay knowledge, written accounts of events, and of history itself. Knowledge that has been mediated is regarded with doubt. True knowledge is considered to be that which one derives from experience. As a result, our work and this report have been treated very skeptically. How could we know anything unless we had lived in the country for a lifetime?

A man told R. Scollon of how he learned to operate a road grader. He sat for several days at the side of the road watching a grader in operation. He watched carefully, and when given the opportunity to take charge, he drove it well and without difficulty. When the man finished this part of the story, he emphasized that he could not say how he did it. This was the point. Learning comes by direct experience and perception, not through the mediation of thought or conscious planning.

This attitude toward learning was frequently reiterated. One learned Chipewyan in the bush by speaking about trapping, it could not be taught. It was said that a dictionary of Chipewyan could not be made. Many attempts to begin classes in Cree and Chipewyan were thwarted, and though in each case a different reason was advanced, the overall pattern indicated that it was felt that learning through conscious teaching either could not be accomplished at all or could be accomplished only for things that it was useless to learn.

In contrast one can look at how people learn bush skills. First one watches the process. Then one tries to do it alone. If it comes out wrong the whole object is discarded and one begins again. The moccasin or snowshoe is not fixed up from where it went bad but thrown away so the learner can start fresh.

It often happens that outsiders find it virtually impossible to follow a discussion or argument. The outsider's description is usually that the discussants lacked logic or that they did not stick to the point. A closer look at several arguments has shown, however, that it is simply a different mode of argumentation. Whereas the modern consciousness focuses on the outcome of the argument, someone wins and someone acquiesces, the bush consciousness focuses on the process of argumentation and seeks consensus throughout. For this reason it often takes very long for a decision to be reached.

In one discussion that we observed, the reason for the discussion was the approaching vote on shortening the tenure of the Chipewyan chief from life to 2 years at a time. This vote would be tantamount to questioning the chiefdom of the current chief. Several members of the group were known to favor electing a new chief and of course this vote would be the first step. In an hour or so of discussion, however, the topic of the vote was never directly broached. In fact, an overt disagreement was never allowed to surface.

The method of argument was for one to say first something like, "We have a good chief." The second would then agree saying, "I agree that we have a good chief but there are other good people." Thus it was only implied that this chief might be replaceable. The first would then say, "I agree that there are other good people but they don't know how to speak for the people." This would be answered by "People should tell their chief what they think, then he can speak for them."

The discussion proceeded in a very circular and holistic way. Much of what had been said before was repeated with only subtle changes in detail. On the whole, these changed details were not of importance except to the extent that they presupposed new underlying assumptions, and that was the ground on which the argument was being carried out. The method was to integrate new details and to shift presuppositions no more rapidly than could be fully assimilated as the discussion progressed.

The bush consciousness looks at history from a similarly integrated point of view. The Chipewyan version of the first contact with Europeans projects the modern importance of French-speaking Europeans back onto the first Europeans contacted. Thus it is said that Chipewyan first contacted the French. This view of the past assumes as Hedden (1975) has said that things are the same as they have always been and is critical of attempts to change the understood order of things.

Some time in the early 1950s a herd of caribou came through the center of the settlement. A number of people told us that people went out and killed them with clubs. It is explained that the caribou do not like to be clubbed and that is why since that year they have not come back to the area. It is assumed that there is a correct and traditional way of doing things that is challenged only at the risk of major destructive changes in the world.

The integrative aspect of the bush consciousness gives a highly ordered view of reality. This view is centered on the life of the individual and alternately takes on faces of ethnocentrism and egocentrism. It highly values its own view of the world and consequently rejects either attempts to change this view or attempts to intrude knowledge that cannot be easily assimilated to this view. It can be seen now that the integrative aspect and the entropic aspect of bush consciousness are deeply related. The entropic aspect is the reaction of the integrative aspect to the intrusion of institutions and structures that are felt to be foreign. To the extent that these institutions and structures cannot be immediately assimilated, they are either ignored or destroyed.

HOLISTIC LEARNING AND TACITURNITY: THE NONINTERVENING ASPECT

There is a third aspect of the bush consciousness which we have chosen to call "nonintervening," though not without misgivings. Where this aspect is displayed, the modern consciousness often views it as "unresponsive," "passive," "sullen," or "withdrawn." These labels may be misleading because they represent a negative reaction to this aspect. We see it as related to the overall preference for a holistic view of the world and human activity. This results in both greater and lesser involvement in activities than the modern consciousness experiences. Since we feel that the focus of the term "intervening" is on the breaking up of whole structures with outside interference, we have used "nonintervening" for this aspect.

The man who watched the road grader for days before attempting to intervene in its operation displayed this aspect of bush consciousness. His approach can be most easily seen by contrast with the way the modern consciousness would approach the same task. The whole activity would be dismantled into component activities and each activity mastered separately before the student would be allowed to attempt the whole task. This massive intervention in the structure of grader operation is foreign to the bush consciousness. One either observes a grader or operates it. There is no middle ground.

Children are trained in nonintervention by being allowed to observe a wide range of activity in the adult world and by having very little restriction placed on their attempts to integrate their activities into this world. They are physically restrained only when there is a danger of major injury. Minor injuries, such as those received from touching hot stoves or falling, are tolerated. They are allowed to learn whatever they can assimilate in this way.

This mode of child rearing is effective for producing the integrative consciousness as well as nonintervention. By rarely intervening in the activities of their children, adults constantly display a model of nonintervention to the children that they are expected to emulate in their own lives. As a result, any intervention by adults is taken as a very serious matter.

When we first began receiving visits from children in our home we were surprised at times by how quickly they would leave. Looking carefully at the situations in which this happened we found that these truncated visits always occurred when we had become excessively interventionist for their taste. An offhand but negative command, such as "Let him play with that now" was enough intervention to send them away convinced that we were very angry with them.

It is important to emphasize that the nonintervening consciousness is applied not only to intervention in the activities of others but to all conscious intervention. In this way it relates very closely to the integrative aspect. It is wrong from this point of view to take any distance from oneself. In one case we knew of a mother who taped over a mirror on a baby's toy because the baby was looking at herself in it. This reflexiveness is discouraged.

People who if necessary would undertake to walk 20 miles without preparation find it hard to understand such activities as walking or running for exercise. What is incomprehensible is that one would analyze an activity such as walking as being conducive to good health and then consciously set about trying to maximize that goal. In one case the jogging of the school principal was given as the cause for all the game disappearing along his route. The animals had easily tolerated any number of cars, trucks, motorcycles, bicycles, and even walking hunters, but one man jogging for his health was thought to have driven them deep into the bush.

Finally, three linguistic manifestations of the nonintervening aspect of bush consciousness can be mentioned. The reading of Chipewyan and Cree syllabics was widespread in the older generation. Nevertheless there were very few people who could write in syllabics. Our own experience is that it only takes several days of active, interventionist study to learn this system of writing, and yet there are very few who have done this.

Here a partial explanation can be found in the nature of the texts being read. The introduction of syllabic writing was with liturgical texts and, at least in this community, syllabic writing was rarely used for any other purpose. People then may have come to view these texts and writing itself as inviolable, something to be received but not interfered with.

In another case this explanation cannot be advanced. This is in the phenomenon called dual-lingualism by Lincoln (1975). It is common for one speaker to be speaking in, say, Cree while the listener responds in Chipewyan. Each understands the other language but does not speak in it. This kind of receptive knowledge of a language has often been called "passive," but here we would prefer to call it nonintervening. One hears and understands structures in the language but does not actively take a role in producing them.

Finally we can comment on a quite general taciturnity we encountered at Fort Chipewyan. Talk is sparse and slowly paced. Where we made attempts to control topics or increase the pace, the conversation would be truncated much as were the visits with children. There is a general avoidance of such negotiated social encounters as conversations, which we take as further evidence of the nonintervening aspect of the bush consciousness.

PERSONAL VIABILITY:
THE INDIVIDUALISTIC ASPECT

To the outsider the integrative aspect of bush consciousness sometimes has the appearance of simple egocentrism. The individual places a high value on his or her own view of the world and in extreme cases even denies that any other view is possible. The world is integrated to the point of view of the individual. This position then leads us to the individualistic aspect of bush consciousness. The central characteristic here is that the individual is considered to be a fully viable unit of survival. Any form of dependence on others is avoided. Freedom is expressed as the highest value. As an aspect of bush consciousness this belief in one's own viability without any sustenance from other members of the society is the central, organizing aspect.

A recent reaction to this individualistic consciousness was the physical education teacher's complaint that it was impossible to teach teamwork in basketball: "They're five individuals out there." At the same time other members of the community were complaining that in an election some people had not been individualistic enough and actually voted for a member of their own family.

This individualistic aspect is not the individualism of the modern consciousness. The emphasis on personal gain and the display of personal power and wealth in relation to the society is lacking. What is emphasized is the freedom from dependence on other people and from society, and this freedom is felt most strongly in the bush. This aspect of course is strongly related to the frequent trips into the bush even where these trips are unmotivated by the need to hunt or gain an income through trapping. In the bush one can continually reassert the ability to live on one's own resources.

It is important to bring up at this point a pervasive feeling of being in harmony with what is called nature. This includes everything in the world with the exception of modern society and its products. Society in general is felt as unnatural in anything larger than very small groups. People returning from the bush frequently mention the feeling of disharmony they feel in the town and say that they are only able to regain their equilibrium by going back into the bush. In spite of the amount of time now spent in town, the bush consciousness feels at home only in the bush.

THE UNITY OF THE FOUR ASPECTS

The bush consciousness can be characterized as individualistic, nonintervening, integrative, and entropic. As we have suggested, these aspects are closely interrelated, and we have suggested that the individualistic aspect is the organizing principle. In some cases, however, there appears to be a contradiction produced by an individual's behavior strongly intervening in the life and affairs of another person. The entropic activity "jewing" is a good case to illustrate the problem. Here the goal is to be disruptive and intervening and yet a great deal of "jewing" is tolerated. On the other hand there is resistance to any attempts to control one's life. Appointments are kept late or not kept at all. Contracts are violated. Jobs are quit.

To reconcile this apparent contradiction we have to look at motive. When the intervening behavior is part of an intentional plan to introduce structure into the activities of another person, it is fully resisted. When the intervening behavior is either entropic in that it is intended only to reduce the existing regularity of one's plans, or individualistic in that it is motivated by the perpetrator's personal considerations, it is tolerated as normal behavior for the individual perpetrating the entropy or individualism.

It is possible to illustrate that it is the motive that makes the difference with a case in which a woman was upset with the social assistance officer over his absence from his office. He had not been in his office and the woman was attributing it to an interest in reducing his contact with the clients he was supposed to serve. That is, she attributed his absence to an attempt to control her access to social assistance. Yet when she confronted him and sought an appointment and he said he would also not be in his office that afternoon because he was going out to the bush, the woman's approach changed entirely into understanding acceptance.

In another case, during the winter, a man had left his pickup truck running outside when he went in to visit a friend. When he went back out, the truck was gone and he was not able to find it until the next day. It had been abandoned where the person who had taken it had run into something. Although the owner of the truck was certainly not pleased with this event, he had no interest in reporting it to the police or in pressing charges against the man who had taken the truck. He said he knew the man had no money and anyway he did not like the police very much himself. The point is that the other man's individualism was tolerated, and allowing it to go unchecked was preferred to the introduction of the legal structuring of a foreign institution.

We may now return to the term we are suggesting, "reality set." The first word of the term is chosen from the phrase "the social construction of reality" and is meant to suggest this theoretical framework. At the same time the term suggests the relativism of reality when it is used as a modifier to the second word, "set." By this we mean to capture the point Bateson (1958) has made of the importance of learning sets or secondary learning. That is, one not only learns the content of one's reality, one learns a way of learning specific to that reality, and thus it forms a learning set. In the term "reality set" we hope both to capture the relative nature of reality from the point of view of the perceiver and also to indicate that a reality implies a mode of learning or adaptation to the known and know-able world.

REALITY SET, ALTERNATE VIEWS

There have been various ways of speaking of world view in the anthropological, sociological, and psychological literatures. This has led to the association of terminology with the theoretical focus of each of these disciplines. Since, again, we have developed a new term, reality set, it is important now for us to review briefly our reasons for not using existing terms in our discussion.

Perhaps the earliest work of relevance to this study is that of Benedict (1934) and Bateson (1958). We could also include Honigmann's work (1946, 1949) in this group and characterize this body of work as ethologi-cal in nature. Benedict was concerned with developing ways of speaking of the whole that was culture, emphasizing especially that this whole was not a simple summation of the parts. The term she preferred was the "configuration" of the culture, and this term has remained to some extent in the literature where researchers have sought a holistic view of culture.

Bateson became aware of Benedict's work while still in the field and it was no doubt influential in his development of the concept of the "ethos" and "eidos" of the Iatmul. He nevertheless preferred to use his own terms because they allowed him to focus separately on two aspects of the Iatmul "configuration," the affective (ethos) and cognitive (eidos). Bate-son's warning here should be remembered as well. He emphasizes the danger of reifying these aspects as separate entities. They are two ways of viewing the same thing, that is, the cultural behavior of the Iatmul.

Following on Bateson's study were Honigmann's studies of first the Fort Nelson Slave (1946) and then the Kaska (1949). These two studies are of particular importance to us not only because of their concern with ethological matters but also because the groups Honigmann studied are quite comparable to the people at Fort Chipewyan. To Bateson's concern with ethos, however, Honigmann added a critical concern with the de-velopment of ethos, that is, socialization. Of course Bateson himself in his 1958 epilogue to *Naven* sees this interest in the development of ethos as crucial to the whole enterprise.

As useful as the work of Benedict, Bateson, and Honigmann is to us, we are unable to use it directly for one important reason. The focus in all of this work is cultural. That is, an attempt has been made to relate an ethos (eidos, configuration, worldview) to a cultural group. On the whole, the group is taken as given. It is true that there is not an insistence on a one-ethos–one-group view. That is, Bateson speaks of the male and female ethoses of the Iatmul as two separate positions. They are, however, in a fixed relationship of complementarity within a larger whole which is the Iatmul culture. Honigmann, on the other hand, does speak of acculturation for the Fort Nelson Slave. But for the Slave as well as for the Kaska, Honigmann's ultimate goal was historical reconstruction, and this led him to seek a reconstructed ethos which would be free from the effects of contact.

The work of Honigmann remains of central importance in spite of his vacillation between wanting to reconstruct an unaffected aboriginal ethos for a discrete cultural group, the Kaska, and his later realization that this ethos is characteristic of many (if not all) northern Athabaskan groups (1975). The explanation that would be advanced, we presume, would be that this ethos was characteristic of some protogroup, since it is found in the descended modern northern groups today. We should like to advance an alternative explanation which relates this "ethos" to the social conditions found at least throughout the subarctic transitional forest and thus found in all of the groups inhabiting that zone to some extent. Since "ethos" has been used by Honigmann and Bateson to refer to some cognitive–affective reflections of specific cultures, we feel it is better to avoid this term in the case of Fort Chipewyan since we ultimately intend to suggest a much broader distribution of the worldview we are seeking to characterize.

A second reason we are interested in Honigmann's work is because of the emphasis he places on the ontogenetic development of ethos. In this we see an important correlation with the work of Jean Piaget. Piaget's studies of what he calls intelligence are crucially tied to cognitive development (Flavell 1963). His position is that our understanding of what is known cannot be divorced from an understanding of how it comes to be known. At first it may appear to be unfortunate for our purposes that the work of Piaget is ethnocentric in the extreme. If we consider Piaget's work to be a careful study of the eidos of the modern consciousness from the inside view of a person who himself holds this position, however, we can still find it quite useful for our purposes. We are especially interested in his concept of adaptation, which we will need in speaking of the nonintervening aspect of the bush consciousness.

We have thus, on the one hand, the ethological literature, which is overly restricted to the study of discrete cultural groups to be useful for our purposes, and Piaget's cognitive psychology, which is too falsely universalistic to be taken at face value on the other. The approach that we have found to suit our needs most closely is that which has been called the sociology of knowledge. This field concerns itself with the social construction of reality (Berger and Luckmann 1966) and as such is centered in the philosophical tradition of phenomenology. We have found this work useful for several reasons. First in Berger, Berger, and Kellner's (1973) *The Homeless Mind* there is an insightful exposition of the way of thinking associated with modern technological society which they have called the "modern consciousness." This description is rather important because of the high level of generality at which it is developed. At this level of generality, there is much held in common among all societies in which there is modern, technological, industrial production. Thus at least the United States, Japan, the Soviet Union, and Western Europe hold this basic position in contrast to the so-called developing countries. It is because we would also want to mark worldview distinctions between these groups that the term worldview is too specific for our purposes.

Second, Berger, Berger, and Kellner have tied the development of the modern consciousness to modern technology and the institutions of this technology, and thus there is differential participation by individuals in the society. This is especially true in developing nations where the central problem of their work, the conflict of consciousness, is focused.

A third reason why this framework is of use to us is because it is our concern to relate linguistic convergence to the way in which language is known by speakers. For this reason we require a point of view that allows us to focus centrally on knowledge. In its relation to phenomenological philosophy, the social construction of reality emphasizes the study of the everyday reality as expressed by people as the "world as usual." It is this "world as usual" that we are seeking to characterize for Fort Chipewyan.

A fourth reason for using this framework is the close connection to the work of the various people studying conversation and other linguistic social interaction. Because of the philosophical connections among ethnomethodologists, cognitive sociologists, and cognitive anthropologists, it is possible to relate our discussion quite directly to that body of work.

Finally, this framework is well suited to developmental formulation. Even where primary socialization is not specifically studied, it is implied as a central and interesting aspect of the social construction of reality.

THE MODERN CONSCIOUSNESS

In fixing the stove, R. Scollon approached an object and a problem that were, in most respects, the same object and problem that the former tenant had faced. It is clear from their different actions on the object and from their different solutions to the problem that they were perceiving this very ordinary oil stove in radically different ways. The difference lies not in the object but in the actors' conceptions of the world in which this object is included. Our experience of this world is as an ordinary everyday world. We are sure the former tenant's experience of his world is equally unexceptional. This ordinary everyday consciousness of the world we live in constitutes our reality set. We will first briefly characterize our reality set, the modern consciousness, and then discuss the reality set that we are calling the bush consciousness.

The first of these has been treated at length by Berger, Berger, and Kellner (1973). The modern consciousness that they discuss is widely held throughout European technological society. This is the reality set with which R. Scollon approached his oil stove, dismantled it, and reassembled it, as well as the reality set with which we use that activity as an example here. To begin with, Berger, Berger, and Kellner (1975) have defined modernization as "the institutional concomitants of technologically induced economic growth [p. 9]." The modern consciousness derives from this in that it makes a deep assertion of the superiority of modern, technological life over any other. The primary carriers of this modernization are the institutions of technology and bureaucracy. Cities and sociocultural pluralism are secondary carriers. There are three aspects which are central to the modern consciousness. The first of these derives from the technology. To the modern consciousness it appears that there is a vast store of technological and other knowledge. From the individual point of view it is assumed that although one does not know everything, one could acquire this knowledge, given the appropriate training. For the things not known by the individual it is assumed that there is an expert who does know and who could be consulted. To a great extent our presence at Fort Chipewyan was a manifestation of this aspect. This volume further displays this view in making available to members of the society the results of our fieldwork and the putative benefits of our presumed expertise.

Modern technology is founded on a production principle of the separation of labor into its component activities. This gives to the person a sense of being a part in a much larger organization, the ultimate goals of which are largely out of his control but which depend on his activity. The result of this separation of labor is a principle of componentiality. The world is viewed as being separable into distinct parts. Furthermore, any part is understood as replaceable by another similar part. On the part of the individual we assume equivalence of training, background and knowledge. In schools, children are age graded, skill graded, and intelligence graded. In jobs, workers are hired, trained, and replaced by categories, not as unique individuals. And thus the individual is seen as consisting of component roles, a worker by day, a parent by night, and a tourist on holidays. Thus the componentiality of the assembly line reflects back onto the role structure of the person. This componentiality is systematized by the bureaucratic organization of the modern consciousness that views the world as orderly and predictable. Everything is placed in order in a taxonomic arrangement. Nothing is allowed to remain as an exception. Miscellaneous categories are eschewed.

A great deal more could be said about this reality set if it were our primary focus. There are two reasons, however, for not engaging in a long discourse on the modern consciousness. The first is that it has been well described by Berger, Berger, and Kellner (1973) and here it is our goal simply to sketch in the outline. At the same time we need only to point out that this is the reality set of the reader, the authors, and of the body of literature to which this volume seeks to be a contribution. Our second reason then for not engaging in a full discussion of this reality set is that wherever the psychological, sociological, linguistic, or anthropological literatures have been involved in ethnocentric discussions of the nature of the individual, society, language, or man, they have unwittingly been elaborating our own reality set. As an example of our meaning here we will look briefly at two areas of research in our society, Piaget's concept of intelligence, and ethnomethodological conversational analysis.

Piaget argues that the two central factors of intelligence are organization and adaptation (Flavell 1963, Piaget 1972). He seeks in his work to describe on the one hand the structures of intelligence, that is, its organization, and on the other, the development of structures, that is, adaptation of the individual over time to the environment. For Piaget, of course, the earliest intelligence is sensorimotor and derives from the child's experience with the physical world. The highest development of the adult's intelligence is, of course, Piaget's own philosophic concern with epistemology—as he puts it, "genetic epistemology."

In this work we see Piaget as offering a classical example of the view that the modern consciousness takes of knowledge. He is concerned not only with the contents of intelligence, but also with the structure and development of intelligence. Not only does he want to study what we know, he also wants to study how we come to know it. In this Piaget does not take a culturally relativistic perspective. One can search his writings in vain for suggestions that it is possible for adult intelligence to be organized in alternate ways. The closest one comes is in early suggestions of analogies between so-called "primitive" thinking and that of children (Piaget 1969).

As we have suggested above, then, Piaget's view of intelligence as organization and adaptation can be taken as an expression of the view that the modern consciousness takes of itself. That is, Piaget's work studies the eidos (to use Bateson's term) of the modern consciousness. We would now like to look more closely at his concept of adaptation because of the use we will make of it later in contrasting with the nonintervening aspect of the bush consciousness.

Piaget sees adaptation as consisting of two indissociable components, assimilation and accommodation. Any act of adaptation involves both components. Piaget's first insight came in the study of mollusks where he noticed that the very primary process of ingestion required both modification in the structure of the ingested substance (assimilation) and modification in the structure of the organism (accommodation). From this he developed the analogous concept that any act of knowing (adapting to the knowable world) required both changes in the structure of what was known (assimilation) and changes in the internal structure of the knower, the intelligence. These latter changes he refers to as accommodation.

In his work with children, Piaget (1962) then related the ascendancy of assimilation over accommodation to play, and the ascendancy of accommodation over assimilation to imitation. That is, where the child restructures the world so strongly that it loses its pragmatic grounding as "real world," we consider the activity to be play. Where the child restructures his or her own internal mental organization so strongly as to lose individuality, we consider it imitation. Piaget then discusses the swing from play to imitation and back, the swing between assimilation and accommodation, in the seeking of equilibrium states that are the structures of intelligence.

Piaget's view of adaptation in regards to intelligence or knowledge is important to us because of its dual emphasis on the organism or individual on the one hand and the environment or society on the other. In our concern with the social construction of reality we are putting a greater emphasis on the environment than Piaget would choose to do, no doubt, but our central concern requires a mechanism for change or adaptation as does Piaget's. We wish, then, to add Piaget's view of adaptation to Berger, Berger, and Kellner's view of the modern consciousness.

Having added Piaget, we now have a mechanism for interaction with the knowable world. To round out the view of the modern consciousness, we need to introduce the recent body of work generally known as conversational analysis. In this work researchers with anthropological, sociological, linguistic, and psychological perspectives have sought to develop our knowledge of the negotiated exchange of points of view that takes place in conversation. Gumperz's (n.d.) summary of this body of work leads him to suggest its usefulness in attempting to "account for both shared grammatical knowledge and for differences in communicative style and knowledge that characterize our modern culturally diverse societies [p. 26]."

Goffman (1976) uses talk (conversation in its most general sense) as "an example of that arrangement by which individuals come together and sustain matters having a ratified, joint, current, and running claim upon attention, a claim which lodges them together in some sort of intersubjective mental world [p. 308]."

Conversational analysis, then, reflects the importance of talking in modernized society as a means of negotiating and testing intersubjective reality among other things. Where Piaget has described a general theoretical mechanism of adaptation, the conversational analysts have begun to develop a much fuller understanding of this mechanism in actual interpersonal situations.

We can now summarize the modern consciousness as componential in that it views the vast store of knowledge as separable into component parts and in that it views individuals as components in a much larger social whole. It is bureaucratic in its taxonomic ordering of this social organism. It sees knowledge as being acquired by simultaneous changes both in what is to be known and in the knower. This factor combined with the componentiality of knowledge leads to the development of knowledge in incremental steps. Among the mechanisms by which this reality set is maintained is ordinary talk, in which the conversational partners continually test, modify and develop their intersubjective reality.

THE BUSH CONSCIOUSNESS

In arguing for our choice of a new term, reality set, we said that, among other things, it was the high level of generality of this term that appealed to us. We wanted to consider the reality set held in common by modernized people in technologically developed societies, despite lower-level cultural and worldview differences, in contrast with the bush consciousness. Now we are turning again to the bush consciousness to argue that this reality set is also of considerable generality and not restricted solely to members of some discrete ethnic or cultural group.

Honigmann, who was the first to systematically develop a concept like the bush consciousness, did so in relation first to the Slave (Honigmann 1946) and then to the Kaska (Honigmann 1949) northern Athabaskan groups several hundred miles to the west of Fort Chipewyan. Of course, he did not use our term. At that time he was, as we have said, concerned with characterizing the aboriginal ethos of these Athabaskan people. Some years later (1975) he commented:

> Comparative studies made among the Slave and Dogrib Indians suggest that internal variation is present among the Kaska, but those studies also suggest that the generalization I offer concerning Kaska personality traits are probably reasonably prevalent

in that group, for a number of the same ones recur in the other groups. Hence, they are probably general to the Athapaskan people in western Canada. The high evaluation of personal independence, present-orientedness, suppression of hostility, dependency strivings, and emotional suppression are specific traits that I noted among the Kaska whose recurrence in other Athapaskan groups has been demonstrated by other observers [p. 553].

Thus in the intervening years, descriptions have come forth indicating some generality for these personality traits. VanStone (1963) has commented about the community of Snowdrift to the north that, "Snowdrift is a bush community exhibiting a sort of bush culture that is duplicated many times in many places throughout the Canadian north [p. 109]." Helm *et al.* (1975) have suggested that

In spite of the linguistic break between Algonkian and Athapaskan in the Subarctic, the contact events of the last 250 years, as well as the precontact conditions of the physical and intercultural environment, provide a more immediate comparability of Indian adaptation and experience from the eastern slopes of the Rockies to the Labrador Peninsula than obtains across the Northern Athapaskan domain *per se* [p. 304].

This theme is now being heard in studies throughout the Athabaskan and Algonkian area of North America. Researchers are now declining to draw any sharp discontinuities anywhere in the region, and what is said about one group, however that group may be defined, tends to ring true for another group not originally included. At the same time, researchers are finding it difficult to establish a sense of community even at the local level. Smith (1970) says of Brochet, Saskatchewan, "it is not possible to say that a sense of community exists that embraces all Chipewyan or all Cree, much less the entire village [p. 64]." If it is difficult in a global sense to distinguish an Algonkian and an Athabaskan reality set, we must remember Mandelbaum's (1940) early comment on the mixing of groups:

The "Cree" are a composite of many distinct Indian societies who moved West with the fur forts . . . . The Cree became an amalgam of many different tribal stocks. Not only do we find that the Assiniboin, Monsoni, Ojibway, and the Algonkin to the east and south lived among the Cree, but even their enemies, the Dakota, the Athapascans, and the Blackfoot occasionally camped with and married into the bands of the Cree [p. 180].

This theme, which has been further reiterated by Cunningham (1969), Cox (1969), and Fisher (1969), gives us reason to suspect, at least, that the reality set we are describing as the bush consciousness may in fact be considered one of much generality. As we shall see subsequently, research done throughout the area on northern Athabaskan and Algonkian groups points to much similarity in the reality set of these people.

The first characteristic on which research has focused has been individuality. Mason (1946), who conducted field research in the areas of Fort

Chipewyan and Great Slave Lake in 1913, comments that "individualism seems to be the key to the interpretation of this culture. The individual is bound by few taboos and coerced by no authority [p. 43]." This aspect of the bush consciousness has been reiterated by Honigmann (1946, 1949) for the Fort Nelson Slave and for the Kaska at Lower Post, British Columbia, by VanStone (1963) for the Old Crow Kutchin, by Savishinsky (1970, 1971) for the Colville Lake Hare, and by McClellan (1970) for the Tutchone in the Yukon Territory. McClellan's comments are insightful because of the relationship she draws between the individualistic aspect of the bush consciousness and her own difficulties in understanding ethnic groupings:

> It is my present feeling that among the Indians I know best, most questions about ethnic *groups* are beside the point. I think that the Tutchone, for example, have often restructured my questions about the *group* to which a person belongs, so as to focus much more specifically than I realized on the particular *individual*. My failure to appreciate the Athabascan emphasis on the individual only compounded some of my confusion about ethnic groupings [p. XIV].

We might add here that McClellan's insistence that this individual is an Athabaskan, that is, primarily a member of a linguistic and cultural group, may be further compounding the problem. At least as far as the individualistic aspect of the bush consciousness is concerned, Preston (1975) has considered it central to the Cree character he describes for James Bay Cree, and before him, Hallowell (1946) for the Saulteaux.

These latter two cases are quite informative in that they also point to both the integrative aspect and the nonintervening aspect as further characteristics. That is, this reality set is internally reasonably consistent wherever it is found.

The individualistic aspect of the bush consciousness, then, is its central, organizing aspect. As Honigmann (1949) says for the Kaska, "So long as the Kaska can contain their physical and social environmental participation within narrow limits, they feel resourceful, capable, and safe; trouble is avoided, life is simple, and the individual is supreme [p. 306]."

Knowledge in this reality set is conceived of as the result of the personal experience of the individual. As Preston (1975) has said for the Cree, "In the process of life-long socialization an individual develops increased ability to symbolically integrate the meaning of experiences [p. 278]." This reflects the integrative aspect of the bush consciousness which tends to "view events personally rather than objectively [p. 9]." Honigmann sees this aspect as utilitarian. The aim is toward "mastery of experience via concrete, immediate thinking, sparing a minimum of attention for abstract speculation or non-functional elements of craftsmanship like beauty, decoration, and perfectionism [p. 258].'' Honigmann relates this taste for the concrete and pragmatic to the individualistic aspect in that "the concrete gives the Indian a sense of mastery, while the abstract means losing control [p. 261]."

A further manifestation of both the integrative and individualistic aspects is the lack of specialization of knowledge. This has been mentioned both by Honigmann (1949) and Fisher (1969). Fisher points out that "most of the important economic or social tasks are performed within the family hunting group by non-specialists [p. 15]."

What is known, then, is known pragmatically from the point of view of the experience of the individual. Foreign elements are integrated, and so Vandersteene (1970) says that in putatively traditional Cree legends "it is often difficult to make a distinction between the elements of strictly pagan origins and those which have undergone the influence of Christianity [p. 42]." Gardner (1966) uses the term "memorate knowledge" to characterize knowledge of this sort; this is "knowledge which is held on the idiosyncratic level, the result of personal experience and individual analysis, rather than being derived from group opinion or tradition [p. 390]."

The bush consciousness, then, is individualistic and integrative. These two aspects are closely related in that knowledge is highly personal and idiosyncratic. There is a positive avoidance of social traditions or the specialized knowledge of others which parallels a general avoidance of interference in others' lives. This avoidance is reflected in the third aspect of the reality set, the nonintervening aspect.

We may look at this aspect in two ways. First we can consider it in light of learning or education, and then we can look at interpersonal relationships, especially as mediated by talk. Most researchers have commented on the nonintervening aspect of learning. VanStone (1963) is perhaps typical: "It is difficult to detect the ways in which children learn the techniques of sub-arctic living [p. 44]." When boys are taken on hunting trips the most they are allowed to do is run the outboard motor a while on the way home. "In other words, if a boy learns anything on trips of this kind, he does so entirely from observation [p. 44]."

It is interesting and amusing to compare this with Honigmann's (1949) very similar comment:

> Instruction and direction are rarely explicit. "Do this," is the formula, and the child is left with the task of working out the details of an activity for himself. . . . The same kind of teaching was used with the ethnographer. Activities were illustrated but never explained in detail, the exposition of principles being ignored. On the second day of a journey with dog team and toboggan, the handling of the vehicle was entrusted to the ethnographer without a word of instruction regarding the techniques of managing the dogs [p. 185].

There are two ways in which this mode of learning may be called nonintervening. As educator, the teacher does not directly intervene in the activities of the student. The child (or the ethnographer) is expected to watch and learn without active intervention on the part of the teacher. On the other hand, the learner is expected to learn how to do things without immediately intervening in their operation. That is, learning is holistic and not incremental.

To adapt Piaget's terminology, we can suggest that nonintervening learning is characterized by a dissociation of assimilation and accommodation; where for the modern consciousness learning is characterized by an indissociable equilibrium of assimilation and accomodation, for the bush consciousness it is characterized by first a period of accommodation in which the learner watches and observes, adjusting the structure of his or her knowledge to the object or event being observed. This is followed by a period of a very high level of assimilation. The world is operated on in a total, holistic way, and every attempt is made to restructure it to fit the cognitive structure of the individual. From the point of view of the modern consciousness this initial period appears passive or inactive and some, such as VanStone, fail to see this as part of the process of learning. The second period of assimilation is viewed as too much intervention in the action and structures of the world. Thus in the example we gave in which a man learned to operate a road grader by first watching for 3 days and then beginning to grade a road, no doubt the first period would be taken by the modernized observer as inactivity and the second as over-confident bravado. From the point of view of the highly individualistic bush consciousness, however, this mode of learning that swings from accommodation to assimilation is an integral aspect of the reality.

It is important to recall Honigmann's (1949) point that "in the early years of life it is not so much *what* is learned as *how* learning takes place that is important in patterning the world and self-views [p. 14]." Thus early education is indulgent (Chance 1968; Gardner 1966; Hatt 1969; Honigmann 1946, 1949; McClellan 1970; Sindell 1968) and in being indulgent it displays for the learner a model of the world in which the reality of the individual is supreme and not to be challenged by the intervention in his or her affairs or views by others.

We may also look at nonintervention in terms of interpersonal relations. It has frequently been observed that there is a general taciturnity among holders of the bush consciousness. Honigmann (1949) observes that "in the family as well as in other groups there is a relatively low value on conversation [p. 166]"; "although individual loquacity varies, in general people tend to say little during a visit (to the discomfort of white hosts!), the situation often resembling a roomful of disparate individuals [p. 168]." This behavior is very much like that of Kutchins in Arctic Village (Scollon 1975) and Chipewyan at Snowdrift (VanStone 1963). VanStone has also added the observation that volubility increases with drinking and along with volubility comes the increased use of English.

In order to understand the avoidance of talk as a reflection of the bush consciousness we need to recall Goffman's observation that one of the things going on when people talk is a negotiation of an intersubjective reality (1976). Where the value is placed on a highly individualistic and personal view of reality, it is then at least consonant with this value that individuals should avoid contexts in which this personal reality is open to challenge and negotiation. We can see, then, that nonintervention in the affairs of others is extended to include nonnegotiation of personal, individualistic reality. To the extent that ordinary conversation is concerned with the negotiation of intersubjective reality, it is avoided.

We can now look at what appears to be a contradiction in Honigmann's (1949) observations. He noted that for some two or three individuals he encountered a "rapid flow of more or less chronological detail which contained little in the way of personal attitudes or reactions to life experiences [p. 21]". This rapid flow of talk would stand as a contradiction to the general taciturnity were it not for the fact emphasized by Honigmann that this rapid flow contained little which would commit the speaker on matters of "personal attitudes or reactions to life experiences," that is, to reality set.

The fourth aspect of this reality set we have called entropic. On the whole there are few direct comments about this aspect from linguists and ethnographers. Honigmann (1946) does say about the Slave that "that individualistic goal of the configuration is in conflict with the corporate goal of the white culture [p. 149]"; and about the Kaska he (1968) says that "the Kaska Indians extended profound, deliberately cultivated disrespect to authority symbols which represent the larger Candian society of which the Indians formed a part [p. 222]." He (1949) even gives a rather full anecdote which captures the general distaste for planning and systematicity that we have called entropic:

> The Kaska Indian appears unable to adhere to a sequence of causally related activities whose end lies in the relative present. This was demonstrated when Richard Day and a Tahltan youth announced the intention of setting a brew in the bush. Richard first forgot to buy the ingredients, making it necessary to use the other boy's supplies. It was then discovered that the brew barrel was in Richard's house, where Edward Prince was also living. Because of his tendency to drink unready liquor, Edward could not safely be told of the brew before its completion. The barrel, therefore, had to be secured without Edward's knowledge. A good way of doing this, Richard decided, was to have a dance and, while Edward was fiddling, Richard would slip away and cache the barrel. The dance was held as planned but Richard became

interested in "bothering" June Barre, and as a result never left the dancehouse. The brew was postponed until the following day. Often people do not even try to plan their behavior systematically. Rarely do people come to a store knowing in detail what must be purchased. As a result, shopping is a slow process in which the buyer often uses the mercantile display to remind him of his needs. Actually few activities are undertaken with a plan. Either the individual operates through a series of automatic habits or muddles through by making adjustments as required. Watching Richard and his Tahltan companion finally set brew, one got the impression that they had no clearly conceptualized notion of the total process of which the separate acts were parts. After each step they stopped to discuss what was next in order. Such lack of planning often results in being unprepared to complete an activity. A house begun in the fall is often left unfinished for a year, until the builder can, for example, secure additional materials to complete the roof whose requirements were underestimated. Lack of preparedness was evidenced when Irene Wiley, after heating water to wash clothes, discovered that she lacked soap powder.

All of these behaviors, involving planning for relatively immediate goals, reveal not only utilitarian antipathy to conceptualization and systematization, but are also relaxed, indecisive modes of attending to problems of living. They reveal the operation of a flexible motivation that is not bound by rigorous rules. In packing and storage we find a similar lack of compulsive order, no indication of a notion like: "A place for everything and everything in its place" [p. 271].

On the whole, however, researchers have avoided direct discussion of the entropic aspect of the bush consciousness. There are, nevertheless, frequent indirect indications that this aspect was fully in evidence. This expression normally shows up in a despair fieldworkers have felt in trying to engage in controlled systematic research. When Lowie (1959) went into the area in 1908 he found the people at Fort Chipewyan "highly suspicious" and in cases "uncompromisingly refractory [p. 31]." He considered his trip there to be scientifically the least fruitful trip he had ever made.

Shortly after him in 1913, Mason (1946) undertook a summer's fieldwork in the area and had a similar experience. He reports "many and long periods when linguistic informants or interpreters were not available [p. 3]." At Fort McMurray "conditions for ethnological work were not good [p. 7]." At Forth Smith, "as elsewhere, great difficulty was met in securing the services of an interpreter [p. 7]," and when he finally secured one, "progress was slow and unsatisfactory [p. 7]." At Fort Resolution where he intended to stay, "as everywhere much vexatious difficulty in working was found [p. 7]." When he gave up at Fort Resolution and went on to Fort Rae, "the promised available interpreters did not materialize [p. 9]." Mason's general comment is about as openly condemnatory as an ethnographer is likely to become:

Personally I found the natives with whom I came into close contact generally cleanly, pleasant though retiring and suspicious, comparatively honest, but inclined to be greedy, grasping, and ungrateful. Practically all travelers from Hearne down, as well as traders anathematize their dishonesty, unreliability, ungratefulness, cruelty, incompetence, and general meanness. . . .

> From their former days of impotent terror they have naturally inherited a
> suspicious dislike of all strangers, and a cowardly disposition with its natural concom-
> itants, a bullying contempt for weaker parties, and a selfishness and general unrelia-
> bility. Their principal object is to get the most out of their transactions with all others,
> and in this respect their relations with the earlier fur traders have but rendered them
> sharper. As among all peoples there are individuals of better and of worse characteris-
> tics than the average, the latter class seems to be larger and the general average lower
> among these tribes than usual [p. 30].

It is clear that Mason, as Lowie before him, had had a hard time. This reaction, however, is the ordinary reaction of the modern consciousness to the bush consciousness. One sees it in fur traders, ethnographers, Indian Affairs officials, schoolteachers, and missionaries. The highly individualistic and integrative world of the bush consciousness strikes the modernized person as chaotic where it is not directed toward the person and as hostile and suspicious where it is. This entropic aspect of the bush consciousness is as much a reaction of the modern consciousness as it is a property of the bush consciousness. As such, we may think of it as only existing to the extent there is contact between the two reality sets. This is why it has not appeared frequently in other reports, even where these reports have treated other aspects of this reality set.

Osgood in his 1928 fieldwork undoubtedly experienced the same problem but he did not directly speak of it until recently. He (1975) attributes his difficulties at Colville Lake to inexperience and describes his trip as "an anthropological fiasco [p. 517]." He could find no native interpreters and only very reluctantly produced a final report on his time in the field.

Although Osgood attributes his own difficulties to inexperience he was careful to warn Honigmann (1949) that "certain marked personality features distinguished Athapaskan people which might make it difficult to approach them in interpersonal relations [p. 3]."

Honigmann reports that Osgood's observation was corroborated by his field experience both at Fort Nelson in 1943 and at Lower Post in 1944–1945. In both places he had difficulty finding informants and also experienced most of the general problems associated with the entropic aspect of the bush consciousness.

Finally, we can note that this problem does not seem to be restricted to Northern Athabaskan research. Bloomfield found difficulty in locating "good" Cree informants and found it necessary to give an apology as part of his introduction (1930).

We can see then that what is perhaps the most salient of the aspects of the bush consciousness, the entropic aspect, is experienced by the researcher as difficulty in field method and as such is sometimes not considered to be directly relevant to the content of the fieldwork.

REALITY SET AND THE NATURE OF LANGUAGE

Language as part of the knowable world is susceptible to being affected by the assumptions the knower makes about this world and by the way in which things are learned. Now that we have discussed the two reality sets, the bush consciousness and the modern consciousness, we are in a position to relate each of these to the nature of language as it is understood by each.

To the individualistic and integrative bush consciousness, language is also highly integrated to the personal experience of the speaker. There are no normative standards or higher values placed on the speech of others. One is one's own expert, but at the same time because of the nonintervening aspect, no attempt is made to impose one's own values on others. Thus language is seen as highly individualized and variable. This contrasts, of course, with the normative standards of the modern consciousness. We have our dictionaries, grammars, and good speakers. We also have a whole range of specialists in language, from school teachers to logicians and linguists. Even where the insistence against normative standards is loudest, that is, among linguists, we can see the very fact of professional specialization in the analysis of language as reflecting the view that there is something there to be studied that is at least a constant enough phenomenon to be susceptible to formal treatment.

This leads to a second point which is that the bush consciousness resists any attempt to systematize or organize knowledge beyond the integration of one's own experience. Again, language is seen as not organizable in any global sense and there is a positive resistance to attempts to introduce systematization. This shows up most strongly in the attempts of fieldworkers to get people to make judgmental statements about language or in fact to work at all in the study of language. There is an obvious contrast with the modernized goals of the fieldworker and this contrast produces the "vexatious difficulty in working conditions," mentioned by Mason above.

A third point of comparison relates to the pragmatic nature of knowledge in the bush consciousness. Language that is not of immediate value in the ongoing situation is considered of little or no interest. This contrasts with the extreme forms of decontextualized knowledge found in modernized society. In fact these two views encounter each other nearly at the extreme when a fieldworker seeks to record a text in a language which he or she does not understand for storage in a museum. It is difficult to imagine a use of language more decontextualized than this and as such there is little that is more antithetical to the bush consciousness. It is not surprising that fieldworkers find it difficult to gain cooperation in the field at this task.

A fourth way in which the two reality sets contrast is on the dimension of taciturnity–volubility. This is, as we have suggested, related to the negotiation of intersubjective reality and as such is a very sensitive point for the bush consciousness, especially where it feels under pressure from the modern consciousness. Thus where the fieldworker seeks to increase talk for the purposes of recording either the speech itself or its contents, the opposite effect results. Just here people become reticent and try to avoid such talk-based encounters. To the nonintervening aspect of the bush consciousness, the attempts of the linguist or ethnographer to establish rapport through talk appear as aggression. The more the researcher relies on talk to negotiate this ''rapport,'' the more aggressive he or she is felt to have become and the greater the resistance and general taciturnity become. The nonintervening aspect then produces interpersonal situations in which the most suitable actions for the ethnographer or linguist are the least desirable for the informant, and the mutual understanding which the modern consciousness seeks is avoided by the bush consciousness.

A fifth difference between the two reality sets is in the manner of learning. For the bush consciousness, learning is holistic, characterized by a dissociation of accommodation and assimilation. Language, then, is learned in larger pieces than for the modern consciousness, and immediate feedback is not assumed. For children this shows up as an initial apparent slowness. There is no expectation that children will speak until 4 or 5 years of age (Honigmann 1949; R. Scollon 1975). For adults this shows up as the phenomenon of dual-lingualism (Lincoln 1975). There is no expectation that a person who can understand speech in a language should also be able to speak that language. Where the modern consciousness assumes an indissociability of assimilation and accommodation (or in this case of speaking and hearing) and treats cases of comprehension without production as marginal or transitional, this is taken as a normal possibility by the bush consciousness.

We can now summarize these positions on the nature of language. The bush consciousness, because of the integrative aspect, tends to reduce all experience to an internally integrated whole. Where the speaker has experience with various languages this produces linguistic convergence. At the same time, since the experience of the individual may include speech to others who have not produced such converged models of language, there is some pressure to maintain some diversity. In all cases this knowledge will be holistic and nonspecialized and the individual will resist attempts by others to regularize and systematize this knowledge.

To the modern consciousness, language is thought of as consisting of discrete systems, languages, and within those systems, discrete components (grammars, lexicons, texts, sentences, clauses, words, and segments). The individual speaker and his or her knowledge are thought of as parts of a larger organized whole, the language, and as a result the speech of the individual is considered idiosyncratic and defective, the larger whole being inferred from this imperfect behavior of individuals. The individual will, of course, recognize the possibility of expertise, and even where the opinions of experts may be questioned, the existence of those experts is not.

CONVERGENCE AND THE BUSH CONSCIOUSNESS

We may now return to the linguistic convergence we have observed at Fort Chipewyan and look at it in light of the concept of the bush consciousness. In Chapter 3, we discussed the phonological variation that was present in the various languages at Fort Chipewyan. As an example we look at the shift of s-consonants to ʃ-consonants and suggested that this shift was used by speakers to indicate their position in the conflict between reality sets in the community. We are now in a better position to discuss why these alternations should work in this way.

As we have said, the bush consciousness places a positive value on convergence on the one hand and on the reduction of systematicity on the other. As convergence, the shifting of s-consonants to ʃ-consonants can be seen as a convergence with the Cree phonological system. This is further supported by the fact that these shifts also neutralize underlying distinctions in English and Chipewyan (and French) and operate to reduce the systematicity of these languages, at least in their surface forms. By reducing the discreteness of the historically separate phonological systems, this set of consonant shifts nicely reflects the entropic aspect of the bush consciousness reality set.

A third way in which these shifts manifest reality set is in the domain in which they operate. For the people we have characterized as "bush," the rule s → ʃ is applied as an idiolectal rule. That is, the domain for its application is the speech (in whatever language) of the individual. For the modernized people, this rule is applied to languages as historically discrete varieties. Thus the rule s → ʃ applies to Chipewyan but not to English in the speech of people who were in the process of becoming modernized. We see, then, a phonological rule being treated individualistically in the bush group but systematically in the modernized group.

What we have seen for phonological convergence may also be reiterated for the lexical and clause structure convergence we have discussed above. By reducing historically discrete linguistic systems toward an undifferentiated single system, the bush consciousness is able to maintain a highly individualistic and integrative view of language as part of its world.

5

SOCIAL ATOMISM AND
SPEECH COMMUNITY

We began in Chapter 3 by describing the linguistic convergence that has taken place at Fort Chipewyan, Alberta. In Chapter 4 we argued that this convergence is intimately related to the reality set that we have called the bush consciousness. Because of the integrated and individualistic way in which things are known, the individual does not know languages as discrete historical varieties, but rather the individual seeks to integrate his or her experience with language into a unified and converged whole. Thus the bush consciousness is the cognitive set in which linguistic convergence at Fort Chipewyan occurs. It forms one element in the process of linguistic convergence. The other element in this process is the multiplicity of languages. In this chapter we will look at the linguistic history of the settlement at Fort Chipewyan, focusing on the relationships between the four languages that are spoken there.

At the same time it is necessary to discuss the social conditions that give rise to the bush consciousness. Although we wish to introduce a note of caution into the discussion of social atomism, especially in discussing causal relationships between reality set and social conditions, we feel that the work of Honigmann (1968) and Gardner (1966) gives us reason to believe that a deeper study of these relationships will prove fruitful.

Finally, we will be concerned with the concept of speech community as it might be applied to Fort Chipewyan. It will be necessary to discuss to what extent this concept is relevant to the discussion of language at Fort Chipewyan.

SOCIAL ATOMISM

In his early description of the people of the Great Slave Lake, and including in his description the people at Fort Chipewyan, Mason (1946) says, "individualism seems to be the keynote to the interpretation of this culture. The individual is bound by few taboos and coerced by no authority [p. 43]." Honigmann (1946) echoes this theme of individualism in speaking of the Fort Nelson Slave when he says, "Each man was, to a large extent, a law unto himself, subject only to family pressures and to public opinion within the group from which, however, he was always free to subtract his allegiance [p. 94]." Regarding higher level social order Honigmann cautiously says, "In general community organization is so imperceptible as to warrant the conclusion that it is almost nonexistent [p. 128]."

In his fieldwork at Lower Post, Honigmann (1949) apparently felt more certain that social organization at the community level was virtually nonexistent and reports, "Kaska social culture may be understood once it is realized that the Indians conceive of interpersonal adjustments atomistically, that is, as lying in the avoidance of as many intense and close human relationships as possible [p. 208]."

Or, in another place reports, "It is in keeping with the atomistic character of Kaska society that cooperation within a tribe or within the nation as a whole should be unknown. No mechanisms for bringing about the unified functioning of these groups are available and group sentiment is transient and ephemeral [p. 153]."

Honigmann (1968) traces the term "social atomism" back to Ruth Benedict in her lectures in 1942 at Columbia University. He characterizes atomistic communities as ones in which there is a primacy to individual concerns, where there is reserve or restraint in interpersonal relationships out of respect for the individualism of others, where there is little or no large-scale organization, where alliances shift rapidly and changes are essentially unilateral, and where social relations that do exist are strained, contentious, or hostile. It is interesting for our purposes that he also mentions "a weak and fragmented network of communication [p. 221]."

We could then describe Fort Chipewyan as an atomistic community except for the difficulty we feel in using the term "community" in juxtaposition with "atomistic," and for the important fact that social atomism does not represent all of the people who live at Fort Chipewyan.

These points we will take up again at the end of this chapter. For now, however, we would like to emphasize that the characteristics given by Honigmann do represent a social type that is an integrated way of organizing human interactions, and that this social type relates directly to the reality set we are calling the bush consciousness. That is to say, the bush consciousness is the reality set of socially atomistic people.

In this respect we find Gardner's (1966) report on the Paliyans of India quite interesting. In a setting quite different from that of the Mackenzie River drainage, he has described what is essentially the same social structure and reality set. He characterizes the Paliyans as individualistic and as avoiding cooperation and competition. What we have called the integrative aspect of the bush consciousness, Garner calls "memorate knowledge." This he characterizes as "knowledge which is held on the idiosyncratic level, the result of personal experience and individual analysis, rather than being derived from group opinions or traditions [p. 390]."

Of the nonintervening aspect, we have observed both noninterference in the training of children and a general taciturnity among adults at Fort Chipewyan. Gardner (1966) reports children to be treated with great indulgence and regarding taciturnity says, "Paliyans communicate very little at all times and become almost silent by the age of 40 [p. 398]." Gardner, then, is reporting on a relationship between a type of social organization and a reality set that corresponds well to our observations at Fort Chipewyan. He concludes by saying, "Features such as abandoning the aged, 'toleration' of incest, lack of leadership, individualism, and memorate-level culture are no longer to be seen as exceptions requiring individual and particular explanations. They are integral aspects of the internally consistent culture types of which Paliyan culture is an example [p. 410]." Although Gardner does not specifically mention it in his summary, he might also have included a general taciturnity and a predilection toward multilingualism and linguistic convergence as belonging to this culture type. These he does mention earlier, as does Honigmann (1946).

To retrace our steps a bit, then, we began by describing linguistic convergence at Fort Chipewyan. This was explained as being caused by the reality set, the bush consciousness. This bush consciousness itself might be thought of as being caused by the social atomism of the community at Fort Chipewyan. One would then continue to seek causes by looking for the causes of social atomism. We prefer, however, to avoid this regression of causes by considering that rather than looking at a chain of causation, we are really considering the same phenomenon from different points of view. If we are primarily interested in "explaining" linguistic convergence, then perhaps the bush consciousness and social atomism could be thought of as its explanations. When we shift our focus to social atomism, however, we see that linguistic convergence is one of its manifestations. We are engaged in describing not linear chains of causation but rather a closed and circular causal system. We feel as Bateson (1958) did with his material that it has been useful to describe linguistic convergence, the bush consciousness, and social atomism as three separate phenomena, but at the same time we would like to emphasize that these are, in fact, three views of what is essentially the same phenomenon, the mental world of the people at Fort Chipewyan. To speak of linguistic convergence puts our focus on communication, to speak of the bush consciousness puts our focus on the social construction of reality, and to speak of social atomism puts our focus on a social and cultural description.

In the discussion to follow, then, we do not wish to suggest that the linguistic history of the community at Fort Chipewyan is an "explanation" of the current situation there. We are presenting this discussion to give the reader a fuller feeling for the historical and social context in which the bush consciousness has lived.

THE FIRST CONTACT

One can imagine a past before Europeans had arrived in the subarctic in which Chipewyans inhabited the zone along the edge of the forest between what is now called Hudson Bay and Lake Athabasca. At that time, at the southern edge of their territory they fought with Crees and on the northern edge they fought with the Inuit. To the west, the Beaver and Slavey Indians bounded their territory, and to the northwest the Yellowknives and the Dogribs lived.

This past is largely a reconstruction on the basis of what was learned after these groups had come into contact with Europeans, and its details are still the subject of active research (Gillespie 1975). Krauss (1976) has cautioned us on linguistic grounds that we cannot assume a pure and unbroken residence of Chipewyans in this area for the period preceding European contact, though there is archaeological evidence that some Athabaskans had occupied the territory since the birth of Christ.

Rather than imagining a time preceding contact, we can begin with the event itself. The account given by MacGregor (1974), though written for a popular audience and seriously limited in point of view, is in essential agreement with other written accounts. We have chosen to quote this version over more academic treatments of the history because of the currency MacGregor's book has in Fort Chipewyan itself. It is being read and accepted with enthusiasm as the best account of the area's history:

Like all white explorers, Stewart was led and instructed in the method of living off the Barren Lands by an Indian—in this case a Chipewyan, and, even more remarkably, a woman. In the records her name is not given and she is known to us only as the "slave woman," but she had been a victim of one of the numerous Cree attacks and had been kept as a prisoner. When she escaped, she made her way to York Factory on Hudson Bay, where, using the Cree tongue, she explained to Governor James Knight much of the geography of the vast land lying north and west and then undertook to guide Stewart and a few dubiously peaceful Crees on their remarkable trip towards Great Slave Lake.

Leaving York Factory on June 27, 1715, the little band set out on foot on the round-trip which was to take them until May 7 the following year. All summer long the courageous and capable "slave woman" guided the party and then, urging them over the snowy waste, finally brought them safely to a gathering of her people in the vicinity of Great Slave Lake. There she not only explained the advantages that would accrue to the Chipewyans if they took their furs to the Hudson's Bay Company but also showed them how to prepare their skins for market and induced two youths of the tribe to return with Stewart and herself to the Bay. With the aid of the Slave woman the Chipewyans had been brought into contact with the fur company and the first white man had put in a winter in the Mackenzie watershed [p. 5].

Within 2 years, by 1717, Fort Churchill had been established to accommodate the new trade with the Chipewyans.

There is another account of this event, however, which is also worthy of quotation in full. This is the traditional Chipewyan story of how they first contacted the Europeans. It offers much more detail in some cases as well as some interesting differences. The story that appears below was told by Victoria Mercredi of Fort Chipewyan in Chipewyan and was translated by Lena Piche and the authors. Although it differs in several places from other contemporary versions there is full agreement on the major details:

Fallen Marten (θa náltθ'eri)

At first there was a woman called Fallen Marten. The Crees and the Chipewyans were warring then. The Crees used guns to kill people because they had found the French first. Finally they killed all the people.

One woman called Fallen Marten was a Chipewyan woman. She was a nice looking woman and because she was good looking the Crees took her. While the Crees were keeping her they brought knives, clothes, and kettles from the fort. The Crees were killing beavers then because they were selling them and so they had to pack their beaver pelts. While they were packing the pelts the woman thought, "I'll go along with them." So when they went in the bush she followed behind the Crees.

As she followed the Crees they went into a rock house (Churchill). She just followed them. She thought, "Maybe there are people living there.'' But when she got there she just walked around the house because she didn't know where the door was.

Suddenly the boss saw her. When he saw her he opened the door for her. The Crees were sitting there inside. People were giving them guns, shot, gunpowder, and everything.

Then the woman walked in. ''Where do you come from?'' he asked. ''I live with these Crees,'' she answered.

The woman spoke in Cree. I guess the Frenchman could understand Cree. They say that the Cree first found the French.

''I'm staying with this man,'' she said. ''Where are your relatives?'' he asked. ''They killed all my relatives so I've been staying with them for a long time now.'' So the French boss said, ''From the appearance of this woman her people must also be good looking people. You said that they didn't look like people, but that they looked like monsters, and that they would kill us. That's why we gave you guns, shot, and gunpowder. Now I am not going to give you those things,'' he said and took it all back from them.

After he took the things back the Crees left and the woman stayed with the Frenchmen. Then the French boss asked her, ''Do you have any relatives who are still living?'' ''My relatives are still alive but they live a long way away,'' she answered. ''Could you go get them in the winter time?'' he asked. She answered, ''Yes.''

So when fall came and the ice was real hard the woman left. The Frenchman walked ahead of her and she followed with a dog team. She walked and walked. All of a sudden she came to where there were many trails. ''These are not my relatives' trails. These are the Crees','' she said and just followed the trail. All of a sudden she came to another trail and she said, ''This is my relatives' trail.'' So when she came to her relatives' trail she took the lead.

The people found out that she was coming so they ran away. Fallen Marten went on ahead. Suddenly Fallen Marten met some people. There were two people looking at her and holding weapons. They began to chase her and she fell down. She fell down with a heart attack. When she fell she said to the people, ''Don't bother me,'' and made signs with her hands. So they left her alone. Long after that she was able to say only, ''Marten, Marten, Marten,'' as she signed falling with her hand. After she was well again she told her story. ''I found the French for you. That's why I came to see you, my relatives.'' Only then the people went to her.

The Chipewyans went to her. Then they made a fire and ate. They put all the things in the fire, knives, pails and everything. They made tea in the pails and began to eat with all the things they had brought.

Then the people went off together. So that the Crees, the Chipewyans, and the Frenchmen would all stay together in peace they made five Frenchmen stay with them, they were like policemen. They talked to the poeple.

That woman was called Fallen Marten and she found the Frenchmen. That's why now we're staying here. That's why at the beginning if only the Crees had found the French there would have been only Crees here now.

These two accounts of the original Chipewyan contact with Europeans agree substantially that it was the Crees who blocked the Chipewyan from earlier contact, that the Crees could do this by virtue of their superior ability to make war with guns, and that it was a woman who was the intermediary. Beyond that there are some striking differences.

In the written accounts of this contact history, William Stewart is given the credit for initiating the contact. In the Chipewyan view, it is the Chipewyan woman, Fallen Marten, who first sought out the means of contact. In the European account the native language of the Europeans was English, but in the Chipewyan account this language was French. Stewart is said to have gone out from York Factory, but in Fort Chipewyan people say that the contact was made at Churchill.

Although these differences may be in part reconciled by noting shifts in the meanings of Chipewyan *bálai* ('button', 'French') and *tθeye* ('rock house', 'Churchill'), for the purpose of this study the most important detail of this event was that contact was made possible by Fallen Marten's bilingualism. It was because she could pass herself off as a Cree woman that she was able to plead the case of her own people.

Perhaps the most important difference between the two histories is that the European version focuses on the economic and historical importance of the contact while neglecting to mention the impact felt by the immediate participants. In the Chipewyan version, one is reminded of the confusion felt by Fallen Marten when confronting such a totally foreign structure as the fort and the risk to her life taken in entering and betraying her captors for the sake of her own people. Again, on returning to meet her own people she feels such fear of them that she is unable to speak and has difficulty in identifying herself. Comparing the two versions we see that the European view is that courage was needed to face the *snowy wastes*, whereas in the Chipewyan version it is the contact of cultures and especially her return to her *own* people that tries Fallen Marten's courage.

This history of the contact of the Chipewyans with Europeans has been given in some detail here for three reasons. First, we feel it is rather important to emphasize that there may be important differences between a native, oral history of the speech community and a European, written history. Some of these differences may be reconcilable, especially through European techniques of analysis, but not all.

Second, the native view of the speech community shows a considerably greater concern for the problems of communication in contact situations than European accounts. Since for most of the history of the speech community we have only the European version, this native concern for communicative problems must be assumed even where it is not overtly mentioned.

Third, from the native account we can see an emphasis on the value of bilingualism from the earliest contact. As Chipewyans view their own history, bilingualism brought them the new way of life which they have lived now for nearly 250 years.

SETTLEMENT ON THE LOWER ATHABASCA

Helm and her associates (1975) have argued for viewing the contact history of people in the Mackenzie drainage as having occurred in three phases, the incipient–early contact phase, the contact–traditional phase, and the modern or government–commercial phase. Following their format, then, we can probably consider what we have described above as "the first contact" to be the beginning of the first phase, the incipient–early contact phase. Before Fallen Marten (θa nált θ'eri) made her trip to Hudson Bay, her own people are said to have been without knowledge of the Europeans and their goods.

With the establishment of contact between Chipewyans and Europeans of Churchill came an important linguistic development in the Chipewyans' life. Though they may well have had occasion to speak with other Athabaskans as they do now, each person speaking his own language but understanding the other's, the contact for trade at Churchill probably required that at least some of them speak Cree or English some of the time. This was effectively a shift from being monolinguals to being bilinguals. The development was accompanied by a second development. At least some Chipewyans moved from being hunters to being at least part-time trappers.

Certainly neither of these shifts occurred suddenly, nor did they affect all Chipewyans equally. Nevertheless during the 62 years following Fallen Marten's introduction of trapping and trading to the Chipewyans, more and more of them made the long trip to Churchill to trade. Finally, in 1778, Peter Pond established a post in the Peace–Athabasca delta, close to the present site of Fort Chipewyan, and inaugurated the fur trade in the west; thus the contact–traditional phase could be said to have begun. At the time Pond established his post, both Chipewyans and Crees were present in the area.

From a linguistic point of view, we can see that one major effect of Pond's settlement was to add the English language to the range of possibilities at Lake Athabasca. Since that time the presence of English speakers has remained virtually uninterrupted. As the fur trade developed in the next 70 years or so at the new site of Fort Chipewyan, and as the competition between companies increased, more and more English speakers came to Lake Athabasca. This, of course, would have produced many occasions for direct English–Cree and English–Chipewyan translations. It is likely that, as in Fallen Marten's case, Cree was used by Chipewyans. It is unknown to what extent Crees ever used the Chipewyan language in this period.

The trader George Simpson was certainly not the first to advance the policy of taking native wives in 1820, though he is remembered for his strong recommendation of this solution to European–native relations. 1820, however, was the date of his own first contribution to the creation of a group of native bilinguals, that is, children learning at least two languages as their native languages. We can see then that since at least 170 years ago there has been a growing population of people who would feel equally at home in several languages. Add these to the ones who learned to speak one of the currently available languages as adults for the purposes of trade or in marriage, and we see multilingualism as becoming a stronger force over the years. The possible repertoire would include as its main elements English, Cree, and Chipewyan, but there was also the possibility of Beaver, Slavey, and Dogrib, depending on how far afield a person's travels led.

When Father Taché of the Oblates of Mary Immaculate arrived in Fort Chipewyan in 1847, he was met by people who were well prepared for his coming. Native people had heard for years of the whiteman's medicine and were ready to learn more about it. Europeans in the settlement had regularly celebrated Christian services among themselves and on some occasions had admitted native people as observers. During his stay Father Taché celebrated the first Roman Catholic mass and baptized 194 people. Although Father Taché did not stay long, within 4 years Father Faraud took up permanent residence in the settlement, establishing the Nativity Mission in Fort Chipewyan in 1851.

From our point of view the presence of the Oblate Fathers in Fort Chipewyan is important for two reasons. The subsistence base of the native culture in the area of Lake Athabasca had been effectively shifted from hunting to at least part-time trapping in the course of the preceding 130 years. As Asch (1976) has pointed out, this created a dependence on the world economy of which native people were scarcely aware. Now with the activity of the Roman Catholic missionaries, there began a fairly rapid shift in the cosmology of native people. Christian beliefs and explanations began to replace the native belief system. This appears to have happened much more rapidly than the shift in subsistence patterns.

A second result of the Oblate Fathers' presence is of just as great importance in the linguistic history of Fort Chipewyan. These men were native speakers of French, so French became established as the fourth element in the already abundant repertoire of the settlement.

We need to emphasize that this was not the first time that the French language had been heard in the area. For some years, French-speaking voyageurs had been coming to Fort Chipewyan. The establishment of the Nativity Mission, however, gave French a social importance that is reflected to this day in the native view that the first contact of natives with European culture was with French Europeans. The French presence there within memory has been so strong that it seems they must have been there from the beginning.

The social role taken on indirectly by the French language in the founding of the Nativity Mission was further buttressed within 20 years with the establishment of the Holy Angels School in 1874 by the Grey Nuns. Thus in a small way at first with only 11 children, the eventual replacement of native education with Christian and European education began.

It is important here to recall the comparison of the two versions of the original Chipewyan contact with Europeans. In the European view, the contact which brought guns, clothes, and teapots to the natives in exchange for furs was at a different time, a different place, and in a different language from the contact that brought them the Christian faith. In the Chipewyan view, these events have been merged into one. In the wisdom of the oral tradition, European technology, economy, and religious history are seen to be intimately related. They are not perceived as separable and replaceable components as the European tends to see them. Of course, it is clear that the missionaries themselves saw this essential unity and acknowledged as much in their establishment of an education system which included European secular subjects and even calisthenics as well as religious instruction.

On the CBC North television program "Full Circle" on December 6, 1976, Mrs. Arthur Woodward, now of Fort McMurray, said, "I speak French, English, Chipewyan, and Cree. That's enough for Alberta." This group of four languages is often given by people in the area around Fort Chipewyan when one asks what languages they speak. In this sketch of the history of Fort Chipewyan we have seen the events that led to the presence of these four languages in the area.

Because of the intermarriage between groups beginning as early as the eighteenth century, many people were native bilinguals. By the late nineteenth century it is probable that most of the people coming to the settlement of Fort Chipewyan could communicate to some extent in all four languages, though certainly they would prefer to speak in only one or two. It is likely as well that facility in language and translation decreased with distance from the settlement and the frequency of visits there.

The view we get, then, of the settlement and its surrounding area at the end of the nineteenth century is of a group of people sharing a trapping subsistence, technology, and economy, largely sharing a Christian religion, and sharing some languages. The most radical demarcation between groups would be between the settlement people and the bush people. The first group would include the traders, clerks and their wives, priests and nuns, and any others who lived primarily in the settlement, depending for subsistence on the activities of others. The second group would include all the rest who lived primarily in the bush, gaining their subsistence from trapping and hunting, and who still came to the fort only to trade or to celebrate Christian holidays. By the end of the nineteenth century the people at Lake Athabasca probably shared more with each other than any of them shared with more distant but culturally related groups. Their language was a pragmatic multilingualism. One learned and spoke whatever was necessary to communicate.

TREATY EIGHT AND THE
SECULARIZATION OF EDUCATION

When the Treaty Eight Commission party arrived at Fort Chipewyan in the summer of 1899 to seek the agreement and the signatures of the native people, they brought with them some assumptions about native culture that have had a lasting impact on the structure of the community. The first assumption they made was that there would be a native tribal organization of enough strength that the signature of the leaders of the tribes would be sufficient to guarantee the acquiescence of all tribe members. They assumed they had only to locate the chiefs and headmen and procure their signatures.

Fumoleau (1975) has painstakingly reconstructed the history of this signing, making full use of the testimony of native people who were present. His work has shown that this assumption of native leadership was largely wrong and has left a history of misconceptions about the nature of the agreement reached. At Fort Chipewyan there was, apparently, a person who spoke as the Cree chief, but the commission actually undertook the creation of a Chipewyan chief, as it did in other areas to the east and north of there.

The second assumption the Treaty Eight Commission made was that there were discrete divisions between natives and nonnatives and, among natives, between Chipewyans and Crees. As Richmond (1970) and McClellan (1970) have suggested, these distinctions between ethnic groups may have been spurious or beside the point. That is, in the atomistic society of the people who lived a bush life at Fort Chipewyan by 1899, ethnic distinctions may have largely been lost under the presence of individualism and ethnic convergence.

At the time of the signing of Treaty Eight there were nonnative trappers living a bush life and coming into the settlement only to trade. There were also native people living in the settlement who were not directly engaged in the bush life. Yet there is no doubt that the Treaty Commission had little difficulty deciding who should sign and who should not in most cases. The distinction between Indian and non-Indian was well fixed in their minds and in the goals of the government before arriving at Fort Chipewyan. We can be sure, for example, that when the Treaty Commission requested the presence of the missionaries (Fumoleau 1975:77) it was as witnesses to the event, not as potential signers. A significant distinction emphasized by the treaty, then, was between native and nonnative people, even though in some cases this cut across the social and economic organization of the settlement and surrounding region.

Another division created, of course, is the notorious distinction between Treaty Indian and Non-Treaty Indian or Méti. Before the signing of the treaty a person with European ancestors was free to decide his or her own position in the distinction between settlement or bush life. The treaty forced a decision along new lines which left to this day a complex of problems in social and economic identification for Treaty Indians and Métis alike.

The third division created by the signing of Treaty Eight was between Chipewyan and Cree. In the same way that people of mixed native and European ancestry were made to choose whether or not they would consider themselves to be native, people of mixed Cree and Chipewyan ancestry were made to choose a unique identity. Although in some cases this may not have been difficult, at that time it tended to operate at cross-purposes to an ongoing process of ethnic convergence. At a time when the distinctions between Chipewyans and Crees were rapidly dissolving into a pan-bush identity, the Treaty Commission introduced a discrete distinction between the groups that it required to be perpetuated indefinitely into the future.

Finally, for the sake of completeness it should be mentioned that it was also at this time that the Northwest Mounted Police established a post in Fort Chipewyan. This was the first of many government agencies to become established there. In the following years the distribution of treaty payments and the consequent reinforcement of the social and cultural distinctions created by the treaty were witnessed by a representative group of police.

The linguistic point to be drawn from this discussion of Treaty Eight is that the treaty does not appear to have produced any direct change in the basically multilingual behavior of the people in the area of Fort Chipewyan. Nevertheless, the treaty forced on each Treaty Indian a decision to be officially identified with a unique band. The result of this was that there was no longer any direct correlation between the linguistic and cultural activity of a person and his or her band affiliation as a Chipewyan or Cree.

It is rather easy to lose sight of this fact since the assumptions brought to Fort Chipewyan by the Treaty Eight Commission are widely shared by members of the Euro-Canadian culture the commission represented. The situation is further complicated by the recent development that many people in the community are coming to share the views of the Commission in spite of their own behavior to the contrary. To discuss this latter aspect it is necessary to look further at education in the settlement.

From the founding of the Holy Angels school in 1874 until the establishment of the Indian Affairs school in 1954, education in Fort Chipewyan was religious education. Although both academic and vocational secular subjects were taught, the motivating force behind education was always the spiritual development of the students. Of course, in this case spiritual development meant instruction in the Roman Catholic faith.

In early years the medium of instruction was apparently quite flexible and included all four languages available in the community. Reading of Chipewyan and Cree syllabics developed by the Wesleyan missionary James Evans was quite widespread. Older people now recall spending long nights in the bush reading Biblical stories in Chipewyan, Cree, or French during the early decades of this century. This indicates that the religious instruction of the mission extended well out of the settlement into the bush.

In the several decades preceding the establishment of an Indian Affairs school, however, things were not so flexible in the mission school, at least from a linguistic point of view. There began a period of strong repression of the use of native languages. At least one person recalls as a child being forced to sit in the corner with a large potato in his mouth until his jaws ached because he had spoken Cree at school. Others describe it less graphically as being required to speak only French at school.

Since this was a residential school and the children were left entirely in the care of the staff of the school for most of the year, this emphasis on the homogenization of language has left a strong impression on the community as a whole. There is an important aspect of modern communication which this repressive policy produced. This is a rather negative attitude toward the French language held by those who were forced to speak it in exclusion of other languages.

This policy went against the obvious reality of the community and its history and may also be related to the present strong resistance to any other attempts to do the same wherever they occur. This shows up in many places, from the resistance to the study of English in school to the insistence that it is impossible for a Cree person from another community to teach Cree in Fort Chipewyan.

Thus when Indian Affairs took over education in Fort Chipewyan in 1954 it was taking over a tradition of some 80 years standing. Although some English was used in school before 1954 and some French continued to be used after that date, perhaps the most significant shift in policy for our purposes was linguistic. Now instead of trying to produce monolingual French speakers, the school began to try to produce monolingual English speakers. This, of course, was in keeping with the policy throughout North America of seeking to integrate native people into the mainstream culture as quickly as possible.

ETHNOHISTORY

There is a need for a major study of the ethnohistory of the people of the Fort Chipewyan area. Current sources of information are conflicting and misleading. If you go into the office of the Athabasca Cree–Chipewyan Band in Fort Chipewyan and ask how many Crees and how many Chipewyans are registered there, the answer that is given is "over 700 Crees and over 300 Chipewyans." If you press a little harder for exact figures, the latest ones available as of January 1977 are from August 31, 1976. These figures are 828 Crees and 264 Chipewyans. There are two things that can be noticed in this. The first is that this question is taken as a reasonable question. That is, it is reasonable to think that the entities "Cree" and "Chipewyan" are countable and further that they have been counted and fairly recently at that. And the second thing to notice is that there is a difference of about 100 in the estimate and in the actual figures. The number of Crees is underestimated and the number of Chipewyans is overestimated.

When we arrived in Fort Chipewyan and told people that we had been studying Chipewyan and were interested in studying it further, people told us that we had come to the wrong place, that Fort Chipewyan was "an all Cree town." When questioned further they would agree that there were Chipewyans living in Fort Chipewyan but that most people were Crees. Of course, we were interested in understanding the position of Chipewyan in a community where it was not the only language in use. One of the things we wanted to establish was just who spoke the language, and as a preliminary we wanted to establish the identity of the people in the community. In other words we were looking for more or less straightforward answers to the questions: How many Crees and Chipewyans are there in Fort Chipewyan and who are they?

It is unrealistic to expect a straightforward answer to these questions. Because of the convergence of all groups in the area through intermarriage, many if not most individuals could legitimately call themselves members of any or even all of the four founding groups—Cree, Chipewyan, English, or French. Nevertheless, in Fort Chipewyan it is considered reasonable to ask if someone is Cree or Chipewyan, and so it is necessary for us now to discuss how this apparently contradictory situation could arise.

Table 5.1 gives some population statistics we have selected to illustrate how a demographic approach to identification in Fort Chipewyan can be misleading.

The view of the two native populations of Fort Chipewyan given by

TABLE 5.1. Population Statistics.

	Cree	Chipewyan
Hudson Bay Company[a]		
1821–1822	—900—	
Father Emile Petitot[b]		
1862	300	900
1879–1881	one family	no mention
Treaty Eight[c]		
1899	183	407
Athabasca Cree–		
Chipewyan Band[d]		
1976		
estimated	700+	300+
actual	828	264

[a] Wuetherick (1972:A87).
[b] Wuetherick (1972:A87).
[c] Wuetherick (1972:A136).
[d] Athabasca Cree–Chipewyan Band Statistics.

these statistics indicates that after an early period in which there was a drastic decrease in the population of both groups, the Crees steadily increased their population at a pace more rapid than that of the Chipewyans', until in 1976 the groups have reversed their relative sizes. Given these statistics one would then look for causes inhibiting the growth of the Chipewyan group but not the Cree group.

Thus it has been explained to us that there are so many more Crees than Chipewyans because one of the many influenza epidemics decimated the Chipewyan group. A somewhat more sophisticated explanation that has been given is that in cases of mixed marriages the woman takes the band membership of her husband according to the Indian Act. This implies, of course, that the majority of mixed marriages consists of Chipewyan women and Cree men.

Another explanation which has been advanced is that where mixed marriages occur, the children can choose on which side they will register and the decision is usually made to register under the father's band. This again implies that the fathers are mostly Crees.

Although these explanations do not account for what happens in the cases where mixed marriages occur between Chipewyan men and Cree women, they do point to the major problem with the statistics offered. The counting of the entities "Cree" and "Chipewyan" assumes that they are discrete categories, and yet, as we have mentioned, intermarriage among all groups has occurred in the area going back at least 150 years. This is perhaps what was behind the Hudson's Bay Company's counting all Crees and Chipewyans together in 1821. As we suggested in our historical sketch of the area, it was Treaty Eight that recreated the clear distinction between Chipewyan and Cree that had been blurred in the development of the bush culture. This distinction was, in fact, a paper distinction in that it forced every native person registered under Treaty Eight to consider herself or himself to be either Cree or Chipewyan.

From the record of epidemics in the area it is clear that there were frequent fluctuations in the population (Wuetherick 1972; MacGregor 1974). Adding this to the mixing of historical lines through intermarriage and the blurring of cultural distinctions in the bush culture, we begin to see that in 1977 when a person is registered as a Chipewyan or Cree it expresses something quite different from a pure line of descent from the aboriginal people and culture.

In our first contacts with people in the community, we kept "discovering" Chipewyans. These were mostly women who as far as we had known were Crees. They spoke Cree and had Cree families. Only after some time did we learn that they had been born and raised as Chipewyans and only began to learn Cree upon their marriage to Cree men. This is at least their report. It is likely, however, that they had heard Cree spoken by the time of their marriages and may have understood much of it. In these cases our "discovery" of Chipewyans who had shifted their identity confirmed the view given above that women took the ethnic identity or at least the registry of their husbands.

Perhaps the most extreme case of this shifted identity we knew of was one in which a young woman in her 20s told us her mother had been a Chipewyan but she herself and her sisters had all been raised as Crees. Her father was a Cree, and while he was still living he spoke to them in Cree and her mother spoke to them in Chipewyan. They were learning both languages. But then her father passed away and after that her mother only spoke Cree to them so that they would grow up as Crees.

This case follows both of the principles given. A Chipewyan woman became a Cree because of her marraige to a Cree man, and the children took the Cree identity because of their Cree father. To maintain this in the face of the father's absence in death indicates a rather strong loyalty to these principles.

We then began to discover cases in which Chipewyan men were also registered as Crees. In one case it was in a family we had come to think of as one of the "purest" Chipewyan families. We had only heard English and Chipewyan spoken in their home and the children actually could speak Chipewyan to some extent. We first found out that the children were registered as Crees. We were surprised and asked why. The answer one of the girls gave was, "Too many Chips, I guess." When we found that their grandfather who was raising them in place of their father was also registered as a Cree we began to see that the explanations we had been given did not fully explain why there were more Crees than Chipewyans. In this case the answer appears to be that a group of Chipewyans were quite arbitrarily registered as Crees because of their residence in Wood Buffalo National Park at the time of registry.

In one family a Chipewyan man had married a non-Treaty Indian woman. By the principles people had explained to us, this woman should have become a Chipewyan woman though she spoke Cree and thought of herself as being Cree. Instead, the man had been arbitrarily registered as Cree. The woman then became Cree as well and ultimately served as a councilor of the Cree Band. In this case an "all Cree" family was produced from the union of a Chipewyan man and a non-Treaty woman.

When we began to inquire into this we were told by the social assistance officer that as many as 100 Chipewyans had changed their registry to the Cree Band in the past decade or so. It is curious now to note that this is just the size of the error in estimated band registry we were given. There are at least 100 people now registered as Crees who had once been registered as Chipewyans. There are many more, especially women, who switched upon marriage. Even greater than that is the number of people who could have chosen to be registered as either Chipewyans or Crees because of double ancestry.

Perhaps it is easier to see now why it should not be easy to say whether one is Cree or Chipewyan. Nevertheless it is taken as a reasonable question, and people do assert Cree identity and Chipewyan identity. The great majority who have chosen to be Crees usually express an explanation that is based on kinship, and so it is to kinship that we may look for the first explanation.

Without considering structural differences between aboriginal kinship systems or even modern contrasts between Chipewyan and Cree kinship systems, it is possible to argue that the Crees at Fort Chipewyan place an absolutely higher value on kinship than do the Chipewyans.

In Fort Chipewyan a man was asked to come to speak to schoolchildren. His only restriction was that since it was a Cree language class he should speak in Cree. Otherwise he was considered to be the best judge of his own topic. As it was the first class, he felt it was most important to begin by instructing the students in kinship terminology. He especially wanted to record his displeasure with a growing practice of referring to people by name only and not by the appropriate kinship term. He felt that the appropriate use of kinship terminology was the entrance to a knowledge of Cree language and culture.

This same approach to the learning of Cree has been taken by Tait (n.d.) in her *Introduction to the Cree Language,* where the entire first volume is devoted to kinship terminology. Within the community of Fort Chipewyan the Cree root for 'grandfather', *musom,* is used widely, even in conversations between people who speak very little Cree. This emphasis on appropriate usage was undoubtedly behind a 10-year-old girl's self-correction. This girl, who is as much a Chipewyan as any of the children, who spends much of the year in the bush on the Chipewyan reserve, and who has by self-report fought Cree children who have berated Chipewyans, was referring to the Chipewyan chief's brother, Ben Marcel, who is her grandfather. She said, *He's my grandfather,* and then quickly added, *I should say musom.*

Thus we see that people who regard themselves as Chipewyans have borrowed at least one kinship term from the Crees in their ordinary speech. In their teaching of the Chipewyan language, to the extent that they are willing to teach it at all, they rarely mention kinship terminology. When one specifically seeks to elicit kinship terms, the response is something akin to boredom. In short, Chipewyans do not appear to have the overriding concern with kinship that the Crees do, and this may be a reason behind the rather pervasive swing to Cree identity.

Although we wish to avoid making a very strong claim of variation within the group at Fort Chipewyan that is characterized by the bush consciousness, we would now like to suggest that the distinction between Cree and Chipewyan may relate to a partial polarization within the reality set. Because of the somewhat higher emphasis on social organization among the "Crees," we would like to suggest that this may represent a somewhat less atomisitc, somewhat more modernized position. Whether or not this represents an aboriginal difference, it may represent in the present community a range of choices from more to less "bush." Thus identification as Chipewyan may represent a strong identification with the bush consciousness, but identification as Cree may represent a position somewhat more intermediate between bush and modern. In the modern period when the choice of identity has for many become quite arbitrary from a historical point of view, the choice of identity may be motivated more by the person's reality set than by any other factor.

If this analysis is correct it would argue for a significant increase in identification as Crees as people moved into the settlement from the bush. The previously referred to transfer of registry happened during the last decade or so. This is the period during which there has been a great increase in settlement population. This movement corresponds with a government ruling that social assistance payments cannot be made to families whose children do not attend school. Thus as people are required to move into town by the government, their presence in the settlement and their activities cause them to begin to feel more like Crees than Chipewyans, and the registry reflects this still somewhat subtle shift in identification.

As a shift within the bush consciousness, it is not experienced as a radical change of reality set. It is experienced as a small loss in individuality, perhaps, but also as a corresponding gain in the ability to accept the foreign. This shift in the integrative aspect may in the long run pave the way for the major shift into the modern consciousness.

This account remains incomplete as it stands, however, since it implies, even though it does not state, that Chipewyans are somehow "purer" than Crees in Fort Chipewyan. It implies a continuum from bush consciousness to modern consciousness that places Chipewyans at one extreme in something like their aboriginal position, Europeans at the other extreme as the primary holders of the modern consciousness, with Crees and Métis somewhere in between. And it implies that only the Crees and Métis are involved in the choosing of reality set. This putative continuum could be indicated graphically as follows:

Bush consciousness		Modern	consciousness
Chipewyans	Crees	Métis	Europeans

past +————————————————————————→ future

Because there is a net increase of moves into the settlement in the past several decades, it might also be assumed that this continuum is operating as a historical development in one direction only. Apparently, however, although there has been a net increase in settlement population over bush population, there are some people who have chosen to move farther out. This would suggest movements in both directions on the reality set continuum as well.

It only remained for us to "discover" Crees as we had discovered Chipewyans. It was reported that there was a Cree family of a few generations ago that had been abandoned by the Crees. Although we do not know the circumstances of this abandonment, the response of the head of the family is said to have been to make his children vow that they would never again speak Cree, but that they would consider themselves to be Chipewyans. They took the father's first name as a family name and from then on have lived as Chipewyans. Although it is difficult to establish the veracity of this report, it does suggest that the movement from Chipewyan to Cree identity has been compensated to some extent by movement from Cree to Chipewyan identity.

It turns out that some of the people whom we had come to regard as the "most Chipewyan" have descended from the family about which this story is told. So not only is the choice of being identified as Cree potentially an expression of reality set, the choice of Chipewyan may also be an acquired identity. If we sketch out this history, then, we get what on casual view looks like the same categories before and after the contact–traditional period, the period of the bush culture. The meaning of the terms has changed, though, with "Chipewyan" before the bush culture representing a continuous historical development from the aboriginal culture but after bush culture representing a high degree of identification with the bush consciousness. An individual within one of the new categories may actually trace his or her history back to any or all of the prebush categories:

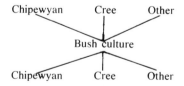

Finally, it is important to emphasize the view the bush consciousness takes of its own past. As we showed earlier, the modern "Chipewyans" trace their past back to the woman called Fallen Marten ($\theta a \ n\acute{a}lt\theta'\rho ri$) and project the recent importance of French Europeans back onto the originally contacted Europeans. It can be seen that the modern "Chipewyans"

are simultaneously projecting their own current identity as Chipewyans back onto the past. This is also true of Crees. Thus the view we are constructing here of a discontinuity between modern groups and aboriginal groups is not held by the members of the speech community. Their view on the whole is of a continuous past and an unbroken tradition.

THE MODERN SPEECH COMMUNITY

On parle le rababou[1]

I went into the Bay the other day and Mrs. Flett was standing there talking to Victoria Mercredi. And Mrs. Flett was talking to her in Cree and she was just talking back in Chip. So I just said in French, "I might as well speak French since we've got everything else here." and Mrs. Flett said, "On parle le rababou." And that's the truth, you know. The way they speak around here just mixes everything in.

At school there is a small gathering after the Cree and Chipewyan classes. The teacher aide (TA) is a Chipewyan woman in her late 30s. One guest speaker (GW) is a woman who was born in a Chipewyan family but married a Cree and has now been at the school to teach girls about sewing in Cree. The other guest speaker (GM) is in his 50s, is a Cree and is married to a Chipewyan woman. We are also present and the people know that we are studying Chipewyan and some Cree.

As this group converses we notice that GM speaks in Cree, mostly to GW. GW speaks in Cree and Chipewyan addressing herself to both GM and TA, that is, not switching sequentially but shifting her gaze as she speaks. Each turn stays within a language. TA speaks in Chipewyan and addresses herself mostly to GM and GW. Perhaps the most remarkable aspect is that there is no faltering or hesitation. The conversation moves fluently with good precision in the alternation of turns and the allocation of speaking rights.

In another case where social distance requires some indirection an older woman asks her peer a question in Chipewyan. This is passed on to that woman's daughter in Cree. This young woman then asks her friend who is the target addressee in English. The answer in English is immediately understood without translation or indirection.

[1] Brouet composé de farine et de pémican [Petitot 1876].

> A joint meeting of the Cree and Chipewyan Bands begins with someone saying to the group waiting outside, "We might as well start." Inside everyone sits as far back in the hall as possible so the Chipewyan chief asks everyone to move up in English. No one moves. He then says something much longer in Cree but still there is no movement. Finally, when he begins to address individuals by name whether in Cree or English they move up.

> The Band manager calls the meeting to order in English and explains that R. Scollon will talk about his work before the regular business begins. Scollon begins to explain in English and shortly the manager asks him to pause so that what he says can be translated. The Chipewyan chief then translates into Cree. It takes much longer and when he finishes he says in English facing the audience but addressing Scollon that he has added some things from what he told him before at his house. Then he asks Scollon to read from his Chipewyan stories. He reads several paragraphs and when he finishes there is applause. The Band manager then calls for a vote to see if they support his work. As some are beginning to raise hands, someone says that maybe that should be said in Cree. So the Chipewyan chief translates into Cree and then the vote is taken.

> Months after the meeting people came up to R. Scollon and ask to hear the rest of the story he had read. They say that he speaks just like their grandfather. At the meeting he was the only one to speak Chipewyan.

> At a general meeting of the town the first speaker, from out of town, is the vice president of the Alberta Métis Association. He speaks to the group in English.

> He is followed by the vice president of the Alberta Indian Association. She speaks first in English and then translates her speech into Cree.

> The third speaker is the Chipewyan chief. He speaks at length in Cree. When he finishes he gives a brief English paraphrase.

> The first speaker then requests the floor and speaks in Cree.

> No Chipewyan is spoken and the Chipewyan chief reports that none of his people are at the meeting because he is speaking for them. In the voting he is counted as 1 not 264.

From these examples of language in use in Fort Chipewyan we would like to draw two points. The first is that the practice called dual-lingualism by Lincoln (1975) is widely used. As we have mentioned earlier, it is considered normal for people to carry on conversation in two or three languages with individual conversants opting to speak only in a single language throughout. Of course, the amount of convergence that has taken place makes these separate "languages" not so highly differentiated as they might be elsewhere.

The second point we wish to discuss is that there is some functional specialization of languages in Fort Chipewyan. We can look, for example, at Chipewyan. One does not hear it spoken at public meetings or even at joint band meetings. It is used only in small groups and familiar settings. When the Chipewyan chief who himself speaks "all four" languages chooses to make his speeches at town meetings and even in meetings of the joint Band in the Cree language, we begin to see that there is some functional specialization of the languages spoken in Fort Chipewyan. Since French began and is ending as the most specialized of the languages, it is perhaps best to begin with it.

We have said above that French entered the speech community in force as the language of the Nativity Mission and of the Holy Angels School. From 1847 until 1975 its domination of religion and morals was almost complete. Until 1954, French was the enforced language of the school and the residence home. Except for a few hours on weekends and 10 days at Christmas, children were taught the 10 basic commandments as well as a host of subsidiary ones in French. No gum chewing. Mouths closed when listening. No talking at meals. Untied hair must be cut short. This more-than-military regimen was the life of many of the people of Fort Chipewyan during their formative years and this formation was all in French. In 1954 when the school was secularized and Anglicized, the mission remained guardian over the students during the hours out of school. Only in 1975 when the residence closed did this full reign of French finally end. A recent view of a woman who considers herself a native speaker of French is that it is "not good for anything anymore."

Another phenomenon may well be related to this religious and moral specialization of French. Many women have told us that they had to learn Cree when they were married because their husbands did not speak Chipewyan and they could not talk to each other. In the same situation now English is used as the common language, and we wondered why French was not used by the earlier couples who had been mostly raised in the mission and who were all French speakers.

The answer may lie in the normal marriage pattern. Generally couples live together and consider marriage only sometime after a first child is born. This practice, which is viewed as the normal way of doing things, would certainly be viewed with displeasure by the personnel of the Roman Catholic mission. Because of the close association of French with moral instruction, we suggest that it was effectively disqualified as a common language for a couple who had not yet married. In the interim between meeting and marrying a number of years would pass during which time some less morally colored means of communication was needed. In most cases Cree was chosen. In more recent times, because of schooling in English, these communications can be conducted in English without any sense of immorality and without the necessity of learning another language. Thus it seems that the functional specialization of French may be bringing about its current disappearance from use in the community.

Of the European languages, English has been in Fort Chipewyan the longest. It came with Peter Pond in 1778 and has been maintained steadily in some form by traders down to the present. With the secularization and Anglicization of the school in 1954, it became a major part of all the younger speakers' repertoires. In 1976 its position was further strengthened with the first television broadcasting from Vancouver.

Where the specialization of French was the cause of its strength for many years but its ultimate weakness, the strength of English in community use may be its lack of specialization. Rather than describing where English is used, one can describe where it is not used. The only situation we know of where there is any attempt to restrict the use of English is in classes in the school in the Cree and Chipewyan languages. Its use is naturally limited in situations where participants do not understand English, but these participants are rare and it is understood that they would allow English to be used if they could understand it. In one case a young woman told us that her grandmother understands only Chipewyan, Cree, and French, so when she talks English to her it sometimes takes 5 minutes "to get through." It is not implied though that either the grandmother should learn English or that the young woman should learn one of her grandmother's languages. This communication, even though slow, is good enough.

People in Fort Chipewyan mention two kinds of language, "high" and "the way we talk here." One reason advanced for why a dictionary could not be made of Chipewyan was that there was no "high" language as there was for English and French. As we have said before, the Chipewyan chief feels he can speak high Cree but not high Chipewyan. On one occasion the Chipewyan reporter, Evelyn Cook, of the CBC Mackenzie Network's "Dene News" called him on the phone. He said later that he did not realize he was going to be speaking on the radio and appeared to be embarrassed by the dissemination of "the way we talk."

Another person said that a priest had come from Fond du Lac who spoke Chipewyan better than she did. He spoke in high language and she could not understand him sometimes. At the same time she did not feel this was in any way shameful. She was only reporting the differences between ways of speaking. From her point of view the high language is found in the biblical and other liturgical texts that have been written in syllabics. She felt we would learn good Chipewyan from studying these texts.

In some cases high language is equated with the way people speak elsewhere. Fond du Lac, La Loche, and Cold Lake are often mentioned as being places where "good Chip" is spoken. R. Scollon found that his own speech in Chipewyan, which was inevitably modeled after François Mandeville's texts and pronounced rather slowly and awkwardly, was taken as the way they speak at Cold Lake. In Cree, good language is the way they speak "down south." Usually where a location is mentioned, this is the Saddle Lake Reserve.

Within the community, then, we see that Chipewyan is viewed as not having a high variety. Cree has both high and low, and both English and French have both. Comparing the community with other places, it is felt that both Cree and Chipewyan are low, or at least a higher variety is available elsewhere (see Table 5.2). Before presenting the table, however, several things need to be mentioned. First, it is necessary to distinguish production and comprehension. People who speak Chipewyan recognize the speech of the Chipewyan reporters on the radio as a high variety but do not themselves attempt to speak that way. They also point out that it took these reporters some time to develop this ability. In the same way French speakers can understand the French of the well-educated missionaries but make no attempt to speak high French themselves.

STYLE AND THE GOOD SPEAKER

When the earliest Europeans met the Chipewyans, they noticed the lack of oratory or more elaborate forms of speech that they had seen in the native groups to the south (MacGregor 1974). When the Treaty Eight Commission was at Fort Chipewyan in 1899 they noticed that the Cree

TABLE 5.2. Status of the Varieties of the Four Languages.[a]

Style	Mode	Cree	Chipewyan	English	French
"the way we talk"	P	+	+	+	(+)
	C	+	+	+	(+)
"high"	P	+	−	+!	−
	C	+	+	+!	+

[a] Parentheses indicate that this usage is decreasing. Exclamation marks indicate a strong increase which we expect will continue in the near future. P is production, and C is comprehension.

chief made a speech in which the conditions of their signing were given. The Chipewyans presented a long list of conditions and would not cooperate in signing until all the items had been argued out in detail. In 1977 the Chipewyan chief gives his speeches in Cree. Although there has been much linguistic convergence accompanying the switching, mixing, and blurring of lines of native identity, a distinction in what we might call styles of interacting has been maintained between Chipewyans and Crees to the present.

We observed this difference in style, for example, when a short announcement had to be translated into Cree and Chipewyan. The announcement of the new program in native languages was about one paragraph long in English. It was to be written in Chipewyan and Cree in alphabetic and syllabic writing if possible. The approach taken by the Chipewyan person was to translate line by line or phrase by phrase in fairly short units. When the paragraph had been finished, it was taken to a woman who knew syllabics. Again the text was read a piece at a time and written down. Changes that occurred in this process were not noticed overtly and they were left in the finished text. The whole process took about an hour and the full text was never read through from beginning to end. The Cree version was quite different. It was first decided that the whole task should be done by one person. First there was about an hour of discussion explaining the task and especially filling in the background of the text. Before the person would be asked to undertake the task, it was felt he should know the purpose of the announcement and who wrote it. It was also explained how the announcement fit into the language program in the school and how that program fit into community educational goals. When this background had been established, the person was asked if he would be willing to write out the announcement. He agreed.

Then the approach was to read and discuss the English text. When the translator felt he fully understood the original, he then began to recreate the text in Cree syllabics. It was felt that a line-by-line translation would be accurate enough but basically unintelligible in some deeper way.

In this example we can see a clear difference in the attitude toward the creation of text. We have further observed that whenever tape recordings were made, the Cree speakers asked to hear the tape played back and listened to the whole with great attention. They commented on points where they were especially pleased with their own phrasing or with the content. In contrast to this, the Chipewyan speakers rarely showed any interest in these replayings of their own speech.

In making requests there is also a difference in style. The Cree method is quite indirect. One gives all of the background detail first, and where the listener is astute or willing, he or she will anticipate the request.

On the other hand, the Chipewyan method is to ask directly. Where further details are needed they are supplied later in a type of cross-examination.

The final example we can call "speaking for." Although both groups would say that the role of their leaders is to speak for them, there seems to be a difference in how this is done. We have discussed before arguments in which there is a constant attempt to achieve and to maintain consensus. This largely characterizes Chipewyan arguments. A leader must talk frequently with his people so that he is confident that he shares the same presuppositional foundations as they. Where this foundation is shared, whatever is said is thought of as "speaking for" the people.

In contrast to this is the Cree oratorical style of speaking for one's people. The leader's view is understood to be essentially and originally his own, but through his ability to be convincing he is able to bring others along with him. Thus where he succeeds he speaks for the people.

We can now characterize the Chipewyan interaction style as direct, particularistic, and argumentative. The Cree style by contrast is indirect, holistic, and oratorical. Although these styles can often be used to describe the actions of individuals, it is also possible for the same person to make use of both of these styles. An astute switching of interactive styles is often used as the basis for an effective political technique.

Finally, it can now be asked: What counts as a good speaker in the speech community of Fort Chipewyan? Perhaps the central quality is versatility. One person was singled out as a good speaker because he can tell stories "from both sides," that is, he could tell Cree and Chipewyan stories. Another man told his nephew that it was good to know several languages so that when the people began warring again he could understand his enemies. Another person emphasized being able to "get down to the way we talk." Where people are acknowledged to be good speakers, they can be seen to control the minimum four Chipewyan, Cree, English, and French, and usually will claim to understand several other languages as well. Further, they also control both the Chipewyan and Cree styles of interaction. Such considerations as correctness and elegance rarely are mentioned in discussions of good speakers.

COMMUNICATION ROUTES

To a certain extent the settlement at Fort Chipewyan may be seen as a terminal for communications with groups and institutions outside of the community. In trying to get a well-rounded view of language and communication at Fort Chipewyan, then, we feel it will be useful to think of communications outside of the community as taking place along communication routes. For our purposes here we will look at 11 of these routes.

The first route at which we will look is a commercial route. Most of the goods that are bought and sold in Fort Chipewyan come from or through Edmonton. It is the route used by the Hudson's Bay Company, the Cremetchip Cooperative, and several other smaller entrepreneurs. Although private parties do a large volume of business by mail order from Simpsons–Sears out of Regina, this is also routed through Edmonton and Fort McMurray. The actual transportation route depends on the time of year, with heavy goods arriving by barge when the lake is free of ice and by road through Fort Smith in the winter. Lighter items arrive by air. In return, furs that have been trapped and prepared in the bush around Fort Chipewyan are shipped out along this route.

The linguistic point to be made here is that the use of this route requires the use of English. There are such things as wholesale catalogues, bills of lading, invoices, and checks to be handled. One must read, write, and speak English to some extent to use this route. This fact is captured in the joke about the barely literate storekeeper who ordered 30 cases of "This Side Up." It is not surprising that most of the movement along this route is made by people who are quite modernized.

The second route we wish to consider is the political route of Band affairs. The office of Indian Affairs that has jurisdiction over Fort Chipewyan was located at St. Paul at the time of our fieldwork. At the same time a very influential group of Indians in Alberta is located at Saddle Lake near St. Paul. Traffic along this route is largely restricted to influential members of the two treaty Indian bands. Because of the Cree influence of the people at Saddle Lake, there is a tendency for this route to have emphasized the use of Cree and, especially, to have developed an awareness of a high variety of Cree. It is common for people at Fort Chipewyan to say they are 20 years behind the people at Saddle Lake, expressing both the actual time difference between the signing of treaties in the two areas and an attitude of being somewhat backward in the development of modern native awareness.

The third route is also political, but this one involves provincial politics. In some cases offices in Fort McMurray have jurisdiction over Fort Chipewyan, and in others the offices are in Edmonton. On the whole this route is one-way into Fort Chipewyan, since there is no political body in the community with any more than advisory powers. This route is perhaps the most exclusively English route. Public meetings held to gain a view of community interest or to announce governmental policy are attended by no more than the several people who feel they can endure an encounter with elaborated government English. Government publications are virtually unintelligible to most community members and thus often the only real communication along this route comes in terms of regulations which are enforced by the Royal Canadian Mounted Police. In some cases the offender first becomes aware of the violation when being arrested. The net result of this condition is an entropic distrust of all communications along this route.

The fourth route is the communication among family and friends. The most important connections appear to be at Fort McMurray and Fort Smith, but there are some connections with Fond du Lac and most of the other smaller communities in the area. There is frequent movement along this route and there is little linguistic restriction except for Fond du Lac. There are said to be no Crees there. Movement to the other places takes place among all members of the community.

There may be a channel restriction along this route, however. Most communication among friends and family is by word of mouth. Phone bills of $80 to $150 indicate frequent telephoning. One woman says her son called home every night during the first several years he was in high school at Fort Smith. On the other hand relatively few personal letters come through the post office. This channel restriction may reflect the prevailing lack of interest in writing.

The fifth route is like the fourth except there is a specific goal in its use. During the summer there are softball tournaments between teams from Fort Chipewyan and Fort Smith. During the winter the games are bingo and basketball. Even more important in the winter is the shopping available at Fort Smith; there is a larger variety of meats and fresh fruits and vegetables, and of dry goods as well. But perhaps the most important commodity available at Fort Smith is liquor. There is no provincial liquor outlet in Fort Chipewyan and this provides a strong motive for some people to drive or hire a taxi at $20 a trip to go to Fort Smith. Although there seems to be no overt linguistic restriction on this route, modernized, Euro-Canadians tend to look on these trips with disparagement.

The sixth route is the radio. The CBC Mackenzie Network comes from Yellowknife and is broadcast with few changes from Fort Chipewyan to Coppermine on the Arctic Coast. Perhaps the most interesting aspect of this radio broadcasting is that there are regular programs in the "Dene languages" (Chipewyan, Dogrib, and Slavey), which add up to as much as 2 hours a day during the week. There is only one half-hour show on Saturday in Cree. This means that Chipewyan is receiving a much higher representation than Cree on the radio. The program which is listened to most is the "Dene News." During the summer of 1976 this was on mornings at 11:00. It was played over the loudspeakers in the Bay (Hudson's Bay Company Retail Store) and in the Cremetchip Cooperative store.

One person, a Chipewyan, said "everyone listens" to the news. At first we took this to mean only the Chipewyans, but later found that many Crees listen to this news and understand this variety of Chipewyan. This program was switched in the fall of 1976 to afternoons at 3:00. Shortly after television braodcasting began, the program "All in the Family," which is programmed at 3:00, replaced the "Dene News" in the Bay, the Coop, and in many homes as well.

Most of the programming on the CBC is in English. It includes a mixture of programs from all over Canada and programs prepared in the Yellowknife studio. There are frequent community announcements and weather reports. From this programming one gets a strong feeling of community with the Northwest Territories.

In addition to the one CBC station, several others are available if antennas are erected. Many people erect these antennas and thereby gain access to the news, weather, and music of the south. Without an antenna at night in good weather, stations from as far south as Utah and as far west as Vancouver are available, and though we have not observed many people listening to these stations, some have reported that they do.

Until television became available in November of 1976, the only operation of the seventh route was in the movies shown at Mah's Hall. These films run from Walt Disney to Bruce Lee's *Kung Fu*. When television began, people were ready with a television set in nearly every home. There is little doubt that in the long run this steady input of regular television programming from Vancouver will be an important influence toward the development of the modern consciousness in Fort Chipewyan. The children now compete with each other in the memorization of commercials and slogans and have, as a result, moved directly into the advertising jargon of the technological culture of Canada and the United States.

The eighth route is the occupational route. One of the worst dilemmas faced by modernized, working people in Fort Chipewyan is that there is practically no employment in the settlement. One can either work and leave or be unemployed and stay. Most of the employment is at Fort McMurray, beginning in the form of vocational training and ending in the various semiskilled jobs in the oil development there. There are many programs through which people go out to Fort McMurray for training and then, upon completion of their training, are placed in jobs. They do not often stay long in the jobs.

One man explained his problem. His wife drinks heavily. When he went to Fort McMurray he took his wife and family. He was busy with his training and work but his wife began drinking. Finally, he was forced to choose between staying there and having good employment but losing his family, or returning to Fort Chipewyan where he could help to keep his wife from drinking but where he would have no work. Fort Chipewyan and Fort McMurray are the two horns of this occupational dilemma.

For most of the available jobs it is necessary for the employee to use English. So in addition to requiring residence away from Fort Chipewyan, this route usually requires a shift toward monolingualism.

The ninth route is the medical route. Since there is only a small nursing station in Fort Chipewyan, all complicated medical procedures are done either in Fort McMurray or Edmonton. We have found very few people who have not had to go out to the hospital for something. At Fort Chipewyan even childbirth is considered a complicated medical problem. Because of an airline regulation prohibiting women 9-months pregnant from flying, women are sent out to a boarding home in the eighth month to wait until delivery. The inconvenience and dislocation caused by this policy is apparently of less concern to Health and Welfare, than inconveniencing the medical personnel.

Within the community, communication between the nursing station and other people is equally unidirectional. Misunderstandings are frequent, and health authorities view their announcements as having the force of law while people native to the community prefer to ignore them (in the cases where they can understand them).

The tenth communication route consists of the two schools. The Bishop Piche School is the Indian Affairs school which now has all students in grades 4 through 12. The "Public School" is part of the Northland School Division and has all students from grades 1 through 3. Curriculum in both schools is developed outside the community, and the schools are staffed from outside the community. The school committee of the Athabasca Cree–Chipewyan Band has virtually no input to the activities or programs of the schools, and as a result the schools may be regarded as the single most important communication route of the modern consciousness into the community.

Finally, the eleventh route is into the bush. As the milieu of the bush consciousness, the bush remains the nutrient source. When the other routes of communication fail or threaten to exhaust the person, one only need go out into the bush to recover. It is the bush that gives whatever sense of community there is at Fort Chipewyan: The other routes tend to fragment the community into a network of communications with outside institutions. It becomes ironic, then, that as on the surface of it people appear to be moving together into the settlement, in actuality they are using the settlement as a route to outside institutions. The settlement is not the center of social and cultural focus but the terminal for contact with other, outside institutions. If there is a speech community at Fort Chipewyan, it is found only out of the settlement in the bush. This is the background of the common life experienced as home.

THE CONCEPT OF SPEECH COMMUNITY AT FORT CHIPEWYAN

Throughout our discussion we have regarded the concepts of community and speech community somewhat loosely. Now it will be useful to speak specifically of the concept of the speech community. We may take Gumperz's (1968) definition of the speech community as our starting point: "Any human aggregate characterized by regular and frequent interaction by means of a shared body of verbal signs and set off from similar aggregates by significant differences in language use [p. 381]." In our previous discussion we have characterized the people living and trading at or around Fort Chipewyan as consisting of two basic groups, the settlement group and the bush group, and as having two basic reality sets which at least roughly correspond to these groups, the modern consciousness and the bush consciousness. The bush group we have also characterized as atomistic, and as such we should expect very little in the way of community or speech community. Communications are, in fact, irregular and confused. Generally, speech interaction is avoided and so we feel there is, in fact, little support for the concept of a speech community among the holders of the bush consciousness. The community that exists must be thought of as atomistic and so not well organized at the community level. At the same time we have suggested that this general social atomism is characteristic of an area much larger than the immediate Fort Chipewyan area, and so, in the very loosest sense, the speech community might be thought of as including most of the Mackenzie drainage area or even more. Obviously, in either view, it is difficult to maintain the concept of speech community advanced by Gumperz for the Fort Chipewyan area.

It is important now to consider community from the point of view of the modern consciousness. Berger, Berger, and Kellner (1973) have tied their concept of the modern consciousness to the institutions that are its carriers. The primary carriers are the institutions of technological production, such as factories. These are largely absent at Fort Chipewyan. In a pervasive way, however, this technology is present throughout the community. Snowmobiles and power tools are sold at the Hudson's Bay store. There are numerous classes in various forms of technology from the construction of boats to heavy-equipment operation. In the school, students have shop classes in which they learn to manipulate some of the more basic tools of the technology. The fruits of the technology are also abundantly present through the Bay, Simpsons–Sears mail order, and television.

The principal carriers of the modern consciousness in Fort Chipewyan, however, are the government bureaucracies which populate the settlement. Moncrieff, Montgomery, and Associates (1973) report that there are 24 federal and provincial governmental agencies or programs operating in the community of Fort Chipewyan. As we have suggested earlier, Indian Affairs may be, in the long run, the most influential of these because of its control of the school, which as of 1976 has integrated all students whether Indian or not from grades 4 through 12 into one program.

For our current discussion, however, it is perhaps most interesting to focus on the secondary carriers of the modern consciousness. Berger, Berger, and Kellner (1973) have suggested that these are the cities and sociocultural pluralism. As Fort Chipewyan names its roadways, introduces settlement-wide water and plumbing, and unrolls its planned development, it does so as an important carrier of the modern consciousness. As outsiders take up residence at Fort Chipewyan, they (we!) do so as carriers of the modern consciousness, both in that outsiders view the world in this way and in that their presence produces greater pluralization. At the same time, television broadcasting has become the strongest single carrier of sociocultural pluralism, as viewers in Fort Chipewyan watch the lives of Archie Bunker and others being acted out before them.

To return now to the concept of the community, not only do the modernized people living at Fort Chipewyan have a different concept of community, this concept of community is in itself an important carrier of the modern consciousness. It is not simply a matter of two groups viewing the community in different ways, **how** they view community and social organization is crucial to the view they take of reality. Thus it is essential to the modern consciousness to have communities and for communities to become cities by developing industries, a tax base, and a political organization. By the same token it is essential to the bush consciousness to maintain atomistic social relations and to resist organization into groups and communities.

In our view of Fort Chipewyan, whose view of community is it appropriate to take? Since there are essentially two groups with conflicting views, we would like to avoid prejudicing the discussion toward either of the groups. Referring to the people in and around Fort Chipewyan as a community or a speech community favors the modernized group. On the other hand scrupulous avoidance of reference to groups makes what is after all a highly modernized discussion quite awkward. This problem, then, is the source of our very loose use of the concept of community in regard to Fort Chipewyan.

What is of more interest than definitions is the relationship between the two groups at Fort Chipewyan. As we have said, their two views of reality and community are fundamentally opposed. This is much as Honigmann (1949) observed for the Kaska at Lower Post, British Columbia: "In terms of the prevailing atomism of Kaska social life, it is almost inevitable that any activities of the Dominican and local governments in pursuit of their regulative functions should be resented and productive of anxiety [p. 146]." This conflict between reality sets and their corresponding social institutions permeates life at Fort Chipewyan. The bureaucratic ordering of the world has reached out onto the traplines and defined how many animals may be caught, where those animals may be caught, and by whom. In the production of Treaty Eight, the bureaucratic ordering extended to the creation of a new status of social membership for every individual in the area. It is not surprising to see, then, that there is a direct relation between the increase of government intervention in the lives of bush people and the increase in the amount of entropic behavior that has as its goal the subversion of the government imposed order.

It may be seen that the conflict of these two reality sets is largely responsible for the rather frequent examples of entropic behavior. It is important to emphasize that a reality set is experienced by its holder as simply the world as usual. The activities of a person holding a different reality set are not understood as deriving from a different base. They are understood as erratic and unaccountable where they do not affect oneself, and where they do impinge on one's life, they are most often understood as being hostile.

It is possible now to look at the four characteristics of bush consciousness to see how they may be perceived by those sharing this reality set and by those holding the modern consciousness. Table 5.3 suggests how these characteristics might be described.

The relationship between the two groups at Fort Chipewyan may be described as schismogenic (Bateson 1958, 1972). The two groups are in a system of complementary schismogenesis, particularly in regards to concepts of order and bureaucratization. As the modernized group introduces organization into the community, the bush group reacts to this entropically in order to reduce the effects of this order. This entropic reaction is taken by the institutions of modernization—the schools, the mission, and the police—as evidence for the need of greater organization, more programs, and a higher level of socialization to modern life, which when

TABLE 5.3.   The Perception of the Four Characteristics of Bush Consciousness.

	Modern	Bush
Entropic	Destructive "Drag-um down" Treacherous	Revolutionary
Individualistic	Uncooperative Antisocial Selfish Egocentric	Independent Self-reliant
Nonintervening	Passive Sullen Withdrawn Unresponsive Lazy	Observant Quiet
Integrative	Backward Primitive Stupid Illiterate	Native Natural Organic Tribal Oral Nonliterate

instituted produce even greater entropic attacks upon the establishment of order.

Within a schismogenic system there are often internal restraints, places where the rapid acceleration of the split is controlled. Within the system at Fort Chipewyan there appear to have been such checks up until perhaps two decades ago. On the side of the modern consciousness there was simple unconcern coupled perhaps with racism. Fumoleau (1975) quotes Prime Minister St. Laurent as saying that during the period of 1922 to 1939, "Apparently we have administered the vast Territories of the North in a continuous state of absence of mind [p. 20]." This state of affairs was not seriously altered at Fort Chipewyan until the early 1950s, when we may take the secularization of the school as an indication of a newly developed governmental concern. Thus in earlier times, just because the government basically did not care, there was relatively little intervention in the lives of people at Fort Chipewyan.

On the other side, the integrative aspect of the bush consciousness works to internalize foreign institutions, but at a rather slow pace. While outside intervention remained slow and limited, the entropic reaction remained vestigial. Outside institutions, such as the Catholic Church and the trapping economy, were fully integrated into the lives of the holders of the bush consciousness. As government concern increased, however, a rate of change was reached at which the bush consciousness could no longer assimilate the changes. The result was the modern situation of apparently runaway complementary schismogenesis. Rather than getting closer to a general, community-wide organization, the rifts appear to be deepening. The modernized "cures" for community ills are service organizations, education, newspapers, wage employment, and political involvement. The bush responses to these "cures" are vandalism, dropping out, alcoholism, and drugs.

These, then, are the two reality sets available at Fort Chipewyan. It only remains now for us to suggest that although these reality sets on the whole represent the positions of individuals at Fort Chipewyan, it is becoming increasingly common for individuals to seek a personal negotiation of these two positions. That is, some few have sought to develop a modernized reality set for some part of their experience while maintaining contact with the bush consciousness. While it is quite beyond the scope of our research to attempt to discuss these individual situations, it is our observation that the negotiation of the two reality sets which is problematic at the level of the community is very difficult at the personal level. It remains to be seen if a successful negotiation of the bush consciousness and the modern consciousness can be achieved.

6

SOME NEW PROBLEMS

In undertaking our fieldwork at Fort Chipewyan we were interested in placing in context the Chipewyan work of Fang-Kuei Li which had been done in the same community 48 years earlier in 1928. As our period in the field passed, we became particularly interested in two problems, one linguistic and one methodological. The linguistic problem was the convergence of the four languages in use in the community. Because our primary interest had been in Chipewyan, at first we saw this as a problem of accounting for various changes in the structure of Chipewyan. We saw these changes from the Chipewyan as recorded in 1928 by Li and so presumed them to be to a large extent historical developments.

At the same time we were concerned with a second problem, the difficulty of doing linguistic research at Fort Chipewyan. We found it impossible to find a "good informant." Where we sought to work with people toward developing an interest in linguistic work, we also found a general lack of interest, if not actual resistance. As we worked with this second problem, we began to understand some of the characteristics that we have come to call the bush consciousness. Thus it was our methodological problem of finding a way to work at all that gave us the understanding we needed to return to look at the content of our research. Once we were able to account reasonably well for reality set and especially for the conflict between our modern consciousness and the bush consciousness of the people with whom we were trying to work, we were in a position to view the "changes" in Chipewyan as part of a more general process of linguistic convergence. This led us to take a greater interest in the other languages in use in the community. As a problem in community language use we saw it as of as much interest to look, for example, at how Marcel's English was related to Chipewyan and Cree as to look at how his Chipewyan had been "changed."

Our starting point, then, for this fieldwork was the work of Fang-Kuei Li. As we began to place this work in the context of the speech community, we saw that structurally there were important differences between Chipewyan as described by Li and Chipewyan as we would describe it on the basis of our experience in the field. The differences we observed could be accounted for by the fact of linguistic convergence. In a few words, Chipewyan had become in some ways like the other languages spoken at Fort Chipewyan. Our explanation for this was that the reality set of the people who speak Chipewyan had led to a general integration or convergence of experience. Our explanation for the reality set is the social structure of the community, that is, social atomism. The explanation of the linguistic problem of convergence is also consonant with the explanation of our methodological problem. That is, the bush consciousness explains not only linguistic convergence but also the difficulties we experienced in finding out about linguistic convergence.

This twofold problem of linguistic convergence and field method might be thought of as our first-level problem. It is basically a synchronic problem of understanding the relationships among languages currently in use in the speech community. At the same time, the necessity of referring to a standard, in this case François Mandeville's dictated speech, to speak of "changes" in the Chipewyan language, has brought us to a second problem. This is the diachronic problem of seeking to understand how long the present situation has existed at Fort Chipewyan. Has this linguistic convergence been stable for some time or does it represent a development in the 48 years since Li and Mandeville worked together?

We have very little to offer as evidence for the earlier linguistic situation. At the same time, however, we can recapitulate our own method to some extent to see that there is reason to believe that the situation in the Fort Chipewyan area has been reasonably stable for perhaps 100 or more years. Since the two basic conditions for linguistic convergence are the presence of multiple languages and the bush consciousness reality set, if these can be shown to be present, we may presume that linguistic convergence might well have taken place.

In Chapter 5 we presented a sketch of the linguistic history of the Fort Chipewyan area. When Peter Pond established his post nearly 200 years ago in 1778, there were both Chipewyan and Cree speakers present in the area. French was no doubt represented in the speech of the voyageurs but became officially emphasized with the arrival of the missionaries in 1847. Thus the four languages, Chipewyan, Cree, English, and French, have been strongly represented in the area for at least 130 years. We feel it is fair to assume, then, that for at least that length of time the potential for linguistic convergence among these four languages has been present at Fort Chipewyan.

In our own case it was the entropic aspect of the bush consciousness that we first observed, and in the end it may still be the strongest indicator of the bush consciousness for an outside observer. As early as the 1820s the Scottish trader George Simpson displayed his reaction to this aspect of the bush consciousness. MacGregor (1974) quotes Simpson as saying about the Chipewyans,

> I cannot point out a solidary good trait . . . all their dealings are tainted with a degree of low Cunning which one would think it difficult for an uncultivated savage to acquire; they are covetous to an extreme, false and cowardly; . . . the whole Tribe does not possess one particle of honor and to the feelings of gratitude they are total Strangers; . . . such Wretches are only fit to inhabit the inhospitable clime they live in and no one who has had an opportunity of knowing them will commiserate their situation [p. 24].

As historical background, then, we feel that at Fort Chipewyan there were multiple languages in use as early as 100 or more years ago, and evidence that the reality set we have called the bush consciousness was present as early as perhaps 150 years ago. We would now like to consider more closely the history of linguistic and ethnographic work in the area, particularly as it relates to Fang-Kuei Li's presence in 1928.

In Chapter 4 we mentioned in connection with the entropic aspect of the bush consciousness that quite a number of linguists and ethnographers experienced trying difficulties in working in the area. Lowie (1959) in 1908 found it to be the least fruitful scientific trip he had ever made. Mason (1946) in 1913 experienced "much vexatious difficulty in working [p. 7]." Mason explicitly refers to traits that "practically all travelers from Hearne down, as well as traders anathematize [p. 30]." Osgood (1975) in 1928 felt his trip was "an anthropological fiasco [p. 517]," and later cautioned his student Honigmann (1949) about "certain marked personality features [p. 3]." In short, it seems clear that most of the linguistic and ethnographic work done in the Mackenzie drainage has been done against a background of conflict in reality set.

If we look more closely now at the content of some of this research we find, as we might expect, evidence for linguistic convergence. Lowie published his texts in English (Lowie 1912), and so there is no direct evidence for linguistic convergence. He does, however, make several interesting comments about the speech community:

> Tiny as was the settlement at Fort Chipewyan, it was polyglot and socially many faceted. I could speak German to an Alsatian priest and hear French, English, Chipewyan, and Cree, the last two being totally diverse forms of Indian speech. The English I heard naturally varied with the speaker's education and provenience; I was shocked once to hear a physician pronounce "case" in unalloyed cockney as "kyse." The Orkney brogue was not uncommon throughout the region; and French was of course usually of the Quebec variety. French folkways and etiquette were not wanting either; and it was entertaining to watch native women seated on the ground bandying polite "messieurs" and "mesdames" with passersby [p. 33].

Notice that Lowie does not indicate a social stratification of French but rather is surprised to find native women to have assimilated "French folkways." Regarding Chipewyan and Cree, Lowie (1959) records "that the Chipewyans had adopted a good many stories of a Cree cycle that centered in the adventures of a trickster-hero [p. 32]." Incidentally, this Cree character, (wīsahkēcahk, Wolfart 1973; Wisahketchahk, Bloomfield 1930) has been found as far into Athabaskan territory as Arctic Village, Alaska, as Sagithuk (McKennan 1965) or Vasaagihdzak (Peter 1973). This penetration of the Cree trickster into the interior of Alaska speaks for a widespread diffusion of Algonkian characteristics, not just a localized effect at Fort Chipewyan.

The picture Lowie gives us, then, is of a community in which the four languages, English, French, Chipewyan, and Cree, are fully established and in use by many members of the community. He also gives us reason to believe that the bush consciousness was also well established because of the difficulties he experienced in his fieldwork. It is useful to bear in mind the goals of Lowie's research since in the end our argument will seek to relate the recording of linguistic data in the field to the theoretical goals of the researcher. Lowie himself comments: "If the Indians were only of moderate interest, the half-breeds and whites of Lake Athabaska would have formed a fascinating object of systematic research; but in those days "community studies" of this kind had not yet become fashionable and I made only random observations [p. 32]."

It is clearly implied that Lowie at the time of undertaking his 1908 research was seeking out a view of the "pristine" native Chipewyans that apparently was impossible to develop at Fort Chipewyan. He fully acknowledges the linguistically complex and many-faceted social climate of the community he encountered, but noted that **at that time** there was not the theoretical interest in such situations.

From Lowie's record, then, we are at least partially supported in our belief that the social and cultural conditions which would support linguistic convergence were, in fact, well established as of the time of his visit in 1908. Three years after Lowie's rather unsuccessful "reconnaissance trip," Pliny Earle Goddard (1912) spent slightly less than 1 month at Cold Lake, Alberta, where he was concerned with "obtaining at first hand some definite knowledge of the sounds and structure of a northern or Dene dialect of an Athapascan language for the purpose of comparison with Pacific coast and southern dialects [p. 1]." We can begin, then, by noticing Goddard's explicit interest in historical reconstruction and the implication that what would be of interest would be that which would facilitate the construction of a genetic tree or Stammbaum model of the Athabaskan family.

Goddard (1912) does not report any great difficulties in obtaining his material, which may perhaps be explained by the distance of Cold Lake from the center, Fort Chipewyan. On the other hand, the short period he spent at Cold Lake may indicate some difficulties. He does say, though, that the Chipewyans at Cold Lake were "closely associated with the Cree [p. 3]," and that "the entire band are faithful Catholics [p. 3]." He found no instances of "old religious practice or beliefs [p. 3]." We can suggest, then, that at Cold Lake there had been significant contact among Chipewyan, Cree, and French (as represented by the fathers of the Oblates of Mary Immaculate).

In view of the Chipewyan–Cree association at Cold Lake and our earlier suggestion in Chapter 3 that the variation of the s- and ʃ-consonants had as its source the free variation of the Cree consonants /c/ and /s/, it is with great interest that we read that Goddard (1912) was quite puzzled by the variation among the consonants of the s-series and the c-series. (We will now use the symbol for c for [ʃ].) It will be useful to quote his full discussion:

> A series of spirants and affricatives is formed between the front of the tongue and the palate not far back of the teeth. These are very similar to English z and s, but were written *even in the same words* as j (zh) and c (sh). In the texts they have been printed as originally recorded. It was hoped some reason might appear for this variation although it was recognized that they always corresponded to dj, j, c, tc, and tc' as they occur in other Athapaskan dialects recorded. It may be that the sounds are really intermediate between z and zh as they exist in English and therefore heard alternately [p. 75, italics added].

This comment of Goddard's expresses the hope that an explanation would be found for the variation which we have characterized as a variation between s-series consonants and c-series consonants. He suggests that the explanation might be auditory and perceptual. That is, he suggests that it might just be a matter of his inability to adjust his hearing to perceive a point of articulation that is intermediate between an alveopalatal position and a dental position. Fortunately for our purposes he has left the texts just as he originally recorded them in this respect and we are able to observe in Goddard's material just the variation we have observed in 1976–77 at Fort Chipewyan.

It is particularly significant that in Goddard's texts we are able to find shifts of s-consonants to c-consonants (*sū na gī* and *cū na Gī*, cf. Mandeville's *sunaɣî*·'my grandson'; *be djī ya ze* 'young caribou', cf. Mandeville's *bɛdzitcoɣ* 'full grown caribou'), but not shifts of c-consonants to s-consonants. This argues for an underlying distinction between the c-series and the s-series, which is merged variably by shifts of s-consonants to c-consonants. That is, Goddard's evidence argues for assuming a contrast between c- and s-consonants that is neutralized in some contexts.

We can see, then, in Goddard's report the convergence of language which we observed at Fort Chipewyan in 1976–77. We would suggest from Goddard's report and from our own work that Goddard did, in fact, hear these consonants correctly but, as with Lowie, it was the theoretical framework within which he was working that did not allow for a speech community or diffusion-based explanation.

We do not know if Sapir knew of Goddard's work at Cold Lake when in 1913 he asked John Alden Mason (1946) to make a linguistic reconnaissance of the "Athapaskan Indians of the Great Slave Lake region." Sapir, who at that time was the Chief of the Anthropological Division of the Geological Survey of Canada, is known to have had less than full respect for the work of Goddard (Li, personal communication). Apparently, Sapir's doubts about Goddard stemmed from a mistrust of Goddard's ability to hear Athabaskan consonants. We suggest that it was, among other things, Goddard's accurate though unfashionable recording of the shifts of s-consonants to c-consonants in Chipewyan that led to Sapir's doubts about Goddard's transcriptions. We might add parenthetically that the long-standing difficulty with the Beaver consonants of the same series probably stems from the same convergence. Goddard's Beaver informants were able to speak Cree (Goddard 1917) and we must assume similar effects on the Beaver they spoke.

At any rate, Sapir's interest in learning about Chipewyan and other Mackenzie drainage languages fared no better with Mason. As we have discussed above, Mason encountered many difficulties in working wherever he went and he returned quite unsure of his material. When Mason returned he turned over his material to Sapir and copies of the texts are still in the Archives of the National Museum of Man in Ottawa. In time,

Sapir turned over Mason's original texts and notes to Fang-Kuei Li who then passed them on to R. Scollon. No attempt that we know of has been made in these some 50 years to publish the Mason texts. As with Goddard, the resistance to Mason's work appears to be based on a mistrust of his hearing and his transcriptions. One does not have to search far to see the problem. In the first short text recorded at Fort McMurray from an unnamed informant, we find in the fourth line *betc!į* 'he had'. Transliterated into Li's orthography this is *bεtc'į*, which we may compare with Mandeville's *bets'į*. That is, one sees very quickly that Mason encountered in his first four lines of text in the field the variation that Goddard hoped to explain, that Sapir mistrusted, and that continues to the present day. It is clear from Mason's notes on his field material that he was both aware of this variation and concerned about finding an explanation. His notes may be quoted in full on this point (Mason, n.d.):

c – Not quite so clear as Eng sh & less common than s, sometimes confused with s, less commonly with j.

j – Rare in Chip. in others cognate rather with y than with c. Study carefully as all 4 sounds have intermediate tendency & probably are variations of 2 if not of 1 sound. s often written s..

ts	common.	
dz	less common.	
ts!	common	These four sounds may be cognate; may be variants of one sound.
tc	common	Review carefully & try to get system out of it.
dj	common	
tc!	common	

It is clear from the limbo in which Mason's Chipewyan work has remained until today that rather than trust now two reports on this variation, Sapir assumed that Mason's hearing was as unreliable as he felt Goddard's to be. Saville-Troike (1975) has also commented about Sapir's tendency overly to narrow the range of data he would accept as reliable.

Here it is worth quoting Sapir himself. In his book *Language* Sapir (1921) takes a firm position on the conservatism of Athabaskan languages: "The Athabaskan languages of America are spoken by peoples that have had astonishingly varied cultural contacts, yet nowhere do we find that an Athabaskan dialect has borrowed at all freely from a neighboring language [p. 196]."

In 1921 Sapir was aware of the work of Lowie, Goddard, and Mason, and yet rather than accept that an Athabaskan language could be affected phonologically by an Algonkian language (or an Indo-European one), he had preferred to assume that his colleagues lacked the necessary perceptual acuity to do Chipewyan justice. His solution to the problem was apparently to send a person for whom he had a high regard and whom he himself had trained in the field, Fang-Kuei Li. Thus in 1928 Li arrived at Fort Chipewyan.

It is well known in Athabaskan linguistics that Li found in Chipewyan a remarkably conservative Northern Athabaskan language. His work established beyond question a clear distinction between the s-series (<PA *c) and the c-series (<PA *xy) in Chipewyan. His work appears to have vindicated Sapir's mistrust of his colleagues' hearing and established Chipewyan as of 1928 as a language remarkably unaffected by the forces of linguistic diffusion.

From Sapir's point of view the work of Li established the conservatism of the Chipewyan language and at the same time established the unreliability of Lowie's, Goddard's, and Mason's work. From our perspective, however, we see that the observations of Lowie, Goddard, and Mason confirm our belief that the current linguistic convergence at Fort Chipewyan was well established before Li arrived there to do his fieldwork. From our point of view, it is Li's work that is exceptional, and this raises the third general problem we wish to discuss. In a speech community characterized by the bush consciousness and linguistic convergence, how did such a conservative, historically discrete variety of Chipewyan as Mandeville's come to be recorded and analyzed? Now rather than accounting for changes in Chipewyan since 1928, we are seeking to account for the unusual nature of the language recorded in 1928 by Mandeville and Li.

In our solution to this problem we may look at two elements, the informant and the linguist. In Chapter 3 we gave a sketch of François Mandeville's personal history. There are several details of this personal history of interest to us. The first is that he did not arrive at Fort Chipewyan until about 1925, when he was some 47 years old, and so he was certainly not a native of that community. The second detail of interest is Mandeville's considerable experience with other dialects of Chipewyan and with other Mackenzie-drainage Athabaskan languages. It is said he could speak Chipewyan, Dogrib, Slavey, Hare, Loucheux, and some Beaver. Marcel told us that the reason "old François" could speak so clearly was that he had lived in different places where they spoke in different ways. Mandeville could say things so that anybody could understand them, according to Marcel. We take this to mean that to some extent, Mandeville had, in fact, "reconstructed" a maximally differentiated variety of Chipewyan out of his experiences in different speech communities.

This leads us to the third factor. Why should Mandeville have taken such an analytical view of language? The answer is relatively straightforward in our current framework. Mandeville was modernized. There are a number of indicators of this. He worked steadily throughout his lifetime in responsible positions as a trader. He is known to this day for his meticulous craftsmanship. From his own point of view, he considered himself to be French, not native, which we take to mark identification with the modern consciousness. Finally, his very willingness to work so intensively with Li is a strong indication of a modernized view of reality.

A fourth detail that is of importance in Mandeville's personal history is his long-standing interest in writing. He had learned to write in both the ``ABCs'' and in syllabics but was quite dissatisfied with these writing systems in the representation of Chipewyan. When Li began recording his dictations in phonetic script, Mandeville immediately realized that this was the writing system he was seeking. According to his son, P. X. Mandeville, Mandeville kept notes on their sessions and it is quite likely that these notes would have included attempts at writing in Li's phonetic script.

We can see, then, that Li's informant was well prepared to understand his linguistic goals and to sympathize with his method of achieving them. Li, for his part, was of course well prepared with a knowledge of Athabaskan gained in study with Sapir. In light of our knowledge of this informant and this linguist, it is not surprising that they should have produced between them a very conservative view of the Chipewyan language. We were puzzled on the other hand to find no trace of this pervasive and problematic linguistic convergence in Li's material. Two additional reports of interest are Mandeville's son's statement to us that at Fort Chipewyan people mix up their consonants, and François Mandeville's own statement to Li that younger people in the community ``slur consonants [Li, personal communication].'' So we returned to Li's originals to see if there was any evidence at all of this convergence in his original transcriptions. We especially looked for evidence of shifts of s-consonants to c-consonants.

Li has often mentioned that the earlier texts in the collection may be unreliable. He has said that his ear was not ``well tuned'' to the language. Indeed there are in the first two texts many places where segments are rewritten. The cases in which consonants of the s- and c-series are rewritten are of special interest to this discussion. We found that frequently a consonant that was first written as a member of the c-series was then corrected to the corresponding member of the s-series. Thus there are:

Original		*Corrected to*
nádjèltà	'one moves fast'	*náts'èltà*
bètc'án	'to him'	*bèts'án*
djìné	'day'	*dzìné*
nátc'ù·déł	'they shall go'	*náts'ù·déł*
nìdjídéł	'they get up'	*nìts'ídéł*
cèdíł	'they go'	*sèdíł*
cnì	'it is said'	*snì*

There also occasional shifts of c- to s-consonants, as in

k'áłdzìnɛ	'nearly'	*k'áłdjìnɛ*
dàlts'ùł	'one tears it off from the top'	*dàltc'ùł*

   In short, we saw that at least at first Li had heard some of the same variation that had been heard by Goddard and Mason. Several things need to be pointed out here. First, this overwriting and correcting was done to any great extent only in the first two texts dictated. In later texts where there is overwriting it does not affect consonants of these two series. Secondly, the overwriting was done as Mandeville repeated back carefully to Li the forms as they discussed morphological and paradigmatic questions. That is, the shift of s-consonants to c-consonants appears to have happened primarily in the somewhat more rapid flow of the original dictation of the text. In the second pass through the texts where they focused on each morpheme, the variation disappeared and thus it appears at first to have related to a contrast between rapid and careful speech.
   This explanation may be reasonable to some extent, but we must remember that "rapid" in this context is the speed at which Li could write, which never approached even slow conversational speed. A further consideration is that the later texts that were recorded when Li had developed some greater speed do not show this putative "rapid" variation. This returns us to Li's own explanation that at first he was not tuned to the language and could not clearly distinguish s- and c-series consonants.
   We would like to point out that Li had had experience recording in the field for at least four Athabaskan languages before working on Chipewyan. Although these can be argued to be different to some extent, Li was certainly not a novice in his first recording of Chipewyan. Perhaps an even more convincing argument, however, comes out of a text that Li recorded some time after his ear had become "tuned."
   While in the process of recording the story about Raven Head (No. 5

in Li and Scollon 1976), Li recorded a short version of the story *His Grandmother Raised Him (bɛtsuné yɛnéɬcą)*, which was dictated by another informant, Baptiste Forcier. In this story there are several places in which the word 'his grandmother', *bètsùné*, appears as *bètcùné*, which is then corrected to *bètsùné*. That is, even after his ear had been tuned, Li in recording another speaker heard a tc where it "should have been" ts. We feel that the explanation for the progressive phonemicization of the texts lies not in the recorder, Li, at all, but in the narrator, Mandeville.

It is Li's recollection (personal communication) that when he asked Mandeville for stories, Mandeville took it as an opportunity to produce his "highest" liturgical style. He had in that period also written sermons for his cousin, Father Lafferty, and so it is not unusual that in the first text he uses the verb *yastei* rather than *hosni* for 'I say to you'. The first of these conveys an attitude of preaching as against simple description. This is further supported by the content of the first story which is a discourse on native education. We see, then, that Mandeville's long-term interest in developing a "high" or, if you prefer, a literary language was matched well by Li's interest in recording a conservative, maximally differentiated Chipewyan. The facilitating factor was the concept of morphophonemic writing which was represented in Li's "phonetic" transcription.

As they began their work, the variation in Mandeville's speech was evident to Li and he correctly recorded it. We suggest that as they then went over these first texts to correct the transcription and to develop the grammatical notes, Mandeville seized on the possibility of morpho-phonemic representation in writing of the conservative member of each variable pair. He would not have failed to notice that where he had said tc at first and ts later, this later form was the one that Li took as the written representation of the tc–ts set. In short, it did not take Mandeville long to begin saving Li the trouble by simply always giving spelling pronunciations. We suggest that it is no wonder that after the first two texts Li stopped hearing c-series consonants, because Mandeville stopped saying them.

Our first problem, then, was to understand linguistic convergence at Fort Chipewyan, as well as certain methodological problems we encountered. We found that the solution to these problems lay in understanding the reality set, the bush consciousness, and its conflict with the reality set of researchers in the area. This raised the second problem of establishing the historical stability of linguistic convergence and the bush consciousness at Fort Chipewyan. Since our evidence indicates that these have been stable for perhaps 100 or more years, we then were faced with a third problem of understanding how the rather exceptional work of Mandeville and Li could have taken place in this same community. The explanation, we have found, lies in the modernization of the informant and the linguist. They approached the situation with an essentially common point of view on the nature of language as consisting of discrete, isolatable, and systematic varieties with clear historical antecedents.

A secondary result of this line of inquiry raises a fourth problem. There is little doubt that earlier workers in the field took their tasks as being essentially historical reconstruction and considered themselves to have failed to greater and lesser extents. That is, it is apparent that Lowie, Goddard, Mason, and Osgood all would have done an analysis much like Li's had they been able to. Their own comments on the futility of their research efforts indicate that they essentially agreed with Sapir in considering Li to have succeeded where they had not. Lowie's retrospective comment that "community studies" had not yet become fashionable indicates that to a great extent our own ability to continue to work at Fort Chipewyan represents a significant shift in theoretical perspective. The fourth problem, which we would like to briefly consider, then, is why such community-based studies should have emerged.

We see the answer to this historical question as relating to two spheres of interest, one philosophical and one ethical. We see our efforts to understand the bush consciousness as a phenomenological bracketing of our own reality set. In order to understand the relationship between reality set and the nature of language we must first bracket our own assumptions about the nature of language. We must seek to understand what sort of a thing language is within the context of the bush consciousness if we are to understand the structural effects of that reality set upon language. Thus we see our discussion of linguistic convergence and reality set as part of the more general philosophical developments underlying the so-called ethnomethodological work in such areas as conversational analysis (Gumperz, n.d.; Goffman 1976).

At the same time we see our interest in understanding the speech community's own view of language as reflecting an ethical commitment to make linguistic and ethnographic research relevant to the communities in which it is done. It is, perhaps, the first step in a long process, but we feel it is a necessary one. Our experience with the Native American Studies Program at Fort Chipewyan led us to believe that without a deep understanding not only of linguistic structure and even linguistic use in a community, but also of the very nature of language as seen by its users, programs that seek to apply the results of linguistic and ethnographic research may do worse than fail, they may produce lasting damage.

This leads us to our final problem. Research in the Fort Chipewyan area began effectively with the work of Lowie, Goddard, and Mason. Because of their difficulties and also because of Li's success, their

Athabaskan work has been devalued now for half a century. With a shift in theoretical perspectives, however, we find their work to be of considerable interest to us. It is striking to notice the same phenomenon has occurred elsewhere. Gardner (1966) mentions that Bernatzik's (1951) description of an atomistic society was considered by Burling (1965) to be less than competent and even ethnocentric. As with Mason's work, it was the critic who needed to revise his view of what was possible in human society. The problem that arises for us is that of two different views of the nature of language.

In suggesting that we should now reevaluate the earlier work on Chipewyan, especially that of Goddard and Mason, we do not mean to suggest that we should become skeptical about the work of Li. Our experience in the field has only increased our respect for this work. We doubt that there now exists a speaker of Chipewyan with Mandeville's knowledge of the language as well as the ability to express this knowledge, and we highly respect Li's recording of that knowledge. At the same time, however, it is clear that there are very important differences between Chipewyan as recorded by Li and Chipewyan as we have reported it in this book. We can now see that within the perspective of some 100 years these differences should not be understood as historical differences. They are probably better understood as differences in theoretical perspective. As Grace (1977) has argued, we may well be in need of a significant revision in our understanding of the object of linguistic description. To a large extent the object of linguistic description may be a product of the assumptions about the nature of language made by linguists. To the extent that this is true, we see the investigation of those assumptions about the nature of language as the problem of central importance to current linguistic theory.

REFERENCES

Asch, Michael
  1976 Past and present land-use by Slavey Indians of the Mackenzie District. Summary of evidence before the Mackenzie Valley Pipeline Inquiry, Yellowknife, N. W. T.
Balikci, Asen
  1963 *Vunta Kutchin social change.* Publication NCRC-63-3. Ottawa: Northern Coordination and Research Centre, Department of Indian Affairs and Northern Development.
Barth, Fredrik
  1969 *Ethnic groups and boundaries: The social organization of culture difference.* London: Allen and Unwin.
  1972 Ethnic processes on the Pathan–Baluch boundary. In *Directions in sociolinguistics,* edited by John Gumperz and Dell Hymes. New York: Holt, Rinehart and Winston.
Bateson, Gregory
  1958 *Naven.* Stanford: Stanford Univ. Press.
  1972 *Steps to an ecology of mind.* New York: Ballantine.
Bauman, Richard, and Joel Sherzer (Eds.)
  1974 *Explorations in the ethnography of speaking.* New York: Cambridge Univ. Press.
Benedict, Ruth
  1934 *Patterns of culture.* Boston: Houghton Mifflin.
  1959 *An anthropologist at work; writings of Ruth Benedict,* edited by Margaret Mead. Boston: Houghton Mifflin.
Berger, Peter, and Thomas Luckmann
  1966 *The social construction of reality.* Garden City, New York: Doubleday.

Berger, Peter, Brigitte Berger, and Hansfried Kellner
  1973 *The homeless mind, modernization and consciousness.* New York: Random House.
Bernatzik, H. A.
  1951 *The spirits of the yellow leaves.* London: Robert Hale.
Bloomfield, Leonard
  1930 *Sacred stories of the Sweet Grass Cree* Bulletin No. 60. Ottawa: National Museum of Canada.
Burling, R.
  1965 *Hill farms and padi fields: Life in mainland Southeast Asia.* Englewood Cliffs, New Jersey: Prentice-Hall.
Campbell, Ray
  n.d. "Johnny goes hunting." Tape recording. Saskatoon: Saskatchewan Indian Cultural College.
Chance, Norman A.
  1968 Implications of environmental stress for strategies of developmental change among the Cree. In *conflict in culture: Problems of developmental change among the Cree,* Edited by Norman A. Chance. Ottawa: Canadian Research Centre for Anthropology.
Cox, Bruce
  1969 Preface to the Cree Studies Special Issue. *Western Canadian Journal of Anthropology* 1(1):3–6.
Cunningham, Jinkie
  1969 Introduction to the Cree Studies Special Issue. *Western Canadian Journal of Anthropology.* 1(1):iv–vi.
Darnell, Regna
  1971 The bilingual speech community: A Cree example. In *Linguistic diversity in Canadian society,* edited by Regna Darnell. Edmonton: Linguistic Research.
  1974 Correlates of Cree narrative performance. In *Explorations in the ethnography of speaking,* edited by Richard Bauman and Joel Sherzer. New York: Cambridge Univ. Press.
Ferguson, Charles A.
  1959 Diglossia. *Word,* **15**:325–340.
Fillmore, Charles
  1977 Implicit theories of explanation in linguistics. Lecture to the Summer Institute of the Linguistic Society of America, August 3, 1977.
Fisher, A. D.
  1969 The Cree of Canada: Some ecological and evolutionary considerations. *Western Canadian Journal of Anthropology,* 1(1):7–19.
Fishman, Joshua
  1972 The relationship between micro- and macro-sociolinguistics in the study of who speaks what language to whom and when. In *Sociolinguistics,* edited by J. B. Pride and Janet Holmes. Hammondsworth: Penguin.
Flavell, John H.
  1963 *The developmental psychology of Jean Piaget.* New York: Van Nostrand–Reinhold.
Fumoleau, Rene
  1975 *As long as this land shall last.* Toronto: McClelland and Stewart.
Gardner, P.
  1966 Symmetric respect and memorate knowledge: the structure and ecology of individualistic culture. *Southwestern Journal of Anthropology* **22:** 389–415.

Gillespie, Beryl

1975   Territorial expansion of the Chipewyan in the 18th century. *Proceedings: Northern Athapaskan Conference 1971*, edited by A. McFadyen Clark. Canadian Ethnology Service Paper No. 27. Ottawa: National Museums of Canada. pp. 350–385.

Goddard, Pliny Earle

1912   *Chipewyan texts*. Anthropological Papers of the American Museum of Natural History 10. New York: The American Museum of Natural History.

1917   *Beaver texts*. Anthropological Papers of the American Museum of Natural History, Vol. 10, parts V and VI. New York: The American Museum of Natural History.

Goffman, Irving

1974   *Frame analysis*. New York: Harper and Row.

1976   Replies and responses. *Language in Society*, 5(3): 257–313.

Goody, J., and I. Watt

1963   The consequences of literacy. *Comparative Studies in Society and History*, 5:304–345.

Grace, George W.

1977   Language: An ethnolinguistic essay. Unpublished manuscript.

Gumperz, John

1968   The speech community. In *International Encyclopedia of the Social Sciences*. New York: Macmillan. Pp. 381–386.

1977   Lecture to the Language Planning Colloquium. Summer Institute of the Linguistic Society of America, Univ. of Hawaii.

n.d.   Sociocultural knowledge in conversational inference. Forthcoming.

Gumperz, John, and Eduardo Hernandez

1972   Bilingualism, bidialectalism and classroom interaction. In *Functions of language in the classroom*, edited by Courtney Cazden, Dell Hymes, and Vera John. New York: Teachers College Press.

Gumperz, John, and Dell Hymes (Eds.)

1972   *Directions in sociolinguistics*. New York: Holt, Rinehart and Winston.

Gumperz, John, and Robert Wilson

1971   Convergence and creolization: A case from the Indo-Aryan/Dravidian border. In *Pidginization and creolization of languages*. New York: Cambridge Univ. Press.

Halliday, M. A. K.

1976   On the development of texture in child language. In *Proceedings of the First Edinburgh Speech Communication Seminar*, edited by Terry Myers. Edinburgh: Edinburgh Univ. Press.

Halliday, M. A. K., and R. Hasan

1976   *Cohesion in English*. London: Longman.

Hallowell, A. I.

1946   Some psychological characteristics of the Northeastern Indians. In *Man in Northeastern North America*, Papers of the R. S. Peabody Foundation, edited by Frederick Johnson. Andover, Massachusetts: R. S. Peabody Foundation. Pp. 195–225.

Hatt, Judy K.

1969   History, social structure, and life cycle of Beaver Metis colony. *Western Canadian Journal of Anthropology* 1(1): 19–32.

Hedden, Mark

1975   Dispositions on the American neolithic: An introduction. *Alcheringa* (New Series) 1(2): 55–59.

Helm, June, Terry Alliband, Terry Birk, Virginia Lawson, Suzanne Reisner, Craig Sturtevant, and Stanley Witkowski

1975   The contact history of the subarctic Athapaskans: An overview. In *Proceedings:*

Northern Athapaskan Conference, 1971, vol. 1, Service Paper No. 27, edited by A. McFadyen Clark. Ottawa: National Museums of Canada.

Honigmann, John J.
1946 *Ethnography and acculturation of the Fort Nelson Slave*, Yale Univ. Publications in Anthropology, No. 33. New Haven: Yale Univ.
1949 *Culture and ethos of Kaska society*, Yale Univ. Publications in Anthropology, No. 40. New Haven: Yale Univ.
1968 Interpersonal relations in atomistic communities. *Human Organization* 27(3): 220–229.
1975 Psychological traits in Northern Athapaskan culture. In *Proceedings: Northern Athapaskan Conference, 1971*, vol. 2, Canadian Ethnology Service Paper, No. 27, edited by A. McFadyen Clark. Ottawa: National Museums of Canada.

Hymes, Dell
1972 Models of the interaction of language and social life. In *Directions in sociolinguistics*, edited by John Gumperz and Dell Hymes. New York: Holt, Rinehart and Winston.
1974 *Foundations in sociolinguistics*. Philadelphia: Univ. of Pennsylvania Press.
1975 Breakthrough into performance. In *Folklore: Performance and communication*, edited by Dan Ben-Amos and Kenneth S. Goldstein. The Hague: Mouton.

Jackson, Jean
1974 Language identity of the Colombian Vaupés Indians. In *Explorations in the ethnography of speaking*, edited by Richard Bauman and Joel Sherzer. New York: Cambridge Univ. Press.

Jacobs, Melville
1959 *The content and style of an oral literature*. Chicago: Univ. of Chicago Press.

Kari, James
1975 The disjunct boundary in the Navajo and Tanaina verb prefix complexes. *International Journal of American Linguistics* 41(4):330–345.

Kirschenblatt-Gimblett, Barbara
1974 The concept and varieties of narrative performance in East European Jewish culture. In *Explorations in the ethnography of speaking*, edited by Richard Bauman and Joel Sherzer. New York: Cambridge Univ. Press.

Krauss, Michael
1976 Comment at the 9th Annual Calgary Archaeology Association Conference, Problems in the prehistory of the North American sub-Arctic: The Athapaskan question. Nov. 4–7, 1976.

Krauss, Michael, and Jeff Leer
n.d. Proto-Athabaskan *ȳ and the Na-Dene sonorants. Unpublished manuscript.

Labov, William
1970 The study of language in its social context. *Studium Generale* 23:66–84.
1972a On the mechanism of linguistic change. *Directions in sociolinguistics*. New York: Holt, Rinehart and Winston.
1972b The transformation of experience in narrative syntax. *Language in the Inner City*. Philadelphia: Univ. of Pennsylvania Press.

Legoff, Fr. L.
1916 *Dictionaire Francais–Montagnais*. Paris: Desclee, De Brouwer.

Li, Fang-Kuei
1930 *Mattole, an Athabaskan language*. Chicago: Univ. of Chicago Press.
1931 A study of Sarcee verb-stems. *International Journal of American Linguistics* 6:3–27.

1933a Chipewyan consonants. *Bulletin of the Institute of History and Philology of the Academia Sinica* (Supplementary volume) **1**:429–467.

1933b A List of Chipewyan stems. *International Journal of American Linguistics* **7**(3,4):122–151.

1946 Chipewyan. In *Linguistic structures of native America,* Viking Fund Publications in Anthropology, No. 6, edited by H. Hoijer. New York: Viking Fund.

1964 A Chipewyan ethnological text. *International Journal of American Linguistics* **30**(2):132–136.

n.d. Field notes on Chipewyan, 1928. Unpublished manuscript.

Li, Fang-Kuei, and Ronald Scollon

1976 *Chipewyan texts,* Institute of History and Philology, Special Publication No. 71. Nankang, Taipei, Taiwan: Academia Sinica.

Lincoln, Peter C.

1975 Acknowledging dual-lingualism. Paper read at December 1975 meeting of the Linguistic Society of America.

Lowie, R. H.

1912 Chipewyan tales, Anthropological Papers of the American Museum of Natural History No. 10. New York: The American Museum of Natural History. Pp. 171–200.

1959 *Robert H. Lowie, Ethnologist.* Berkeley: Univ. of California Press.

MacGregor, J. G.

1974 *Paddle wheels to bucket-wheels on the Athabasca.* Toronto: McClelland and Stewart.

Mandelbaum, David C.

1940 *The Plains Cree,* American Museum of Natural History Anthropological Papers 37 (2). New York: The American Museum of Natural History.

Mason, J. Alden

1946 *Notes on the Indians of the Great Slave Lake area,* Yale Univ. Publications in Anthropology, No. 34. New Haven: Yale Univ.

n.d. Field notes and texts, 1913. Unpublished manuscript.

McClellan, Catharine

1970 Introduction, Special Issue: Athabascan Studies. *Western Canadian Journal of Anthropology,* **2**(1): vi–xix.

McKennan, Robert

1965 *The Chandalar Kutchin.* Arctic Institute of North America Technical Paper No. 17.

Moncrieff, Montogomery, and Associates

1971 A socio-economic Study of Fort Chipewyan, the Peace Athabasca delta and the Lake Athabasca region. *Supporting Studies, Peace-Athabasca Delta Project.* Technical Appendices 3.

Oblates de Marie Immaculee

1932 *Niołtsi Bedįlise.* Montreal: Librairie Beauchemin Limitee.

Osgood, Cornelius

1975 An ethnographical map of Great Bear Lake. In *Proceedings: Northern Athapaskan Conference,* Canadian Ethnology Service Paper No. 27, vol. 2, edited by A. McFadyen Clark. Ottawa: National Museums of Canada. Pp. 516–544.

Pawley, Andrew, and Frances Syder

n.d. Sentence formulation in spontaneous speech: The one-clause-at-a-time hypothesis. Unpublished manuscript.

Peter, Kathrine

1973 Vasaagihdzak. Unpublished manuscript, Alaska Native Language Center, Univ. of Alaska, Fairbanks.

Petitot, Emile
  1876   *Dictionnaire de la langue Dènè-Dindjié*. Paris: Ernest Leroux.
  1888   *Traditions Indiennes du Canada Nord-ouest*. Alencon: E. Renaut–De Broise.
Piaget, Jean
  1962   *Play, dreams, and imitation in childhood*. New York: W. W. Norton.
  1969   *The child's concept of the world*. Totowa, New Jersey: Littlefield, Adams.
  1972   *The psychology of intelligence*. Totowa, New Jersey: Littlefield, Adams.
Preston, Richard J.
  1975   *Cree narrative: Expressing the personal meanings of events*. Canadian Ethnology
          Service Paper No. 30. Ottawa: National Museums of Canada.
Richardson, Murray
  1968   *Chipewyan grammar*. Cold Lake, Alberta: Northern Canada Evangelical Mission.
Richmond, Sara
  1970   Cognitive and structural bases for group identity: The case of the southern arctic
          drainage Dene. *Western Canadian Journal of Anthropology* 2(1):140–149.
Sankoff, G.
  1972   Language use in multilingual societies: Some alternative approaches. In *Sociolin-
          guistics*, edited by J. B. Pride and Janet Holmes. Hammondsworth: Penguin.
Sapir, Edward
  1921   *Language*. New York: Harcourt, Brace.
  1925   Pitch accent in Sarcee, and Athapaskan language. *Journal de la Societe des
          Americanistes de Paris* 17:185–205.
  1949   *Selected writings of Edward Sapir in language, culture and personality*, edited by
          David G. Mandelbaum. Berkeley: Univ. of California Press.
Saville-Troike, M.
  1975   Sapir's Athabaskan correspondences: Variable data and phonetic law. Paper pre-
          sented at the December 1975 meeting of the Linguistic Society of America.
Savishinsky, Joel S.
  1970   Kinship and the expression of values in an Athabascan bush community. *Western
          Canadian Journal of Anthropology* 2(1):31–59.
  1971   Mobility as an aspect of stress in an arctic community. *American Anthropologist*
          73(3): 604–618.
Scollon, Ronald
  1974   One child's language from one to two: The origins of construction. In *Working
          Papers in Linguistics* 6(5).
  1975   A sketch of Kutchin phonology. *Working Papers in Linguistics* 7(3):17–87.
  1976a   *Conversations with a one year old: A case study of the developmental foundation
          of syntax*. Honolulu: Univ. of Hawaii Press.
  1976b   The framing of Chipewyan narratives in performance: Titles, initials and finals.
          Working Papers in Linguistics 7(4): 97–107.
  1976c   The sequencing of clauses in Chipewyan narratives. *Working Papers in Linguistics*
          7(5):1–16.
  1977   Two discourse markers in Chipewyan narratives. *International Journal of Ameri-
          can Linguistics* 43(1):60–64.
Sindell, Peter S.
  1968   Some discontinuities in the enculturation of Mistassini Cree children. In *Conflict in
          culture: Problems of developmental change among the Cree*, edited by Norman A.
          Chance. Ottawa: Canadian Research Centre for Anthropology.
Smith, J. G. E.
  1970   The Chipewyan hunting group in a village context. *Western Canadian Journal of
          Anthropology* 2(1): 60–66.

Tait, Joyce
  n.d.   *Introduction to the Cree language.* Saskatoon: Indian and Northern Education,
          Univ. of Saskatchewan.
Tedlock, Dennis
  1972a *Finding the center, Narrative poetry of the Zuni Indians.* New York: Dial.
  1972b On the translation of style in oral narrative. In *Toward new perspectives in folklore,*
          edited by Americo Paredes and Richard Bauman. Austin: Univ. of Texas Press.
Toelken, Barre
  1969   The 'pretty language' of Yellowman: Genre, mode, and texture in Navaho coyote
          narratives. *Genre* **2**(3):211–235.
Vandersteene, Roger
  1970   Some Woodland Cree traditions and legends. *Western Canadian Journal of An-
          thropology* **2**(1):40–65.
VanStone, James W.
  1963   *The Snowdrift Chipewyan.* Ottawa: Northern Coordination and Research Centre,
          Department of Northern Affairs and National Resources.
Wolfart, H. Christoph
  1973   *Plains Cree: A grammatical study,* Transactions of the American Philosophical
          Society. Philadelphia: American Philosophical Society.
Wolfart, H. Christoph, and Janet F. Carroll
  1973   *Meet Cree.* Edmonton: The Univ. of Alberta Press.
Wuetherick, R. G.
  1972   A History of Fort Chipewyan and the Peace-Athabasca Delta Region. *Supporting
          Studies, Technical Appendices,* Vol. 3, The Peace–Athabasca Delta Project,
          Canada.

INDEX